Dear Reader:

The book you are about to read is the latest bestseller from the St. Martin's True Crime Library, the imprint *The New York Times* calls "the leader in true crime!" Each month, we offer you a fascinating account of the latest, most sensational crime that has captured the national attention. St. Martin's is the publisher of bestselling true crime author and crime journalist Kieran Crowley, who explores the dark, deadly links between a prominent Manhattan surgeon and the disappearance of his wife fifteen years earlier in THE SURGEON'S WIFE. Suzy Spencer's BREAKING POINT guides readers through the tortuous twists and turns in the case of Andrea Yates, the Houston mother who drowned her five young children in the family's bathtub. In Edgar Award–nominated DARK DREAMS, legendary FBI profiler Roy Hazelwood and bestselling crime author Stephen G. Michaud shine light on the inner workings of America's most violent and depraved murderers. In the book you now hold, ALMOST MIDNIGHT, Michael W. Cuneo tells the story of a convicted triple murderer from Missouri, who rediscovered God and was pardoned by Pope John Paul II.

St. Martin's True Crime Library gives you the stories behind the headlines. Our authors take you right to the scene of the crime and into the minds of the most notorious murderers to show you what really makes them tick. St. Martin's True Crime Library paperbacks are better than the most terrifying thriller, because it's all true! The next time you want a crackling good read, make sure it's got the St. Martin's True Crime Library logo on the spine—you'll be up all night!

Charles E. Spicer

Charles E. Spicer, Jr.
Executive Editor, St. Martin's True Crime Library

DEC 1 2 2005

ALMOST MIDNIGHT

An American Story of Murder and Redemption

MICHAEL W. CUNEO

St. Martin's Paperbacks

Published by arrangement with Broadway Books, a division of Random House, Inc.

ALMOST MIDNIGHT

Copyright © 2004 by Michael W. Cuneo.

Cover photo of highway © Betsie Van der Meer/Getty Images.
Photo of Darrell Mease © Lindner/Springfield/Corbis Sygma.

Library of Congress Catalog Card Number: 2003052202

ISBN: 0-312-93675-3
EAN: 80312-93675-4

Printed in the United States of America

Broadway Books hardcover edition / February 2004
St. Martin's Paperbacks edition / September 2005

St. Martin's Paperbacks are published by St. Martin's Press, 175 Fifth Avenue, New York, NY 10010.

10   9   8   7   6   5   4   3   2   1

To my son, Ryan Cuneo

ALMOST
MIDNIGHT

PROLOGUE

Deputy Jerry Dodd of the Stone County Sheriff's Department was headed up Route 13 on a slow Sunday when the call crackled over the two-way. There was trouble near Reeds Spring Junction. A guy named Tom Woodward had phoned the department, saying a frantic woman was at his house screaming that her parents and twenty-year-old nephew had been murdered. She'd found their bodies just a few minutes earlier. She'd found them, at first not realizing they were dead. But then she'd looked—and she'd seen.

Dodd busted north past the junction and veered to the right off U.S. 160. With the dispatcher barking directions, he tore through a maze of rolling backcountry roads, startling a flock of cranes when he came to a skidding stop on the gravel outside the Woodward place. The woman waiting for him was about thirty, ashen, wearing a jean jacket. Her name was Retha Lawrence. She said she'd found the bodies shortly after two, on a piece of property her parents owned over by West Fork Creek. She'd driven up to the property from the family home in Shell Knob intending to spend the rest of the day.

She told Dodd how to get there. He followed a winding gravel road for a mile and passed through a metal gate, two black-and-orange signs attached to it reading NO HUNTING—NO TRESPASSING. A rough dirt road for several hundred yards, a sharp bend, and he was at the creek, clear and shallow, maybe ten yards across. On the far side, close to where the road picked up again, two all-terrain vehicles sat nudged together, black and shiny blue in the shallow water. On the first, the one closest to Dodd, a woman in pale blue shorts lay sprawled out backward. A man in front of her, in blue jeans and a brown belt, sat with his torso bent far over the side, one arm dangling straight down, the other snagged on the handlebar. On the second vehicle, all Dodd could make out from the opposite bank were a pair of sneaker-clad feet, which seemed tangled up somehow in the front cargo rack.

He cut the engine, got out of the car, and took off his sunglasses. Except for the twittering of birds in the black ash trees, the place was filled with a pale and tremulous quiet. Dodd squinted in the light. Focusing on the first vehicle alone, he could almost imagine it as a favorite photograph in some family album. A couple savoring an intimate moment in a sheltered creek bed—the woman stretching back and enjoying the sun, the man reaching down and running his fingers through the water. Adjusting his gaze to take in the second four-wheeler, the spell was broken. Those feet jutting weirdly from the cargo rack, the body connected to them apparently draped over the other side—nothing dreamily warmhearted about this picture.

Dodd swiped absently at a dragonfly and slowly made his way down the bank and across the creek, the water barely up to his ankles. He walked around the back of the second four-wheeler, the one with the jutting feet. He stood there, looking. He shut his eyes. He opened them again. He thought about putting on his sunglasses. He heard himself breathing. He looked away across the creek and saw the sun glinting off the windshield of his patrol car. He thought he heard a faint buzzing. He looked down again.

It was a kid, a teenager maybe, wearing gray sweatpants and a black T-shirt, splotched with blood. His outstretched arms and upper torso were resting on the gravel next to the creek. The laces of his sneakers were tied to the cargo rack, keeping his feet grotesquely propped up while the rest of his body flopped down the side of the four-wheeler and onto the ground. The upper right portion of his face, above the eye— it was gone, obliterated, reduced to a pulpy mess, red and gray.

Dodd turned away and looked down the road, lush and green on either side, a trail of blood stretching out along the dirt and gravel from around a nearby bend.

He turned back and looked at the two bodies on the other four-wheeler. He saw what he hadn't been able to see from across the creek. The woman was wearing a T-shirt deco-rated with lambs, heart-shaped earrings, and a gold chain around her neck. Her upper torso was caked in a thick reddish-brown. And her head, bent down at a sharp angle to-ward the rear axle—

Dodd put his fist to his mouth. He thought of the woman, the daughter, back at the Woodward place. He hoped she hadn't seen everything he was seeing.

—her head, the top and middle of it, was devastated. An angry, flaming V branched out from her brow to the tips of her skull. Inside the V, there was nothing. Inside the V, everything was gone.

The man in front of her, leaning far over the side, was wearing a gray polo shirt, drenched in blood. His brains were leaking out of a gaping hole in his skull, dripping out bit by bit, forming a viscous, red-and-gray puddle on the wa-ter's surface.

Dodd took a slow look around, scanning the brush in every direction. He walked back across the creek, noticing curdled bits of gray flecked with red floating in the water. He wondered why he hadn't seen this the first time across. He returned to his car and got on the radio. He was told that help was on the way.

He went back across the creek and followed the dirt road to a scruffy farm property a couple of hundred yards along. A big cabin with a tin roof and wide veranda, pretty recent construction. A white school bus that had seen better days. An old flatbed truck with black cab parked alongside a trac-tor and a small trailer. A scattering of outbuildings and chicken pens. Nothing out of the ordinary—Dodd had seen dozens of properties much like it up and down the Ozarks.

He stood frozen on the edge of the property, looking and listening. Nothing. No sign of life beyond the groaning of a door joint somewhere, the clattering of stiff branches in the spring breeze.

He went back to the creek. A dozen lawmen were on hand, hat brims turned low, mouths drawn tight. Some were still wearing their church-going shoes. There was the sound of somebody off in the nearby woods, retching.

The sheriff asked Dodd to videotape the scene.

He retrieved a camera from the trunk of a police car and started filming. He captured everything—the three bodies, the gaping wounds, the bloodstained clothing.

He even captured the flies buzzing in and out of the wrecked skulls.

PART ONE

ONE

Growing up in Reeds Spring, Missouri, Darrell Mease was a tough kid not to like. Ask just about anybody in the small Ozarks town, you'd hear pretty much the same thing. No need to worry about Darrell; R.J. and Lexie's oldest boy was going to turn out just fine.

There was no reason to think otherwise. Darrell was a kid people enjoyed being around. He loved playing the clown, telling stories, joking, and when he teamed up with his younger brother, Larry, at family get-togethers, the two boys tearing it up, they'd have the entire room in stitches. Best of all, Darrell seemed to know when to draw the line. He loved to poke fun, but never to the point where anybody's feelings got hurt.

By all accounts Darrell was a good, perfectly ordinary kid. He was smart enough, scoring decent grades at school, first at the two-roomer up by Mease's Hollow for a year, then straight through grade twelve at the main school in town, but he wasn't cut out for spending much time sitting at a desk. On most days, he could hardly wait for school to end so he could duck into the woods behind his parents' house to hunt for a couple of hours before supper.

Darrell loved the outdoors, hunting and fishing in particular, and he learned almost everything he knew about them from his dad. When he was just two or three, R.J. would take him fishing down by Granny Graves's place at Jackson Hollow and at nighttime tie him to the car with a piece of trout line. Darrell was prone to walking in his sleep, and R.J. didn't want him wandering off into the river. One night R.J. woke up and discovered that Darrell had broken loose, but found him tucked safely into bed at Granny Graves's, just forty yards away. Granny said Darrell had come into her bedroom bragging about fish he must have caught in his dreams.

R.J. was an expert hunter and trapper, and easily one of the best shots in the entire county. He could shoot gray squirrels on the run, and toss walnuts and small rocks into the air and bust them up with his .22 rifle. Darrell admired him for this, but he admired him even more for making the effort to learn how to read so he could keep up with his kids. R.J. had quit school after the third grade, and he'd spend hard evenings working his way through Darrell and Larry's reading primers, with Lexie helping him. Before long, he was reading newspapers and novels like he'd been doing it all his life.

As with most men of that time and place, R.J. wasn't much for advertising his feelings. Darrell and Larry were confident that their dad loved them, but it was something they had to infer from the evidence on hand. R.J. would never come right out and tell them. No hugs and kisses, no sweet words or tender embraces. R.J. preferred to express his affection in other ways—by making things for the boys and, of course, by teaching them how to hunt.

Darrell started out hunting with a BB gun when he was six years old, and when he turned ten he graduated to a single-shot .22, which he bought with money he'd made picking walnuts. He'd go into the woods for hours at a time with his dog, a little mixed-breed terrier named Bull Junk & Iron. He'd learned from R.J. how to bark squirrels, but he'd also hunt groundhogs, rabbits, foxes, opossum, raccoons, and quail. He'd bring the game home and his mom and dad would cook it up for supper. The Meases ate a lot of groundhog burgers when Darrell was a kid.

For a couple of years, Darrell and Larry had a pet goat that R.J. had outfitted with a bridle, a harness, and a two-wheel cart. Their cousin Garth also had a goat he liked to ride around the hollow, and one day the three boys decided they'd hitch Garth's goat to the cart and take a ride over to Aunt Ruby's and watch some TV. Down by the road, the goat threw a tantrum and upended the cart, spilling the boys onto the gravel and tangling the harness. Some people passing in a car, tourists probably, caught sight of this spectacle—*Oh, look at the little hillbilly boys! How adorable! Can you believe it?*—and started taking pictures. The boys were embarrassed. They were scrambling to get their rig set up right, and Darrell told the people if they'd just wait a second they could get some real good photos. The people just kept grinning and snapping away. The boys eventually got everything straightened out and were on their way again, but they were stopped two or three more times along the road by people in cars wanting to take pictures. Some of the people gave them nickels, one big spender tossed them a couple of dimes, and by the time they reached Aunt Ruby's they'd pulled in fifty cents—not a bad haul for a few kids just going down the road to watch some TV on the only set in the hollow.

On summer afternoons, Darrell and Larry and some of their cousins would have BB fights over by a part of the property they called shack town, between R.J. and Lexie's house and the old cannery. This is where the hired help from out of town used to live during canning season. During the fifties, when Darrell was growing up, there were just four or five of the little tar-paper shacks still standing, but the kids saw them as their very own playground village.

Shack town and the defunct cannery were remnants of old Frank Mease's legacy. Frank was R.J.'s dad, and one of the real characters in Reeds Spring history. The son of a traveling preacher, Frank moved from Iowa to Reeds Spring in 1890, when the town was little more than a scratch and a hopeful squiggle on the rugged Ozarks landscape. He hurried through two wives before he was thirty, and then, in 1901, he married a local girl named Elizabeth Teeters and settled down to the business of raising children and canning tomatoes.

Before they were done, Frank and Lizzie had a total of seventeen children, twelve of whom survived into adulthood. R.J., born in 1922, was number fifteen. Their canning operation really took off after the railroad was put through Reeds Spring in 1905, and for a stretch in the second decade of the twentieth century they owned six canneries at once and employed hundreds of people during the busy season, some coming all the way down from Springfield and putting up at one of those little one- or two-room shacks for weeks at a time. Tomatoes were always their biggest product, but after a while they branched out into green beans, blackberries, and raspberries. Frank farmed some of the fruit and vegetables for the operation himself, as often as not working the fields wearing nothing but his boots. Anyone with nerve enough to ask why, he'd sit down and give a good talking to on the restorative powers of the sun.

No one could accuse Frank Mease of entrepreneurial complacency. In 1920 he built an eight-story oak tower at Reeds Spring Junction, installed a telescope on the roof, and rented out the floors beneath to tourists. A few years later, he purchased Old Spanish Cave just north of the junction, opened it to the public, and put up a hotel, gas station, and campground with rental cabins on the adjoining property. The cave wasn't quite the commercial success he'd hoped for, but for decades afterward young Meases, including Darrell, found it an enchanting place to bring first dates. During the 1930s, finally, in an effort to beat back the effects of the Depression, Frank went into the beef-canning business and opened up his own slaughterhouse in a hollow half a mile outside of town.

The advancing years weren't kind to Frank Mease's various business ventures. When he died in 1951, eleven years before his wife, most of what he'd started up had fallen into ruin. Through good times and bad, however, he held on to his spunk. Well into his late middle-age, he still got a kick out of putting an arm chair on the roof of a car and then climbing up on it and amusing folks by standing on his head for five or ten minutes at a time. By the time he hit his seventies, he'd given up on this stunt but was still raising eyebrows. Once, in Springfield, he was intercepted in the middle of an illegal U-turn by a cop who told him, "You can't do that." "If you'd get out of my way, I could," Frank retorted.

Toward the end, Frank was forced to surrender his driver's license, but he didn't let this slow him down too much. He just had somebody else drive him to Springfield for fun and games once or twice a week. In his more domestic moments, he enjoyed entertaining relatives at the big white frame house he and Lizzie had built next to the main cannery early in their marriage. There was no shortage of relatives to entertain. Long before Frank's old age, the rocky corridor stretching northwest for two miles from the edge of Reeds Spring to the junction of U.S. 160 and Route 248 had become known as Mease's Hollow. There were so many Meases in the area, it was sometimes said, that you'd be hard-pressed throwing a cat out of a speeding car without hitting one.

It would be asking too much for anyone on Darrell's mom's side to be as colorful as Frank Mease. Ed Graves came pretty close though—on his good days Lexie's dad could give old Frank a pretty good run for his money.

Ed and Clemmie Graves moved about in the Ozarks a fair bit after getting married, once bundling their young children and worldly belongings into an iron-wheeled covered wagon and journeying all the way from Mammoth to Rogersville. They settled down in the Reeds Spring area for good in 1918, where Ed made a living, among other things, running his own butchering and auctioning business. It was some of those other things that got people talking. During Prohibition, Ed had Clemmie sew half- and full-pint-sized pockets into the lining of his coat. He'd fill the pockets with bottles of homebrew and go into town looking for customers. Finding them was never a problem; the only thing Ed could have used was a bigger coat.

Ed was a big man, at six five and 250 pounds, almost as

big as the stories people told about him. There was the story, for example, about how he shot a revenuer to death in Galena but got out of serving serious time because he was related to the trial judge. Or how he once turned such a large profit selling horses and furs that some of the county's most prominent bootleggers wondered if maybe they'd gone into the wrong business. Ed was known, sometimes admiringly, as a scoundrel, a scalawag, and a womanizer. Never one for manual labor, he lived by his wits and his courage. He'd do almost anything to make an easy dollar, and the thing he did best was trading. In the Missouri Ozarks trading in goods was a well-entrenched practice; in Ed's hands it was an art form. Nobody traded more creatively than Ed. He was the kind of guy, his friends liked to say, who could walk into a county fair with nothing more than a pocketknife and then go home hours later with a new wagon and a pair of mules. He'd just keep trading up, swapping one thing for something else more valuable, and on and on. People seemed to find his charm irresistible.

As for Clemmie, almost everyone in town agreed she was as nice and sweet a woman as you'd want to meet—maybe too nice and sweet, some said, for her own good. Staying married to Ed took a certain forbearance, but nobody could recall Clemmie complaining. If anything, she seemed to view the assignment as a special challenge. Clemmie's great passion in life was religion, the Pentecostal faith to which she converted when she was twenty-eight, and in his declining years she finally succeeded in bringing Ed into the fold. Some folks thought big Ed was merely covering his bets; Clemmie didn't much care what folks thought.

Lexie was the baby of the family, the youngest of Clemmie and Ed's ten children. She was sixteen and still in high school when she married R.J., who was four years her senior. With Frank's help, the couple built a new house on a ridge in Mease's Hollow, a modest, comfortable rambling house they figured would be ideal for raising children. R.J. took a job at the garment factory in town while Lexie finished school, and when Darrell was born in 1946, and then

Larry a year and a half later, their life was starting to take on a nice shape. By 1958, when their daughter, Rita, was born, they had everything a young Ozarks couple could reasonably have asked for.

When Darrell was growing up, it was commonly observed that he took after his dad. Like R.J., he loved spending time in the brush, always itching for an opportunity to get back out again. He was a true Ozarks boy, a hillbilly in the best and most complimentary sense of the word. He knew the names of every plant and animal in the area, what you could eat and what you couldn't, and how to hunt and fish and cook his own food beside a mountain stream. If need be, he could live in the brush for weeks at a time, months maybe, without asking for help.

Lexie knew this about Darrell, but she also knew something else. Lexie was a deeply religious woman, raised by her mom in the Pentecostal faith, where spiritual intuition counts for more than abstract dogma, and she thought she sensed certain things about Darrell that most people probably missed.

When Darrell was four years old, Lexie started taking him to the Reeds Spring Free Pentecostal Church. The church was housed in a former feed store just off the main street, right next to the garment factory where R.J. worked and almost directly across from the walled-in spring the town was named after. She took Darrell to services Sunday mornings and Wednesday evenings, and unlike a lot of boys his age he seemed really pleased with the idea of going.

Darrell enjoyed church. It was a whole different world— a rich and mysterious world that gripped his imagination every bit as much as the world of the backwoods. He loved the boisterous shouting and singing, the sweetly intoxicating poetry of tongues; he looked forward to the preaching, the Bible drills, and the revivals. He was born again, or converted, at the age of ten, which was normal procedure for Pentecostal children of that age in the Ozarks, but for Darrell there was nothing routine about the experience, nothing just-getting-it-done-with. He took his conversion with utmost seriousness, believing that somehow, at the inner core of his being, he'd been marked as one of God's very own. He believed that he'd been profoundly changed—and Lexie believed it, too.

It wasn't that his life changed much on the surface after he was born again. He was far too young for drinking and carousing, and he'd never been heard to cuss, so it wasn't as if he needed to do much about mending his ways. On the surface he remained pretty much the same kid as before, reading his Bible a bit more perhaps, but still hanging out in the woods, still cutting up with Larry. No, it was nothing major, nothing plainly visible, but a series of small things that convinced Lexie there was something special about Darrell.

There was the dream, for example. When Darrell was twelve, he came into the kitchen one morning while Lexie was preparing breakfast and told her about a dream he'd had the night before. In the dream, he and Larry and Garth were walking single-file along a precipitous path, with R.J. up ahead telling them to walk straight and take care not to fall over the edge. The boys tried to do as R.J. told them, but it was tough going. The bank along the narrow path was rocky and slippery, and they had trouble keeping their footing. Once or twice Darrell came close to slipping off, and down below, while struggling to regain his balance, he could see deep pits with grass in them and goats nonchalantly munching on the grass. Eventually the boys made it safely to the far end of the path.

Lexie took dreams seriously. She believed they were an important way the Holy Spirit communicated with Christians, and now, having listened to Darrell, she felt certain she knew the spiritual meaning of his dream. Before she could speak, however, Darrell said, "Mama, this is what it means," and he proceeded to interpret the dream himself.

"The straight-and-narrow path we were walking along stands for the life Christians have to lead after they're born again," he said. "The rough rocky bank stands for all that Satan will try and tempt the Christian with to pull him from the path." He went on: "You know, in the Bible goats represent sinners and sheep represent born-again Christians. Well, these goats are in these pits of sin and they're unconcerned about the condition of their souls—just feeding on what Satan has to offer."

Hearing this, Lexie felt a surge of pride; no, it was something more than pride—she felt real spiritual excitement. Darrell, all of twelve, had understood the dream exactly as it had been revealed to her. Who knew what might be in store for her firstborn son?

There were other small things that caught Lexie's notice. On autumn evenings Darrell and Larry and some of their cousins liked to have spear fights by shack town next to the old cannery. They'd yank up dried-out horseweeds, six or seven feet long, and hurl them at one another, trying to score direct hits. The weeds were tough and pointy and potentially dangerous, so the boys had drawn up their own convention of warfare: no hitting above the shoulders. One evening, when Darrell was thirteen, one of his cousins violated the convention and drilled him in the side of the head. Darrell fell to the ground in pain, and when he got back up he realized he could see nothing, nothing at all, out of his left eye. He walked home, dazed and scared, told his mom what had happened, then went straight up to his room and prayed for healing. Three hours later, the sight in his eye returned.

Darrell's high-school years were about as steady as they come: he seemed to breeze right through. While some of his classmates were running into the typical kinds of teenage trouble—heartbreaks, hangovers, the usual teenage blues—Darrell mostly kept doing what he'd always been doing. He started dating a bit, but he wasn't known as a fast mover. Holding hands and talking was the speed he usually felt most comfortable with. As for school, it was just another way of passing the time—nothing to get too worked up about. His grades were fine, almost always above average, and his teachers liked him well enough, but outside of class he very rarely cracked a book.

Watching her oldest boy go through high school, Lexie

remained as proud as ever. She recognized the temptations teenagers faced, and she was pleased with the way Darrell kept up with his religion, long after many of the kids he'd grown up with had stopped giving it anything more than token attention. She watched him reading his Bible, not as often as when he was younger maybe, but still reading it, still staying firm, and she thought to herself, "I've always known it; God has a special ministry in store for that boy. Darrell might become a preacher."

And why not a preacher? In the southwest Missouri Ozarks, becoming a preacher wasn't a bad career option. Long before Darrell's time, the region was known for its religious fervor and its rich mixture of home-brewed pieties. It was sometimes said, with only slight exaggeration, that every hollow had its own minister and just around the next breakneck bend of the county highway there'd always be yet another roadside tabernacle. If you were a young preacher just out of Bible school with a new message of sin and salvation, chances were you'd find an enthusiastic audience, providing you kept the message simple and biblical and free of anything too foreign-sounding—which usually meant anything too Catholic. Simple and biblical: this is how the Missouri hill folk preferred their religion. And entertaining—a little pizzazz couldn't hurt. The best preachers were those who could fire their people up with threats of damnation and promises of salvation and then cool them down with some good country-cured humor.

Yes, it made perfectly good sense that Darrell should become a preacher. And if so, Lexie just naturally assumed it would be a Pentecostal preacher. He was raised in Pentecostalism, after all, and the southwest Missouri Ozarks was thick with Pentecostal churches. But the region was also thick with Holiness, Baptist, and Methodist churches. This was the very heart of the Bible Belt, and Darrell could have become almost any kind of preacher he wanted.

Of course, there was also the chance he could have become an outlaw, though in Darrell's case nobody really took that option seriously. For a lot of local kids, however, it was just as real an option as anything else. Because here was the thing about the southwest Missouri Ozarks: the region was steeped not only in piety but also in criminality. If the hills rang out with the sweet sound of revival, they also crackled with gunfire and simmered with feuds too stubborn to die, scores waiting to be settled. This was the way it had always been, at least as long as anyone cared to remember. The preacher and the outlaw stood side by side in the local Ozarks mythology, the one proclaiming repentance and eternal glory, the other vengeance and going for broke, both promising relief from grievances real and imagined, ancient and new.

The Ozarks had always attracted outlaws, men and women who were out of sorts with mainstream society, who harbored deep grudges and had few if any bridges left to burn. The rough-and-tumble terrain, with its rugged bluffs, lost caves, and steep hillsides, afforded plenty of places for hiding out, digging in, making plans for that one last score, that one last run for happiness. In the turbulent era following the Civil War, ragtag bands of bushwhackers and night raiders wandered throughout the area, terrorizing local communities and forcing homesteaders to pack up and leave for safer pastures in Iowa, Kansas, or even California. Not long afterward, some of the most celebrated outlaws of the American frontier, including Jesse and Frank James, the Daltons, and the Doolin Gang, used the Ozarks as both a staging ground for their criminal operations and a place for giving the slip to pursuing lawmen. Decades later, during the Dirty Thirties, it was much the same story, with out-of-state heavies making strategic detours into the Ozarks and sometimes shooting up the scenery as they passed through. In 1932 a Reeds Spring blacksmith named Joe Gunn experienced the thrill of a lifetime when he was forced into a car occupied by Bonnie and Clyde and two of their gang members. The outlaws were on the run and needed Joe's help navigating some of the local back roads. Joe steered them out of Missouri and to safety in Arkansas, and a grateful Clyde rewarded him with a crisp ten-dollar bill.

And then, of course, there was moonshine. During Prohibition, the region became notorious for its wildcat whiskey stills, many of which were buried so deeply in the hills, most federal agents wouldn't have been able to find them even if they'd had the nerve to go looking. In addition to fueling the local economy, the moonshine racket heightened the region's atmosphere of mystery and danger. Everyone knew about the stills, even if their exact location was frequently a zealously guarded secret, and everyone knew that the men and women tending them could be ruthless in dealing with unwanted visitors.

The region was also famous for its vigilante justice. In the southwest Missouri Ozarks, the traditional way of settling scores was to settle them yourself. If you wanted to right some wrong, redress some grievance, you did so by taking the law into your own hands, frequently with the help of your close kin. This was partly because the Scotch Irish who had moved into the area during the mid-1800s, rapidly becoming its dominant ethnic group, seemed to have an inherited mistrust of established authority. Mainly, however, it was because there was very good reason in the southwest Missouri Ozarks for mistrusting established authority: the region seemed to breed corruption. Among longtime residents, corruption was taken for granted; it was an open secret. It was assumed that county sheriffs were living out of the pockets of local bad guys, that judges would always remember at the moment of truth which side their bread was buttered on, and that crooked politicians would somehow finagle their way to re-election. It was assumed that the law had virtually nothing to do with justice. The law was a matter of connections, whom you were related to, whom you owed money to, whom you were buying favors from; justice was something you took care of yourself.

The most notorious case of vigilantism in the Missouri Ozarks took place right next door to Stone County, just a few miles down the road from where Darrell would grow up more than half a century later. On April 5, 1885, roughly a hundred men, most of them upstanding citizens—lodge members, Republicans, the works—started a secret society aimed at combating the lawlessness that had become an entrenched fact of life in Taney County, a rural tract bordering Stone County all the way from the Arkansas line halfway up to Springfield. The men initially called themselves the Law-and-Order League, but they soon became known as the Bald Knobbers after their practice of holding meetings on Snapp's Bald, a treeless peak located several miles from the Taney County seat of Forsyth. There's little question the Bald Knobbers had legitimate grievances. Over the previous twenty years, close to forty murders had been committed in Taney County, but not a single person had been convicted in connection with any of them. In some cases, county prosecutors had simply counted their blessings and looked the other way, and in others, the ones that actually went to trial, jurors had usually found persuasive reason—fear of reprisal, donations of good whiskey—to vote for acquittal.

The Bald Knobbers were led by Nat Kinney, a giant of a man at six six, close to three hundred pounds, who had previously put in stints as a gunslinger, a street brawler, and a saloonkeeper in Springfield before moving to Taney County in 1883 and opening a Sunday school. Kinney was just about perfect for the Ozarks. At once a preacher and an outlaw, a man of God and of violence, he'd deliver hell-and-thunder sermons from his Sunday school lectern with his two six-shooters ready for action on a table beside him. At the outset, Kinney and his men seemed motivated by the best of intentions. They claimed to be interested only in cleaning up law enforcement in Taney County and assisting the courts in obtaining convictions for serious crimes. The best of intentions, however, proved alarmingly short-lived. In their first official action, just ten days after their initial secret meeting on Snapp's Bald, the Knobbers snatched two local troublemakers, the brothers Frank and Tubal Taylor, straight from the county jail in Forsyth and lynched them from a black oak by a well-traveled road just outside of town. The Taylor boys had been terrorizing townspeople for years with random acts of violence; Kinney and his men were only too happy to make a public example of them.

Over the next three years, the Bald Knobbers took vigilantism to a level unheard of even in the Ozarks. Not content with punishing perpetrators of violent crime, they appointed themselves moral custodians of Taney County, routinely administering beatings and lashings to anyone they suspected of being a philanderer, a deadbeat, or just plain disreputable. Their reign of self-righteous nastiness came to an end in August 1888 when Kinney was gunned down in a confrontation with a local tough named Billy Miles, but not before the frenzy of violence and recrimination they'd set off had spread to several neighboring counties.

The Bald Knobbers may have revived the age-old practice of lynching, but the most famous hanging in the history of the southwest Missouri Ozarks appears to have been an entirely legal affair. Early on a Friday evening in May 1937, a thirty-six-year-old drifter and convicted murderer named Roscoe "Red" Jackson climbed the fourteen steps to the gallows that had been erected next to the back wall of the Stone County Courthouse in Galena. Reaching the top, and looking out over the crowd that had gathered to watch his execution, Jackson decided he might as well close things off with a little speech.

"As far as death is concerned, there is no reason to fear—it's what you leave behind," he said in a clear, calm voice, pausing for a moment while the noose was slipped around his neck. "Well, now, folks, it's not everybody that realizes what it takes to die," he went on, his voice still clear, still calm. "It's easy when it comes accidental, but it's not so easy when it comes gradual. I want you to feel I'm the center of all this public reproach and disturbance. I know it's too much to ask for the gratitude of everyone, but I'm leaving without any ingratitude to anyone."

The executioner pulled a lever and Jackson's body shot down eleven feet to the bottom of a shallow pit that had been dug beneath the hanging platform. This was the last legal public hanging in the United States. It took place just eight miles from Mease's Hollow, less than a decade before Darrell Mease was born.

So this was it: the outlaw culture, the culture of daring and violence, which local Ozarks kids were partly raised in. And for many kids, especially boys, it held considerably more allure than the other culture, the culture of piety and revival, which competed for their attention. They grew up hearing stories of miraculous healings and midnight conversions. But they also grew up hearing of desperadoes and bootleggers, of Big Nat Kinney and the Bald Knobbers taking care of business their own way, the tried-and-true backwoods way, of Red Jackson standing tall to the end, asking no favors, copping no pleas. The desperadoes and Big Nat and Red Jackson usually won out; theirs was the side with the greater romance.

Of course, local Ozarks kids usually didn't have far to go in embracing the romance of the outlaw. As often as not, they only needed look to their own families and they'd find a grandfather who'd made his living bootlegging, a favorite uncle who'd served serious time for something he may or may not have done, a first cousin who'd already been in and out of trouble so often he was first-name familiar with practically every cop in the county. Local Ozarks kids came by their knowledge of outlaw culture honestly; it was part of their lived experience.

They also came by their cynicism and mistrust of established authority honestly. Here again, local kids usually didn't have to stray very far from the front porch to hear the stories that were an integral part of the local folk wisdom. They heard stories of double-dealing prosecutors, judges on the take, sheriffs on the take, the whole damn system on the take; they heard of sheriffs' deputies busting people up just for the hell of it, of justice being auctioned off down at the courthouse like livestock at a county fair. Sometimes the stories featured members of their own families.

Darrell certainly heard his share of such stories growing up, including several featuring his Uncle Otto, a hard-drinking, sly-humored man who was married to Lexie's older sister Walsie. When Lexie was still a schoolgirl, Otto Ray was a justice of the peace in Reeds Spring with a reputation for playing mean and dirty. If he happened to be low on booze and strapped for cash (as was frequently the case), no problem, old Otto would simply send out a deputy to arrest someone, *anyone*, for public drunkenness. After fining the miscreant, he'd have enough money to head on down to the liquor store for a fresh bottle or two.

There were other stories, too—quite a few involving Lexie's brother Herbert, who held several law enforcement jobs in the Reeds Spring area over the years, including a tempestuous stint as town marshal. Herbert rarely missed an opportunity to leave his mark. He'd make his rounds with a leaded glove tucked into his jacket pocket, hoping (practically pleading) for an excuse to demonstrate its effectiveness when smashed against some poor local's skull. One evening, he threw two drunks into the tank and deliberately left the cell door wide open. Sitting at his desk with his feet up, he said, "I'll shoot the first one that comes out that door." One of the drunks later maintained that his buddy pushed him. His buddy denied it, insisting that the fellow walked out on his own. Pushed or not, the drunk came through the open door and Herbert, true to his word, shot him in the stomach with a .38. The fellow lived, but even Herbert's die-hard supporters (who weren't numerous to begin with) wondered whether the time hadn't perhaps arrived for their marshal to move on.

Herbert did eventually move on, taking his family to California and hunkering down in an abandoned saloon in the Independence–Lone Pine area. He prospected for gold and tried his hand at one or two other things, but mostly he gave the local citizenry ample cause to wish he'd never left Missouri. For a while he limited himself to penny-ante mayhem, bullying, brawling, the usual stuff, but then one night he strode into a bar just outside of Independence and blew some guy's arm off with a .300 Magnum. The local authorities must have had a hard time containing their glee. The guy Herbert shot had long been suspected (without evidence to

pin him down) of brutally slaying and then decapitating two kids in the nearby desert several years earlier. And Herbert? Would anyone really object too loudly if Herbert were sent away for a nice stretch, courtesy of the state?

Herbert's stretch, when all was said and done, amounted to two years in the minimum-security Tehachapi Prison near Bakersfield. He was still serving his time when Lexie dropped by with Darrell and Larry in the summer of 1964. As a high-school graduation present for Darrell, Lexie had taken the boys on a road trip to visit relatives in California, leaving R.J., who really didn't like straying too far from Stone County, at home to take care of Rita. Lexie thought this was a good opportunity for the boys to see their Uncle Herbert, maybe even have something to eat with him at the prison, so they picked up some buns and cold cuts in town and stopped by. Herbert was glad to see them. They were relaxing at a shaded picnic table on the prison grounds when Darrell took out his pocketknife to spread some mayonnaise on a sandwich. Herbert chuckled and told him, "You'd better get that back in your pocket or I might never get out of here."

Darrell loved that two-week road trip to California. He thought it was just about the best graduation present he could have received. Lexie was happy giving it to him. She was pleased he'd stuck it out and earned his high-school diploma—and earned it with some distinction. Despite his sporadic study habits, Darrell made the honor roll his senior year, finishing fifth in a class of twenty-seven. Not that Darrell himself put much stock in the accomplishment. The school, he joked with his friends, was probably just hard up for another live body to fill out the roster.

One thing's for sure: no one made more appearances in the senior yearbook than Darrell. Looking at it today, the 1964 Reeds Spring High School annual has a somber, Sunday-schoolish cast to it: no cutesy photo captions, no "voted most likely to" goofiness—behave yourselves now, kids, this is serious business. Nevertheless, turn the page and there's Darrell again, Darrell in black-and-white: Darrell helping two other kids solve a math problem on the blackboard (mathematics was always his best subject); Darrell, gawky and grinning, in his Wolf Pack basketball uniform (he played varsity hoops his senior year); Darrell in his number 74 football jersey (he played the line, going both ways and hardly ever missing a down); Darrell as a cast member in the senior class production of *Hillbilly Weddin'*; Darrell with the track team; Darrell at homecoming; Darrell, Darrell everywhere. And, of course, there's also the photograph of Darrell the honor student, neatly combed hair, thin lips, weak chin, wearing a jacket and tie he'd borrowed from his football coach, not exactly handsome but not homely either, looking like a kid you might expect to grow up and sell insurance or—who knows?—maybe even preach the Gospel in some roadside church.

The truth is, Darrell had no idea what he wanted to do with himself after high school. College? No, there was no serious thought given to that. Hillbilly kids from Stone County didn't generally go to college back then. Bible school perhaps? Well, maybe later, but not now; at eighteen he wasn't even close to making a serious commitment to becoming a preacher. What Darrell dreamed of doing, though he didn't actually get around to exploring the possibility, was becoming a trick shooter for a gun company. No one could have honestly suggested he lacked the talent. He'd always loved shooting, and now, after high school, he was developing a bit of a reputation. He carried an automatic pistol around with him, a .22 Ruger with a wooden handle which his Uncle Gerry had given him, the barrel stuck inside the front of his pants. He'd entertain friends by flicking quarters into the air and then drawing the pistol and shooting them in midair. People were starting to talk. You might be able to outshoot Darrell with a rifle or shotgun, they'd say, but no way with a pistol. Forget about it: you'd be a fool even to think of trying.

Darrell was proud of his shooting, he didn't mind showing off occasionally, but he was never really boastful about it. Actually, he was a shy kid—a bit cocky on the surface maybe, but shy and insecure underneath. There was a vulnerability about Darrell that he didn't always succeed in covering up with his devil-may-care, backwoods-boy manner. He could be touchy at times; he was thin-skinned, easily bruised. He took insults hard; friendly ribbing, if carried past a certain point, could cause him to smolder inside. He had difficulty shrugging it off. He sometimes took offhand remarks, casual gibes, as a personal attack. Lacking confidence, unsure of where he stood in the world, he was acutely sensitive to how others responded to him. If he felt pushed, or challenged, he'd want to push back. He was determined, he once told a friend, "never to allow anyone to run over me." He'd always been this way. When he was just seven or eight, one of his uncles came over for a visit and started teasing him pretty hard. (The Mease clan was famous for rough kidding and teasing.) The uncle had been drinking, and he apparently went too far. Darrell had been taught to respect his elders, but now, wounded, aggrieved, he stood up and told his uncle to be quiet. No more, he said, that was it, no more abuse. The entire room fell quiet. The uncle turned red and soon left. R.J. was mortified. If he was waiting for Darrell to apologize, however, he could have waited forever. Darrell had dug in. He had right on his side, and he wasn't about to retreat. He'd done what he felt needed to be done; he'd shut his abusive uncle down.

His friends didn't often see this side of Darrell; he was usually pretty good at covering it up. What they mostly saw was a sweet-natured, easygoing kid who rarely had a bad word for anybody. It would be an exaggeration to say that Darrell was popular—he was, after all, something of a loner—but he was genuinely liked and respected by just about everyone who knew him.

Lefa Johnson, a striking brunette, was one year ahead of Darrell in high school, but she got to know him quite well, especially after she started dating his best friend Mike Langston. Years later, Lefa would remember Darrell as "absolutely one of the nicest kids" in their entire circle. "You want to talk about Darrell? Pull up a chair—I could say nice things about Darrell all evening," she said. "Ask anybody who knew him back then, Darrell was just a wonderful kid, a model kid, always smiling and joking, and so honest, so humble. I think the girls liked him even better than the guys did because he was so polite and respectful. He'd never try to take advantage of anyone, he was never fast or crude. He was the most decent boy around. Even our high-school teachers thought so."

Not headed anywhere fast after high school, Darrell started in full-time at the garment factory in town. It was tough and sweaty work, operating the heavy steam presses, but he enjoyed having lunch with his dad most days and the sense of responsibility that came with paying his own way. He knew the job wasn't going to make him rich, but he hoped he'd be able to save some money and eventually take a trip to Colorado, maybe even Alaska, for some big-game hunting. Still, at eighteen there was nothing Darrell liked better than hunting.

But now there was something else going on in his life. Toward the end of his senior year, Darrell had started dating a cute, petite girl named Joyce Barnes, and the relationship was getting serious. Joyce was two years younger than Darrell and just in the tenth grade when they started going together. Her father, Roy, ran a general store at the junction of Y Highway and Route 76, on the way to Cape Fair. Roy Barnes was a strict, old-style Pentecostal with strict, old-style ideas about raising kids. Joyce and her sisters weren't allowed to play basketball at school because Roy didn't want them wearing shorts. They weren't allowed to watch movies or put on lipstick or go to dances. It's as if old Roy saw almost everything in the outside world as a gigantic sin just waiting to happen. A lot of local folks thought he was making a big mistake. Try and raise your kids that strict, it would surely backfire. You were just asking for rebellion. Even before she'd started dating Darrell, there were stories about Joyce. One time, apparently, she'd kicked her father in the crotch and then hidden in the brush while he looked for her with a rifle. Most people who knew her said Joyce was too high-spirited to abide by Roy's rules. Joyce was a rebellion waiting to happen.

So Darrell was working at the garment factory in town and getting in deeper and deeper with Joyce Barnes. It was a big adventure for both of them. They'd get together evenings and take off in Darrell's Chevy, cruising and listening to the radio, visiting nearby towns and grabbing something to eat at roadside burger joints. Some nights they had sex in the Chevy's back seat, two Pentecostal kids who knew they were supposed to wait until they got married, and they began to think that maybe they were made for each other.

Finally, in August of 1965, they did get married. Darrell was nineteen; Joyce was just out of the eleventh grade.

TWO

Darrell received his "greetings" letter from the draft board on January 10, 1966. It was waiting for him when he got home from work. The action was really starting to heat up in Southeast Asia, and it was poor kids like Darrell, kids without college prospects or political connections, who were first in line for patriotic duty. There weren't very many middle-class college students protesting the war in Vietnam back in 1966.

Of the thirteen boys from Darrell's senior high-school class, four received their draft notices the same week. There was Darrell, his first cousin Ronnie Mease, his best friend Mike Langston, and another boy who ran with a different crowd. That's four boys from Reeds Spring, whose population in a good year didn't amount to much more than four hundred.

At first Darrell wasn't sure what to make of it. He sat down on the front porch of the little frame house he and Joyce were living in, just across the creek from his mom and dad's, and read and reread the letter until his eyes glazed. The war in Vietnam was a complete mystery to him. He had no idea what the stakes were, which side was in the right, or whether the United States had legitimate business being involved. Not only that, he couldn't even begin picturing himself in the military. The uniforms, the compulsory subservience, the bachelor living: all of this was alien to him. He'd been raised in the hills and was accustomed to having his freedom. No way, he thought, was he cut out for the regimented life of a soldier.

What's more, the timing couldn't have been worse. He and Joyce had been married just over four months, and so far it hadn't been the smoothest of rides. It was tough putting a finger on it, but something was obviously misfiring. The fun, the easy times they'd enjoyed before getting married seemed almost to have vanished, and there was a constant tension in the air. But they were still just newlyweds, and Darrell wasn't even thinking of packing it in. He wasn't happy, but he wasn't entirely unhappy either. He liked the idea of being married, the idea of trying to make a life with somebody else. He was hoping to give it his best shot and get the marriage on course, but the letter changed everything. What chance did he and Joyce have if he was sent overseas for an extended stint in Vietnam? How could they get things on track if he was thousands of miles away fighting in a war nobody at home knew anything about?

He talked it over with Joyce and his parents, and then the next day with Ronnie and Mike Langston. Everybody tried to put a positive slant on it. Sure the boys had been drafted, but maybe they wouldn't even be going to Vietnam. They might just be sent up to Fort Leonard Wood, the army base this side of Rolla, where they'd stay until the whole business blew over. Hell, they'd probably even be able to make it home weekends. One thing they never talked about was running. Dodging the draft, maybe fleeing north and laying low somewhere in Canada—this wasn't even an option. The boys figured they'd simply report and hope for the best.

They took a Greyhound out of Springfield and checked into the induction center in Kansas City. It was a confusing scene. Two thousand draftees were milling about, getting physicals, trying to get their bearings. Guys in uniforms were barking instructions. Half the time you couldn't make out what the hell they were saying. Finally some guy up front called out the names of thirteen draftees and told them to follow him to a room off to the side. Darrell, Mike, and

Ronnie were among those whose names were called. They had no idea what was up. They were led into a room where there were some guys in marine uniforms sitting behind a table. The one who looked to be in charge said, "Congratulations, men. You're going into the Marine Corps." Now Darrell, Mike, and Ronnie were really confused. They'd thought you had to volunteer for the marines. Before it truly had a chance to sink in, they were on a plane for California.

With the war effort picking up, the marines were running new recruits through boot camp quite a bit faster than usual. Darrell and the boys did eight weeks instead of the customary thirteen, then they were hustled off to Camp Pendleton, outside of San Clemente, where they underwent infantry recruit training. Three months of this, and they returned home on a thirty-day leave.

It was a sweet thirty days. Darrell got in some good hunting and did his best to make up for lost time with Joyce. They still weren't hitting on all cylinders, but there were signs they might be able to get the old romance back in gear. They enjoyed some nice quiet intimate moments, and Joyce seemed proud that her young husband was on his way to becoming a full-fledged marine. Darrell began to think that they might get through this rough patch in pretty good shape after all.

Darrell and Ronnie traveled together from Reeds Spring to the Camp Lejeune Marine Corps base in North Carolina. They'd already been told that they'd be serving as combat engineers in Vietnam; Mike Langston had been given a different assignment and didn't accompany them. After several months training in heavy equipment, explosives, and other tools of the trade, Darrell was sent cross-country to Camp Pendleton for final preparations.

He shipped out on December 15, 1966, and in Vietnam he was attached to the First Marine Air Wing at the Marble Mountain base near Da Nang. His unit bounced around, primarily trying to hold bases that the Vietcong had been forced to give up. Darrell put down beach matting for chopper landing pads and erected Quonset huts and strung razor wire and helped build pontoon bridges. Sometimes he swept for mines.

The combat engineers had it pretty tough. They'd be hammering and sawing away, doing tasks that the squadron counted on for day-to-day survival, all the while realizing they could come under enemy fire at any time. The risk was always there. You're out in the open putting down matting, and then one of your buddies, in the blink of an eye, is on the ground dead or wounded. Darrell saw it happen; everybody saw it happen. Sometimes the engineers, fed up with feeling like sitting ducks and bristling for a chance to take fate into their own hands, would volunteer for missions that no one else wanted any part of. Five or six months into his tour, Darrell succeeded in pleading his way onto a six-man team whose mission was to salvage a chopper that had gone down in the jungle. Even the most gung-ho, combat-hardened marines regarded missions of this sort as suicidal. They had a 50 percent survival rate. Chances were the Vietcong would have an ambush set up, or the chopper would be booby-trapped. Everyone figured half the team would be killed. The mission was called off at the last second. Darrell never had an opportunity to volunteer for another one like it.

One night the base came under heavy rocket attack. Darrell woke and ran through the screaming darkness, the concussions from the blasts knocking him to the ground again and again before he finally reached the bunker. The next morning they dug up a rocket that had crashed right beside the hut in which Darrell had been sleeping. It was a dud—the only rocket out of the thirty-three in the attack that hadn't exploded. Otherwise he almost certainly would have been killed. He wrote his mom about it, telling her the exact time the rocket had landed. In her return letter, Lexie said this was the same time she had been saying an intercessory prayer on his behalf. Darrell was convinced that his mom's prayer had saved his life.

No one knew better than Darrell that he could have been having a much worse time of it. His unit came under fire often enough, but it was nothing compared to what some of the frontline combat troops were facing. Plus, he had found ways of tuning out the danger—the persistent fear and dread. Prayer helped, but before long he found that booze and drugs helped just as well.

Darrell discovered booze and drugs—*really* discovered them—about two months into his stint, after having gone through basic training and all the rest of it without so much as a single drink. Most of the other recruits couldn't believe it. Was this hillbilly kid for real? He didn't drink, he didn't swear, he acted as if he'd never even heard of drugs. After two months in Vietnam, however, he was drinking with the best of them, beer mainly, sometimes as many as twelve pints a night. He also got heavily into marijuana, usually laced with opium. Most of the marines he knew smoked it this way. They'd put a drop of peppermint extract on it to knock out the odor. The booze, the opium, the marijuana: it was almost standard-issue ordnance in Vietnam. Getting loaded (and staying loaded) seemed part of the job description. If you were there, it was just something you did to relieve the sense of danger, and the loneliness. Also the tedium, the long aching hours of sitting around waiting for the next move, and then the move after that.

As the months passed, Darrell found still another reason for getting loaded. Things, apparently, weren't going as well on the homefront as he had hoped. While waiting for her husband to ride out his tour, Joyce had moved in with Larry and his wife, Sophia, just newlyweds themselves. In several of her letters to Darrell, Joyce apparently accused Larry of sexually molesting her. Larry had done nothing of the sort, but it still gnawed at Darrell, worrying about Joyce and her state of mind and wondering whether his younger brother was taking advantage of her. The worry wasn't nearly so bad, he discovered, during the hours when he wasn't sober.

Alcohol and drugs were one thing, sexual temptation was something else. Here Darrell was absolutely determined to stand his ground. It wasn't easy—the opportunities were endless and astonishingly cheap. Young Vietnamese women, desperatcly poor, would walk out to the base and spread their pallets on the ground. Their asking price was usually no more than a ten-cent pack of cigarettes or an orange that any marine could pick up free at the mess hall. At one time or another, just about all of his buddies took advantage of these opportunities, but Darrell succeeded in keeping his impulses under control. His dad had always told him that a real man stuck with one woman. He knew he'd be letting both Joyce and R.J. down if he crossed the line.

Darrell was one of the lucky ones. That, at any rate, was how he saw it. He completed his twelve-month tour of duty on December 10, 1967. He left the service a corporal, and with an honorable discharge. Other than a slight burn to his foot from a piece of shrapnel, he was unhurt. Now he could go home and try to resume his life.

Darrell bumped into Ronnie at the airport in Da Nang the afternoon he was scheduled to fly home. They hadn't seen each other since North Carolina. Ronnie's flight wasn't due out until the next day, and Darrell changed his ticket so they could travel home together. They spent the evening at a bar near the airport. They had a good time, laughing, swapping war stories. They both got lit up pretty good. Ronnie was grateful for the night out, but he couldn't help wondering about Darrell. He'd never seen his cousin drinking before, much less as drunk as he was now. There was no question about it: Darrell had changed.

When he got back home just about everyone thought the same thing. After two years in the marines, Darrell wasn't the same. There were the obvious things you couldn't help noticing. Like a lot of returning vets, he now wore his hair long and had grown a beard. In outward appearance Darrell the clean-cut preacher boy had given way to Darrell the scraggly outlaw. To Lexie's chagrin, moreover, he was drinking, sometimes heavily, and not making much of an effort to hide it. Within a short while of getting back, he'd become familiar with the interiors of half a dozen local bars he'd previously known only by name. After a few beers he'd sometimes say things people didn't quite know how to take.

One night, not long after his discharge, he was with some cronies at a place called the Queen of Clubs, just south of Kimberling City. "You know, the Marine Corps spent thousands of dollars teaching me how to kill and I still haven't killed anyone," he said. He was probably kidding, but no one could tell for sure.

The drinking and the long hair, these were just two of the more obvious ways Darrell had changed. But people back home suspected there was something else too, something that was tough putting into words. It wasn't anything that jumped out at you, but it was there nonetheless. You could sense it especially in his more sober moments, when he'd had only a beer or two, or hadn't been drinking at all. He seemed less carefree than before, a bit reserved, and there was a certain tension in his shoulders, like he was straining under the weight of some secret burden. People didn't know whether it was Vietnam, his marriage, or maybe something else entirely.

In truth, it was probably a combination of things. Darrell didn't like talking about it, but he was having nightmares after returning from Vietnam. They were always alike, just different versions of the same thing. He was being chased, alone and unarmed, by Vietcong through the jungle, or he was scrambling for cover during a rocket attack. Some nights he'd wake up in a panic, and it would take several moments before he realized he'd been dreaming. He'd grab a pistol and go searching for his tormenters, opening dresser drawers, looking through closets, checking under the bed. Darrell suffered nightmares of this sort intermittently for more than a decade, but he kept them a closely guarded secret. He thought there was something shameful, almost cowardly, about the entire business. After all, he was one of the lucky ones.

The marriage was another matter. He and Joyce weren't getting along, and it was easy to see. They weren't very good at concealing their differences. Darrell wasn't even a month out of uniform and they were already going at it, arguing and fighting about everything and anything. It rapidly became a way of life. Their friends and relatives couldn't help wondering what in the world they'd seen in one another to begin with.

They were still practically newlyweds, of course, and some of the things they fought about, such as money and jobs and sex, more or less went with the territory. When Darrell got back home, Joyce was living near Kansas City with Larry and Sophia. Larry and a couple of cousins, Lonnie and Dale Mease, had gone up a few months earlier looking for work and had found jobs at the big Ford plant in Claycomo. Joyce had then moved and taken a job with the telephone company. After checking in with his folks in Stone County, Darrell went to Kansas City himself, thinking he could take his time looking for a job, maybe find something he really liked. With Joyce working, there was no need to settle for the first thing that came along. It sounded good in theory, but almost as soon as he arrived Joyce quit her job, saying it was now up to him to take care of business. Darrell was flabbergasted. This wasn't the kind of welcome he'd been hoping for. Just out of the service, and now he was under big-time pressure to bring home a paycheck. He tried to convince Joyce that she was being unreasonable, that he deserved some leeway before taking a steady job. She held her ground, however, and Darrell was forced to go knocking on doors.

He caught on at the Ford plant, working the assembly line in the body shop. He figured he might as well try to make the most of it and save some money, so he grabbed as much overtime as he could get. After a while, he and Joyce moved into a little frame house in Winwood Lake, a low-rent community near the plant. Their life settled into a deadening routine. Darrell would drive straight home from work, sometimes stopping along the way to load up on whiskey. He'd then drink until he fell asleep. He'd learned to cope with tension in Vietnam by drinking; now he was hoping for the same results at home. Joyce would hit the bottle pretty hard herself, and several times a week they'd veer off into drunken quarreling. Sometimes it was over money. Why were they always broke? Who was spending how much on stuff they really didn't need? As often as not it was over sex. Now that he was back in Missouri, Darrell was hearing disturbing stories. Joyce, according to some accounts, hadn't kept her end of the bargain. He heard that she'd been playing around while he was over in Vietnam trying his best to walk the line. She insisted that she'd been true to him and that the stories were outright lies. Darrell didn't believe her. Whatever slender trust they'd once shared now lay in shreds.

A couple of months later, Joyce phoned her older brother Robert and asked him to come up to Winwood Lake to get her. She said she'd had enough of Darrell and wanted to come home. Robert Barnes was a small, intense, intelligent man with a reputation for decisive action and unflinching opinions. He loved his sister and he'd known and liked Darrell for years. He was rooting for them to sort out their differences and move on with their marriage. But rooting for them didn't necessarily mean betting on them.

"No one wanted it to work out more than I did," he recalls, "but there wasn't much give in either one of them. Joyce was only five two, but when she got mad her temper was uncontrollable. She wouldn't back down from a mountain lion. She'd go toe-to-toe with Darrell or anyone else who got in her way. Now Darrell, I always thought Darrell was a sweet kid with a real nice disposition. He had some peculiar ideas, but you couldn't hold this against him. He once told me that the Social Security system was all messed up. They give you an old-age pension when you're too old to enjoy it, he said. They should give it to you between the ages of eighteen and thirty-four. He was dead serious. The thing about Darrell was, he changed when he started drinking and doing drugs in Vietnam. When he came home, he was a different guy. The two of them together, Joyce and Darrell, they were a couple sticks of live dynamite."

Robert drove to Winwood Lake and found Joyce, her face puffy and lips swollen, waiting on the front porch with her suitcase. He recalls going inside and finding Darrell sitting on a rocking chair in the living room. "He was drunk out of his gourd. I was mad. I grabbed him by the shoulders and started shaking him violently. 'Goddamn big tough marine,' I said. 'Is this what they taught you in the service, you sonuvabitch?' He didn't say a word because he was ashamed. He knew he did wrong. So I took Joyce home to Stone County, but after a few days Darrell came down and they made up."

Darrell remembers it a bit differently. He thinks he must have been blacked out while all this shaking and berating was going on. Otherwise he almost certainly would have mustered a few words in his defense.

It wasn't long afterward that Darrell came home from work one evening and told Joyce to pack her things. They were moving back home. A year and a half of Kansas City, and he'd had enough. He was sick and tired of the whole scene. He wanted to go home where they could make a fresh beginning, maybe buy a piece of land, build their own house, start living like they were meant to live. Joyce found it hard to disagree. She figured they had nothing to lose.

So they moved back to Mease's Hollow, into the same little house across from R.J. and Lexie, where they'd first started out. In 1969 their daughter, Melissa, was born, and two years later they had a son named Shane. In 1972 Darrell bought forty acres of land for two thousand dollars from the postmaster general of Reeds Spring, a good and honest man named Nelson Holt. It was a nice parcel, just down the road from where Darrell had grown up. Right away he started clearing a space for their dream house.

THREE

The move back home didn't work out as Darrell and Joyce had hoped. After a few years they had a third child, Wesley, but they still weren't anywhere close to realizing domestic bliss. Their battles were becoming the stuff of local legend. They found it tough restraining themselves even at family get-togethers.

Darrell's brother Larry vividly remembers an altercation that took place during dinner one Thanksgiving at R.J. and Lexie's. Darrell reached over and took some food off Joyce's plate. Joyce was incensed and started choking him. Darrell choked her right back. They kept at it, gasping and grimacing, until Larry and a couple of other people at the table jumped in and pulled them apart. Sometimes they'd pull guns on each other. One night Joyce held a .45 Magnum (with a cocked hair trigger) inches from Darrell's face. If she'd so much as twitched, she'd have blown him away. Darrell talked her down, then took out his .22 Ruger semi-automatic, which he'd emptied of bullets the night before, and pointed it at her temple. Joyce broke down and cried, and they declared one of their periodic, and highly fragile, truces.

Money was a constant source of tension. They were almost always broke, stuck in a rut of hard poverty. Good steady work was scarce in Stone County—especially for good ole boys like Darrell almost a decade out of school and without much to show for it. It's not that Darrell was lacking in skills. He was a good carpenter and stonemason—and getting better all the time. R.J. had taught him a lot, and he'd been picking up more along the way from how-to books and on-the-job training. The problem was converting these skills into some kind of a steady income. He was forced to scuffle about, taking odd jobs wherever he found them. Sometimes they had to hit up Joyce's dad for grocery money just to make it through the week. The tough grind wore them down. It frustrated and demoralized them, and they took it out on each other.

Alcohol was another constant—alcohol and, eventually, marijuana. Darrell had stopped using marijuana upon leaving the service, but a couple of years after moving back to Stone County he took it up again. It wasn't tough to find. By the early 1970s marijuana was one of the region's leading cash crops. Backwoods boys who in a previous era might have been tending stills were now busy cultivating "Missouri gold." Everyone knew somebody who was in the business. Simply put out the word that you were interested in buying, and you'd be taken care of. Darrell liked getting stoned. It took his mind off his marital problems and gave him a renewed sense of boyish innocence. Even Joyce figured there were worse things he could be doing. She thought he was less mean when smoking pot than when drinking. Darrell thought Joyce was deadly mean all the time, regardless of her state of incapacitation.

Darrell and Joyce, it might be added, weren't working from an entirely new script. Marital problems such as theirs were hardly rare in Stone County. The stubborn pride and hardscrabble self-reliance of the region's inhabitants frequently made marriage a difficult proposition. Raised to fend for themselves and to take guff from no one, the hill folk tended to chafe at the thousand and one little surrenders and compromises that are the routine stuff of protracted domestic life. Men especially were ill disposed to having their freedom shortened. Marriage was a good and useful thing, providing it didn't get in the way of what you wanted to be doing—and what you considered you had an unfettered right to be doing.

There is a legal case from Stone County that helps color the point. In 1959 a fellow from Galena named Lowell Moore filed a petition for divorce on the grounds that he had suffered "general indignities" at the hands of his wife, Minnie. Lowell told the court that Minnie, who wasn't a native of the region, had occasionally insulted his friends and relatives by calling them "hillbillies." Even worse, she had proven herself less than fully enamored of the Four Freedoms that have traditionally been recognized in Stone County, or the "The Kingdom of the James," as the county, after the James River, has sometimes been referred to. The Four Freedoms, inscribed in the cultural landscape of the region, may be boiled down as follows. A man has the right to be master of his own house, and the rights—without interference from his wife—to hunt and fish, drink, and trade livestock with his friends.

In their six years of marriage, Lowell claimed, Minnie hadn't exactly taken these rights to heart. She had sometimes come looking for him late at night when he was drinking with his buddies. Two or three times she had tried to tag along on his fishing outings. She had occasionally questioned the wisdom of his trading practices. And once she had even had the temerity to tell him, right in front of his friends, that she didn't want him going on a turkey shoot. He went on the shoot anyway, of course, but that was hardly the point. Minnie had humiliated him, made him look almost horsewhipped. His buddies couldn't believe it. Eventually some of his friends stopped calling on him, or stopped calling as often as they were accustomed to, because the reception they were getting from Minnie, as one of them told the court, "was a little on the cool side." Finally, after announcing, "I just want my soul back," Lowell had filed for divorce.

The Circuit Court of Stone County awarded Lowell his divorce, but the judgment was reversed by the Springfield Court of Appeals the following year. The appellate court agreed with Lowell that Minnie hadn't been as respectful of the Four Freedoms of Stone County as she might have been, and that she had sometimes "wanted to tie the stake rope a little too short." Nevertheless, she had not inflicted any great or lasting injury upon Lowell, and her interventions, while not always prudent, had generally been well intentioned. As for calling his friends and relatives "hillbillies," the court concluded, Minnie had likely meant this not as an insult but rather as "an expression of envy."

There's no confusing Lowell and Minnie Moore with Darrell and Joyce. Lowell and Minnie weren't threatening each other with pistols or breaking up family dinners with choking sprees. They weren't accusing each other of horrible betrayals or sending out midnight calls for help to heard-it-all-before relatives. Most of the time, in fact, they seem to have gotten along pretty well. Even Lowell himself, in his courtroom testimony, conceded that Minnie could be "a pretty good lover and a pretty good wife."

But this is precisely the point. Marriage in Stone County, even under the blandest of circumstances, could be a tough haul. Men in general didn't think it should cut into their freedom, and women who thought otherwise were sometimes in for a rude awakening. If mild-mannered Minnie Moore could run into so much trouble, then what about Joyce? By almost all accounts, Joyce was volatile and tempestuous and ferociously stubborn. No way was Joyce going to kowtow to Darrell or anyone else. And no way was bullheaded Darrell going to dance to Joyce's tune. Their marriage was damned by cultural circumstance, and damned again by a fundamental clash of personalities.

There was one thing that might have been able to save them. If Darrell or Joyce, either of them, were still going to church, it may have made a difference. Pentecostalism in the Ozarks was a religion of repentance, redemption, and reconciliation. Over the years it had helped more than just a few unhappy couples survive the nasty weather. But Darrell and Joyce had both left their religion far behind. They were out in the cold now, with nothing but booze and drugs to see them through.

So they kept fighting. Sometimes it was serious stuff: Darrell attacking Joyce, Joyce attacking Darrell, the two of them attacking each other. Sometimes it was just petty arguing: Darrell getting on Joyce for her constant carping, Joyce getting on Darrell for his drinking and whatnot. Darrell thought Joyce was always putting him down and sabotaging his plans. Joyce thought Darrell was flaky and unreliable.

Things finally fell apart completely when Darrell came home one evening just as Joyce was packing the three kids into her old Pontiac. She told him she was leaving for good this time. Her dad had given her some money and she was going to Houston where she planned on staying with relatives. Darrell blew his stack. He took out his pistol and sprayed the hood of the Pontiac with bullets. He was aiming for the carburetor, trying to put the car out of commission, but he was drunk and couldn't find the mark. Joyce drove over to her dad's and showed him the bullet holes in the hood. Old Roy was infuriated. He wanted to go after Darrell but was talked out of it by Joyce's brother, Robert.

Joyce went to Houston and not long afterward, in June of 1978, she and Darrell got a divorce. Darrell wanted the kids but he didn't even think of fighting for them, so Joyce got custody. The father almost never got custody in Stone County.

The divorce was rough on Darrell. He missed his kids desperately. He knew they'd gotten a rotten deal growing up with Joyce and him fighting all the time. He regretted not showing them more love and affection. As a father he'd been stingy with his emotions, distant, brusque, revealing just the tough outer shell of himself. He'd been raised thinking this was the proper way for fathers to behave. But now, having lost his kids, he wanted another chance. He wanted to make things right with them.

For a couple of years before Darrell and Joyce split up for good, they were living in a little two-room house Darrell had built on his forty acres in the hollow. The house was tiny and ramshackle, and the rust-streaked trailer Darrell had attached to an outside wall for extra space didn't add much in the way of glamour. But Darrell had meant this as a temporary arrangement only. During the waning months of his marriage he'd dug out a basement and laid a concrete foundation for the dream house he'd long planned on building. When the divorce was finalized he buried himself in the project, putting up walls, making a fireplace and a bathroom, trying to see the project through. He took carpentry work around the county whenever it came along, but mostly he could be found at his property, atop a steep rut road leading off Route 248, hammering and sawing away, drinking whiskey, listening to the Eagles and Creedence Clearwater Revival on a transistor radio. Anybody dropping by unexpectedly did so at his or her own risk. Like his grandfather Frank, Darrell didn't believe in overdressing for the occasion. His work boots and a tool belt: If the weather cooperated, why bother with anything else?

For entertainment there were always the cockfights, with an atmosphere straight out of a hillbilly's dream. The tangy smell of sweat and reefer, burgers on the grill, the friendly roughhousing, the calling and matching of bets—"Twenty on the red," "Fifty on black hat." And then the bouts themselves: the ten-second flurry, a riot of brown and red, the quick strike to the head maybe, lightning fast, long knife or gaff, payoff time. Or the drawn-out fight-to-the-finish down in the drag pit, the referee counting, marking the dirt with a stick, the birds beat up and bloodied, wobbling, pecking halfheartedly, too gone now for spur action, their handlers picking them up and sweet-talking them, cooing, cooing, blowing on their necks. Then back in the pit, the real test of mettle—*Bring it on, baby, let's see what you've got left*—more side bets all around.

Darrell loved the action and would go as often as two or three times a week. The open-air pit at Travis Clark's spread in Lampe, Lloyd Lawrence's arena down in Blue Eye on the Arkansas line, weekend jaunts to arenas in Oklahoma, occasionally all the way to Kellyville south of Tulsa, thirty to forty bouts on a card, up all night drinking, betting, kibitzing. Always the feeling that you were right in the thick of it, not missing a beat, hanging with the bad boys. Darrell knew all the big-time cockfighters in the area: Travis and Bush Clark, Wally Hall, Darrell's cousin Joe Dean Davis, who lived right across Route 248 in the hollow. And Lloyd Lawrence, the biggest operator of them all, a tough and wickedly gregarious guy from over near Shell Knob with deep connections to the game-bird racket nationwide. Most of them were dangerous men, working side deals, drugs, guns, testing the margins, seeing how much they could get away with, sometimes paying for their miscalculations with stints of state or federal time.

For sheer down-and-dirty kicks, the dogfights ran a close second. Most of the cockfighters also raised and trained pit bulls for contract fighting. There was nothing like it for speed and power: two highly conditioned forty-pound snarlers getting it on in a dirt ring over at Joe Dean's, maybe, or down at Travis Clark's. Darrell had always liked pit bulls, their spunk, their fearlessness, the real good ones, the gamers, with absolutely no quit in them. He'd raised several of the dogs himself over the years and he knew that the real champs always fought just as hard from the bottom as from the top. Something to keep in mind, he'd tell himself: a lesson worth drawing on somewhere down the line.

Life after Joyce, then, followed a predictable pattern: hanging out at the cock- and dogfights, getting high on whiskey and grass, working on his house in the hollow, taking paying jobs whenever opportunity came calling. And, of course, the old standbys: hunting, fishing, and shooting. This was pretty much the sum of it. Single again, his kids a thousand miles away in Houston, with no prospects and no plans, Darrell was living with a straitened sense of time, without thought for yesterday or tomorrow. Each day he faced the challenge of making ends meet, drumming up some fun and excitement, getting through the day—the challenge, quite simply, of being Darrell.

Being Darrell. In the years after Joyce this meant several things. There was, first of all, the Darrell open to public scrutiny, the Darrell most everyone thought they knew: Darrell the wisecracking hillbilly, curly black hair and beard, humorous, adventuresome, inveterate prankster, the life of the party, never one to turn down a dare. Darrell the good ole boy. But there was another, less obvious side to him that his buddies and the women he occasionally dated very rarely saw, and that he worked assiduously at covering up. Beneath the happy-go-lucky façade, Darrell was bleeding bitterness and resentment. He'd always been sensitive, alert to the tiniest of slights, but now he felt thoroughly put upon. He existed in an almost perpetual state of grievance. The marriage, Vietnam, the broken promises and lost opportunities: What had he done to deserve all this? What might he have done to prevent it? And the stupefying poverty—always broke, just scraping by. Was this what he had to look forward to? More of the same—and nothing else?

But this was stuff Darrell mostly kept to himself. More often than not, he played his good-ole-boy role to the hilt, drinking and carousing—nothing in moderation, everything to excess. Like the infamous donkey basketball game in Spokane, just a few miles up the road from Reeds Spring.

Playing donkey basketball was one of the ways good ole boys earned their stripes in the Ozarks, and so after finishing work and getting juiced one Friday evening Darrell and five of his pals swung by the school gym in Spokane and challenged the hometown boys to a contest. The hometown boys weren't impressed; these Reeds Spring castaways thinking they could beat them on their own turf, with the bleachers full and their wives and girlfriends cheering them on, no less. There was only one thing to do: accept the challenge and put the intruders in their place; make quick work of them. It shouldn't be too difficult. Just look at those clowns: too drunk, half of them, even to climb up on their donkeys.

Indeed, it was true. Of the Reeds Spring contingent, only Darrell and two other guys, Bruce Broomfield and Bobby Lewis, were able to answer the bell. Outnumbered by the hometown side seven to three, they looked to be in for a good thrashing. Fifteen minutes into the contest, however, Darrell knew his team couldn't lose. Pouring it on, up six to zip already, they were an unstoppable force. Everything was clicking; they'd taken only three shots—not so easy getting into position for a decent shot while commandeering a donkey—but made all three. Their donkeys, clad in the usual rubber boots to protect the hardwood floor, seemed to have a nose for the opposition basket. Normally it was a major accomplishment simply getting the animals pointed in the right direction, but tonight donkey and player, at least on Darrell's side, seemed almost of one mind.

Twenty minutes in, eight to zip now, Darrell's team was threatening to run away with it. Hooting and hollering, laughing and scratching—the rout was on. The fifth basket was the one that did it. When Bruce sank the shot that ran the score to ten to nothing, the scene turned ugly. Apparently the hometown side had taken as much humiliation as they could stand. Somebody knocked Bruce off his donkey with a straight-arm smash and then two other dudes started pummeling him on the floor. Darrell ran over to his buddy's rescue and got in a few good licks of his own before he, too, found himself on the floor with a tough dude named Wild Bill sitting on top of him windmilling at his face. Then half the bleachers emptied and a few dozen guys swarmed the court, everybody looking for a piece of the action. Darrell and his pals, bloodied and bruised, eventually made their way out to the parking lot and escaped in their pickups, but not before being warned against coming back. The local townsfolk didn't want heathen of their sort showing their faces in the Spokane school gym again.

In the spring of 1983 Darrell's cousin Joe Dean heard that the Shepherd of the Hills, an outdoor theater in Branson, was hiring new cast members. He suggested that the two of them drive down and see about signing on. Darrell figured he had nothing to lose.

Keith Thurman, the director of Shepherd of the Hills, was looking for extras to flesh out the scenery, real-lifers, guys who could more or less play themselves as authentic hillbillies. Darrell and Joe Dean were about as authentic as could be, but Thurman needed some convincing that they were the right men for the job.

"I guess I was particularly concerned about Darrell," he recalled. "I didn't know Darrell from Adam but the Mease boys from up around Reeds Spring had a reputation as being bad dudes, real ornery bastards. So at first I was a bit leery of Darrell. I thought we might have trouble with him. But I sat down and talked with him for ten or fifteen minutes, and then I knew for sure that we'd have no problems. He was as easygoing as anything, a real good guy. I liked him a lot right off."

Joe Dean quit after a few rehearsals but Darrell stuck it out for almost two full seasons. He played a Bald Knobber, which consisted mostly of riding horseback onto the open-air set in a cloud of menace. He was perfect for the role—so perfect, in fact, that during his second season the company featured his picture on the front cover of its promotional brochures. It was quite a picture, Darrell wearing a black cowboy hat, overalls, and a faded orange-and-white shirt, and looking down the bores of a cracked-open, double-barreled shotgun.

His second season was cut short when his horse bucked offstage, pinning him against a wall and fracturing his leg. The injury kept him from performing but not from whooping it up at the nightly cast parties. The parties were something to behold. When it came to letting their hair down, the Shepherd of the Hills folks took a back seat to no one. They'd close the bars in Branson as a warm-up and then really let loose at Big Rock on Bull Creek, a picnic and swimming spot near Walnut Shade. One night on the creek, the liquor flowing, someone started shooting off some powerful firecrackers, taking just about everybody by surprise. Keith Thurman remembers almost jumping out of his skin when the first firecracker went off and then finding Darrell huddled on the ground next to a pickup, screaming "Incoming! Incoming! Incoming!"

It was at one of these late-night boozefests on Bull Creek

that Darrell met Donna May. A large, attractive woman, about six feet and almost two hundred pounds, with bright eyes, long brown hair, and sculptured features, Donna wasn't difficult to pick out in a crowd. She inherited her size from her father, Bill, a giant of a man and a notorious quick-buck schemer, and her good looks from her mother, Jeanie, a sweet and elegant woman who played bass in a local swing combo. She'd come to the party with several friends from the cast but spent most of the night hanging out with Darrell. They hit it off pretty well, both of them big drinkers and big talkers, and before the week was through Donna had moved into Darrell's house in the hollow. A year later their daughter, Amanda, was born, and a second child, Tyler, was on the way by the time they finally got around to tying the knot.

Darrell's sister, Rita, who was married by this point and living in Michigan, remembers the wedding as a happy and hopeful occasion. "I'd been away for a while and kind of lost touch with my brother. I didn't really know Donna. She was a big woman, about ten years younger than Darrell, and really quite pretty. They got married on Halloween and the reception was in a big cave with a beautiful bonfire. They seemed really happy—almost shining."

It didn't take long for the shine to wear off. A month or so after the wedding Joyce phoned Lexie from Houston saying Darrell was welcome to come and pick up Melissa, Shane, and Wesley. She'd gotten remarried and was struggling to build a new life. The kids were more than she could handle. Darrell drove down to Houston with his cousin Dale, eager to get his kids back but determined to take no chances. Suspecting Joyce might be setting him up for an ambush, he arrived on her doorstep—in the scalding Houston heat, no less—wearing a military field coat with a bulletproof vest underneath. The precautions proved unnecessary. Joyce was grateful that he'd come and the three kids ran happily from the swimming pool in the yard to greet and hug him. They couldn't wait to get back home with their dad.

Back home—it wasn't what the three kids had been hoping for. Within a matter of weeks Darrell's forty acres in the hollow had become a militarized zone. Donna made it perfectly clear that she didn't want this added responsibility. She hadn't signed on to be cleaning up after Darrell's first marriage. They were crowded and destitute enough as it was without three more kids thrown into the bargain. But it *was* part of the bargain, Darrell insisted. Donna had always known that he'd jump at any chance to be reunited with his first three kids. He'd been up front with her about this from day one. Sure it was awkward, but they'd just have to make the best of it.

Instead of making the best of it, however, Donna and Darrell fell into endless bickering and all pretense of domestic civility soon vanished. Sometimes Darrell would try to cope with the tension by going emotionally AWOL, firing up a joint after work and hiding out in his bedroom. It was tough on Melissa and her two brothers, knowing full well that they were living where they weren't wanted. And it was tough on Donna, Darrell brooding half the time, fuming the other half, the kids—not even her own kids!—openly defying her, stretching her to the breaking point. Finally, Darrell arrived home from work one evening to discover that the kids were gone. There had been one altercation too many, and Melissa had phoned Lexie asking her to come get them and bring them to her and R.J.'s house.

And so that was that. The reunification experiment had ended up a dismal failure. Over the next few years Melissa and her brothers led a nomadic existence, shuttling back and forth between Lexie's place and Larry's, moving to Houston for a month here, a couple of months there, sometimes spending a troubled week or two (but not longer) with Darrell and Donna at the two-room house in the hollow.

It's difficult for Melissa, almost twenty years later, to think back on these unsettled times. Some of the details are scrambled, others mercifully forgotten. She remembers feeling most at home at R.J. and Lexie's house and wishing she and her brothers could have stayed there year-round. She also remembers silently rooting for her dad, this troubled man she'd never really gotten to know, all the while sensing he was fighting a losing battle. "Donna was big and strong and she'd fly off the handle and slug him. I never saw him hit her back, but there was probably a lot going on that I wasn't aware of. The thing was, I really couldn't discuss the situation with my dad. I couldn't confide in him. I loved him, and I knew he loved me, but we didn't have a bond of trust. He was gruff, drunk a lot of the time, stoned. So we were like strangers—father and daughter, but strangers. It's funny the things that stick in your mind, little things, stuff that stays with you. He had a pit bull named Diablo—I remember that. And the skull—he had a human skull on a ledge of the stonework in the basement of the new house he was building. It was wearing a purple knit hat and sunglasses and had a necklace draped around its base and a joint stuck in its mouth. That was my dad—I guess he had his own way of doing things."

Neither Darrell nor Donna had seen it coming, this onset of hostilities; it took them both by surprise. They'd actually been getting along quite well since hooking up at Bull Creek, not exactly lovebirds, but respectful and solicitous, neither one wanting to mess up what seemed a good thing. Darrell was happy to have a woman who gave every indication of being supportive and sympathetic; and Donna was pleased to have a man who, in her own words, was "sweet and witty and very thoughtful—a really considerate guy." But then the crash came and no more sweetness, no more sympathy, nothing but rancor and recrimination and a flaunting ugliness. There were the predictable scenes, booze-fueled, mouth-foaming confrontations—nothing quite so bad as Darrell and Joyce at their most harrowing, but nasty and unnerving enough. It eventually reached the point where simply spending time together proved, for both of them, an unendurable ordeal.

Looking back, Donna says that Darrell changed colors once they'd gotten married and the first blush of romance had faded, revealing a dark side that she hadn't imagined existed. He would sometimes fall prey to bottomless depression, burrowing into his bed for days at a time. Once she apparently found him lying naked, clutching a red wasp by the wings and stinging himself all over his body. Those days when he succeeded in rousing himself were hardly much better. He'd talk endlessly about Vietnam, getting shot at, never having a chance to shoot back, or else hunker down with his latest issue of *Soldier of Fortune* and fantasize aloud about becoming a mercenary or a hit man.

But living with Donna toward the end couldn't have been much fun either. By most accounts she had a ferocious temper and was fully capable, especially when drunk, of fighting like a man. She had a formidable arsenal, at one time or another breaking Darrell's nose with a head butt, blackening his eye with a sucker punch, and coming close to crowning him with a bowling pin. Only once did he return fire, an open-handed blow to the side of her head after she'd hit him from behind with a heavy purse. A friend once asked Darrell if what he'd heard was true, that Darrell had said he could whip Donna in a fair fight. "Nah, I never said that," Darrell answered. "What I said was *maybe* I could."

The embattled couple had plenty of people rooting for them to sort out their problems. Darrell's brother Larry thought that Donna was a fine person and just about everybody in Donna's family thought the same of Darrell. Her mother was especially fond of him. "I always really liked Darrell," Jeanie recalled. "I thought he was very, very nice— a sweet guy. I always got along well with him even though I knew he and Donna were having troubles." At Jeanie's suggestion, the couple gave marriage counseling a brief shot but by this point they were already too far gone for it to make any difference. In the spring of 1986 Donna finally called it quits, checking out of the little house in the hollow with her two kids, vowing never to return.

Once again it hit Darrell hard, maybe even harder than the first time with Joyce. A two-time loser in the marriage department, he now felt thoroughly defeated, a failure to his family and friends, a joke to himself. But even a failure and a joke has to carry on somehow, and the circumstances of

Darrell's life presented two obvious options: he could either take refuge in religion or throw in with the local outlaws. The second option won out easily. It didn't even require a change of clothes; Darrell was already almost there.

If an outlaw was what you were, or what you wanted to be, you couldn't go wrong hanging out at Joe Dean Davis's place, just a quarter mile down the hollow from the edge of town. Joe Dean knew practically every desperado in southwest Missouri, all of whom seemed to enjoy his company. And little wonder. He was a colorful guy, with a rich fund of amusing and lusty stories, and a talent for bending himself to the occasion, interacting with people on terms they felt most at ease with. He may have inherited this talent from his dad, Green Berry Davis, who was a born talker with an itch for politics. On those occasions when he was running for some local office or another, Green Berry would go canvassing door-to-door with a bag containing his campaign props: a Bible and a bottle of whiskey. Once invited inside he'd quickly size up the situation and then, depending on the proclivities of his hosts, he'd either take out the Good Book for some impromptu sermonizing or crack open the whiskey and settle in for an exchange of ribaldry. Either way, Green Berry would usually come off as a guy whom you'd feel comfortable trusting with your vote.

Joe Dean was a guy whom local outlaws felt comfortable trusting with their secrets. Cockfighters, bootleggers, drug dealers, gunslingers, counterfeiters: drop by his place often enough, you'd be sure to catch them all. It was a rare day when there weren't at least two or three dudes from the nether side of the law hanging out—sipping home brew, smoking grass, hatching schemes. And it was rare nowadays that Darrell wasn't hanging out with them. Darrell had always enjoyed visiting Joe Dean, one of his favorite cousins, and after his breakup with Donna, he was visiting more often and sticking around longer. Coming across the rickety old bridge onto Joe Dean's property and wending his way past the one-room log cabin, the fighting roosters in cages or tied up to leashes and scrabbling on the ground, the horses nickering in the makeshift corral—wending his way past all this glorious scruffiness and plopping down on the front porch of the little frame house set out back, he felt like he was exactly where he was supposed to be. He enjoyed rubbing shoulders with Joe Dean's outlaw pals, many of whom he'd known half his life anyway, and the outlaws seemed to enjoy rubbing shoulders with him. And why not? It wasn't as if he was lacking in outlaw credentials himself. Darrell had a reputation for being tough and fearless, and everybody knew he could shoot a pistol like ringing a bell. Everybody knew he was someone you'd want on your side in the rough going; definitely not a guy you'd want to risk antagonizing.

Some days Darrell would check into Joe Dean's in the early evening and then go out honky-tonking, hitting roadside joints all the way down to the Arkansas line. He might start out at the Nite Hawk in downtown Reeds Spring, a creaky old dive with a leaky roof, a place that only the rowdiest of townsfolk mourned when it finally burned to the ground. Then on to Betty's Tavern on Route 13 just south of town, a hard-core joint with a sign above the bar—CUSTOMERS MUST CHECK GUNS AND KNIVES WITH BARTENDER BEFORE BEING SERVED—that no one with any sense paid the slightest attention to. Just about everyone knew that sitting in Betty's unarmed was a serious health risk. He might wrap things up at Hoppy's, an outlaw hangout south of Kimberling City, with a few beers, a couple of games of pool, quarters in the jukebox, a little George Jones, some Allman Brothers, Stevie Ray Vaughan, Lynyrd Skynyrd. And then home, usually alone, Darrell not much of a lady's man at this point, with a little bit of a buzz on, just enough to beat back the demons for the night and hopefully grab some sleep.

As often as not these days Darrell was grabbing his sleep at Rocky Redford's house, about half a mile north of Reeds Spring Junction off U.S. 160. Rocky was a big, brash, good-looking guy with jet-black hair and smooth, clean features. He was also a full-time operator, sneaky smart, too smart maybe for his own good, working so many side deals that the main deal sometimes got lost in the shuffle. He'd moved to southwest Missouri from Hutchinson, Kansas, in the early 1980s and wound up dating Donna's mom for a spell, which is how he got to know Darrell. When things blew up with Donna, Darrell was stone-broke and depressed, and Rocky offered to put him up until he got back on his feet. The arrangement worked out pretty well for both men. Rocky provided the living expenses and the dope, and Darrell afforded Rocky the thrill of spending quality time with a bona fide Ozarks hillbilly.

Rocky had never come across anyone quite like Darrell. Even today, reflecting back on their times together, he can't help speaking of his old buddy in anything but near-mythic terms. "Darrell was one of the most impressive guys I've ever met—a free spirit, fiercely independent, the kind of guy who'll be there when the last dog gets killed. He used to say, 'What is, is; what ain't, ain't.' I've got these words written on my bedroom wall—a motto to live by. He was the best with pistols, *the best*; nobody else was even close. A lot of people—mean people—were afraid of Darrell because of his reputation. They assumed he was a tough guy, a hit man. It wasn't something Darrell cultivated. I doubt he was even aware he had this reputation. It's just the way he was—reckless and brave and the best shooter around. The word was out—everybody knew about Darrell. Once a guy from Louisiana owed my sister money and she asked me to collect for her. I went and told the guy to write a check. The guy said no. I said, okay, today's Tuesday, if I don't get paid by tomorrow, on Thursday I'll talk to Darrell about it. The guy paid right off."

Rocky's younger brother, Rick, a brash, sweet-talking hotshot in his own right, was also down from Kansas trying his luck in the Missouri Ozarks at the time. Rick and Darrell would eventually become the best of friends, but their initial encounter, as Rick recounts in a recent letter from prison, was a real eye-opener.

"Darrell walked into the living room of my brother's house, wearing a pair of boots that didn't match. We smoked some agricultural products. I then witnessed Darrell eat what I remember to be a gallon of chocolate ice cream, while simultaneously sipping on a cheap bottle of wine. To this very day, I can still envision within the framework of my mind those different colored boots; the carton of ice cream; the purple-colored wine; and Darrell with long, scraggly hair, with a full beard the length of Jeremiah Johnson's. Although I do not remember the precise year, I can tell you this: It was shortly after I had seen the movie *Deliverance* about a trio of companions taking a canoe trip together in 'hillbilly country.' That night at my brother's house, as I kept looking over at Darrell devouring his ice cream, continuing to inhale, it dawned on me. Darrell reminded me an awful lot of the pair of hillbillies in *Deliverance*—the same mountain men who ended up buggering Ned Beatty. Needless to say, even if Darrell had asked, there was no way in Dante's Inferno that I was canoeing that night."

Mismatched boots and all, Darrell seems to have attracted a great deal more admiration than scorn during these rough-and-tumble days. Rick and Rocky's brother-in-law, Jae Jones, who currently manages the radio station at the College of the Ozarks, wasn't alone in seeing him as a kind of hillbilly icon, a throwback to a simpler, more primitive era.

"I was working at Silver Dollar City and dating Rocky's sister, Debbie, when I got to know Darrell," Jae said recently. "He was a real character, a real colorful figure in the Ozarks. I found him amazing. Darrell intimidated some people but to me he was more of a protector. He said to me, 'Jae, I'm going to be your friend whether you like it or not.' He was a complex guy. He would talk to me about poetry and history but he was also an outlaw, a by-God Rambo. Don't think Darrell couldn't hand you your heart in a second. Darrell could walk the walk. People weren't inclined to mess with him. But once you got to know Darrell, you couldn't help being fond of him. There was nobody like him. We'd be canoeing on Swan Creek and Darrell would go swimming and catch two or three little turtles and put them in his mouth and then swim back and stick his tongue out and show them to us. I could sit here all day telling you stories about Darrell. Because here's the thing: Darrell was one of the last true hill people. He exemplified the best of hill culture. He was honest and quick-witted. He could live off the land. He was good with his hands, a hell of a stonemason and carpenter, an excellent horseman. He knew so much about animal and plant life. This is a precious, dying culture down here. The old-time hillbillies are dying out. Darrell was one of the last of the old breed. I sometimes think he was born fifty years too late, a hundred years too late."

A funny and loyal friend. A larger-than-life, honest-to-goodness hillbilly. A reckless and dangerous dude. Darrell was all of these things. He was so unselfconscious, however, and so stoked up half the time on drugs and booze, that he wasn't fully aware of being any of them. He had little idea what kind of impact he was having on the people around him. He was a legend in the making, and maybe one of the only people in Stone County not clued in to it. And the stories abounded.

"Say, did you hear about the three pilgrims dropping by Darrell's house up in the hollow? They're all pretty tanked and, anyway, the talk soon turns to guns or shooting or some such. Well, Darrell's always got guns close at hand, loaded to the brim, and he reaches under a cushion on the sofa and pulls out a .22 pistol. The pilgrims follow suit and before you know it they're each holding a pistol of Darrell's. Old Darrell—he says, 'Boys, these pistols are all loaded. Let's put them back now.' One guy's waving a .44 Magnum in the air and he says, 'No, they're not.' Now Darrell wants to prove his point before somebody gets hurt so he fires a shot through his front window. Takes the pane right out. The pilgrims meekly put the guns down and slink on out of there. That's Darrell, boy, seizing control of the situation."

"Hey, and what about Canadian Pete? Now there's a guy who bit off more than he could chew. They're sitting at Rocky's kitchen table cleaning guns and Pete takes up a pistol and aims it at Darrell's head. Darrell looks at him hard and says point it somewhere else but Pete just chuckles and says, 'What's your problem, man? This one ain't even loaded.' 'Yeah, but this one is,' Darrell says, cocking a .22 and drawing a bead on Pete's forehead. Pete's not the fastest learner but this speeded him right up."

At any given time there were always at least a dozen Darrell-isms making the rounds. Some were apocryphal; most were true. Even those that perhaps weren't literally true just as well could have been. No one would have been surprised by anything Darrell did.

In early 1987 Darrell started using crank, methamphetamine. He bought his first line from his cousin Leonard Joe Graves, and before long he was snorting as often as he could. The sense of exhilaration, the surge of energy: Where had this stuff been all his life? He'd get high and then come down and scuffle about for money so he could afford to get high again.

Darrell and crank: no big surprise—in some ways, it was a connection just waiting to happen. By 1987 half the guys Darrell knew were into meth. He couldn't have avoided the stuff even if he'd wanted to. Everywhere he went somebody was bound to be cranking. Joe Dean Davis, just out from a nine-month stint behind bars for growing marijuana, was doing it. So were Rocky Redford and a dozen of Darrell's other running buddies. Almost overnight meth had become the drug of choice for outlaws in southwest Missouri and the easiest thing in the world to score. You wanted a gram of high-grade stuff for a hundred bucks or less? No problem: show up at the cock- or dogfights, or sidle into a broken-down jukejoint—you'd be taken care of, guaranteed.

Something else guaranteed: the crank you purchased at the cock- or dogfights or the local jukejoint was certain to have been produced locally. There was no need to import the stuff. By the late 1980s the Ozarks were jumping with illegal meth labs. They were everywhere and nowhere, tucked into the mist-shrouded hills, hidden away on rancid farm property, invisible to everyone save the outlaws who ran them and the few dedicated lawmen who sought to root them out.

The main wheel behind all this illegal meth production was Lloyd Lawrence, the region's most prominent cock-fighting promoter. It was through cockfighting, apparently, that Lloyd first became involved with meth. He'd feed the stuff to his game birds to get them hyped up for their bouts. There was obviously an untapped market out there—if the chickens dug it so much, what about humans? A risky business, to be sure, but since when had Lloyd been averse to risk?

According to the people who hung out with him, Lloyd was a junkie for risks. He loved the action, rolling the dice, camping out on the precipice. Most of all, he loved getting his own way, and heaven help the person who tried to stop him. A lifelong resident of the Shell Knob area, near the border between Stone and Barry Counties, and an army veteran of World War II and Korea, he'd made a name for himself locally doing whatever he wanted, however he wanted. You'd never guess it from his appearance, short and chunky and grandfatherly, but Lloyd commanded the respect of even the meanest outlaws in the area. He was a bully, tough and ruthless, but he also possessed a certain noblesse oblige. Swaggering through the Ozarks, lord of the realm, he'd routinely dispense favors to anyone fortunate enough to be in his good graces. He'd buy cars and trucks and four-wheelers for family members and friends, he'd take people on weekend jaunts to the cockfights in Oklahoma and put them up in his trailer, he'd drop off gifts of money or booze to old cronies he knew were down on their luck. He had connections in the construction business, and once he took Joe Dean Davis up to Springfield, got him signed on with the carpentry union, and landed him a job paying four hundred dollars a week. Joe Dean had never had a regular job that paid as much as fifty dollars a week. But Lloyd was Lloyd, and sooner or later there was always a price to pay. He rarely lost track of who was in his debt.

Lloyd wasn't averse to risk, but when running his crank empire he was smart enough to parcel out as much of it as he could. He provided the working capital, the lab equipment and raw materials, and the recipe for cooking meth, leaving most of the actual production to others. He franchised, setting up various associates in clandestine meth labs throughout the region. Once the cooking was done he'd arrange for pickup and distribution. It seemed an almost foolproof system. The authorities weren't likely to get in the way. Law enforcement in most parts of southwest Missouri was sparse, shoddy, and corrupt. In any event, if a problem should arise in this direction, Lloyd knew which levers to pull to smooth things over. And if any of his own people should be so reckless as to think of ripping him off, Lloyd had plenty of muscle at his disposal. A late-night visit from Kendall Schwyhart or some other five-star enforcer was not something to look forward to. The anticipation alone could kill you.

Rocky couldn't be faulted for showing an interest. He was in a transitional phase, working at the Radio Shack down in Branson while plotting his next move. The job itself wasn't much but his new co-worker certainly made clocking in easier. Mary Epps was very pretty. Not yet nineteen, with light brown hair and pouty lips, she was a delightful nine-to-five bonus Rocky hadn't been counting on.

Mary seemed kind of in transition herself. She'd been raised in Branson, on the right side of the tracks, the oldest of two kids. Her parents were fixtures in the area. Fred Epps was smart and gruff—a shrewd businessman. His wife, Barbara, was strong-willed, bold, and brassy—and a tireless worker. Together, practically from scratch, they'd built a highly successful trash and recycling business in town. Growing up, Mary hadn't presented many problems beyond the usual, but in her last year at Branson High she'd started ruffling the waters. Nothing too serious, typical teenage strut-about, but enough to earn her notice as something of a wild child. In the 1986 edition of the *Buccaneer*, her high-school yearbook, there was a "Who's Who" section dedicated to graduating seniors. Among the timid photographs with their earnest captions ("Most Likely to Succeed,"

"Most Athletic," "Most Studious"—the usual sort of thing),
Mary stood out like a gangster at a garden party. There she
was, posing in a faux mug shot behind a Branson Police Department sign, with the caption underneath reading "Most
Unpredictable."

A tough caption to live up to, but Mary seemed determined to give it her best shot. After graduating high school
she took some courses at the College of the Ozarks and also
at Crowder College near Neosho and then, in early 1987, she
found herself working at the Radio Shack alongside Rocky.
Ever alert to romantic possibilities, Rocky wasted little time
chatting Mary up, and he soon discovered that she was fascinated by, among other things, guns and outlaws. She even
had a couple of outlaws in her own family. Her Uncle Dave,
on her mom's side, had ridden with a tough biker gang at
one point, and her cousin Red Stephens would eventually receive a life sentence for killing a Reeds Spring deputy. Guns
and outlaws: subjects with which Rocky had more than a
passing familiarity. Attempting to impress her, he regaled
Mary with stories of his best friend, Darrell. Now there was
an outlaw, an outlaw to beat all outlaws—Darrell, fearless,
reckless, way out there, beyond the pale, the last of the true
wild men. And guns? Nobody knew more about guns than
Darrell. Nobody was a better shot. Darrell was Davy Crock-
ett and Jesse James and Wild Bill Hickok rolled up into one.

Rocky succeeded in impressing Mary all right, but not in
precisely the direction he'd intended. Forget about Rocky:
Mary now had her heart set on meeting Darrell. She got her
chance in early March 1987 when the wild man himself
dropped by Radio Shack. Mary came out of the back room,
sure of herself, playing it coy, and walked right up to Darrell
and looked him in the eye. Darrell shot her a smile, which
she didn't return. He thought she might be sizing him up.
She went behind the counter and he followed her over and
they had a nice chat. Her nineteenth birthday was coming up
and some friends were throwing her a party. She invited
Darrell to come by.

Which he did—a week or so afterward. He came by and

wished her a happy birthday and she gave him a big hug. Darrell was pleased but at the same time he didn't want to get his hopes up too high. She hadn't as yet singled him out for special attention. He couldn't help noticing that she was hugging just about everybody in sight.

Then Mary started visiting Rocky's house and hanging out for hours at a time with the ragtag band of outlaws and country grifters that was usually knocking about. One evening she announced that she was going over by Crowder College to look up some old acquaintances. She said that she wouldn't mind some company. "I bet Darrell's not afraid to come with me," she added. Indeed he wasn't, though he thought it best not to go unprepared. From the way she'd put it, he suspected there was trouble at the other end and she wanted him along to fight somebody. He brought a pair of black leather sap gloves packed with lead dust—just in case. As it turned out, he didn't need the gloves. They drove to Neosho and met some of Mary's friends in a bar. It was a nice time. They didn't get back to the Branson area until the wee hours.

A couple of weeks later Darrell finally worked up the nerve to ask Mary out on a real honest-to-goodness date. He took her to Old Spanish Cave north of the junction, the very same cave that his grandfather Frank had opened to the public decades before. They smoked a little dope, walked with a flashlight through the damp and murky chambers, and then sat on a flat-topped rock near the entrance holding hands and talking. Toward three in the morning, just before he took her home, he tried kissing her, but Mary playfully moved her head from side to side, preventing him from making flush contact with her mouth. Incredible, Darrell thought. He wasn't even getting a kiss out of the deal and yet he couldn't remember feeling so happy, so satisfied.

Over the next several months they were rarely apart for longer than a day. Mary would come to Darrell's house after work and usually wouldn't get back to her folks' place in Branson until well past midnight. Their fledgling romance soon became the subject of considerable speculation. What could pretty, young, middle-class Mary possibly see in Darrell? Here was a guy with five kids and two disastrous marriages in his past, a guy more than twenty years her senior with no money and no game plan. So why was she interested in an unkempt, down-on-his-heels hillbilly? Quite a few people in the area chalked it up to meth. Darrell was into meth in a big way and, probably, so was she. Darrell was her ticket to a regular supply of the stuff. Trading sex for drugs—that would explain it. They had Mary pegged as a crank whore.

Actually, this was far from explaining it. Mary sampled crank a few times after taking up with Darrell—but that was it. She didn't really like the stuff and she couldn't understand its big attraction. And even if she were a crankhead looking to swap sex for drugs, there were plenty of other guys in the area who would have been thrilled to oblige her. No need to settle for Darrell: she could have taken her pick.

Crank, it would seem, was only a small part of it. In all likelihood Mary found Darrell attractive for some of the same reasons others did. He was smart and witty and still capable, despite all his rough mileage, of turning on the boyish charm. And for Mary, of course, there was an added inducement: outlaws fascinated her, and Darrell happened to be one of the more engaging outlaws around. So engaging, in fact, that she was soon entertaining fantasies of becoming an outlaw herself. Some nights they'd sit up late talking about partnering in a life of crime, hitting the road as a latter-day Bonnie and Clyde. It's possible, of course, that such talk was only so much bluff and blather. Perhaps even Darrell and Mary weren't sure how seriously to take it.

For all of his shenanigans over the years, Darrell had somehow managed to keep himself impressively, if not quite spotlessly, clean. There'd been a drunk-driving incident, one or two other minor scrapes—nothing much else. In his most memorable run-in with the law prior to 1987 he'd actually been the victim of someone else's craziness.

One evening during their first summer together Darrell

and Donna had joined Larry and Sophia for a picnic at Big Rock on Bull Creek. Sophia's two sisters were there also, and a whole flock of kids. They were relaxing in lawn chairs around a small fire on a gravel bar by the water when two men in a pickup blustered in and drove right through their camp, giving Darrell and Larry the evil eye while passing by. Darrell recognized the driver, a low-grade troublemaker named John Wright III who'd recently moved into a place just up the creek. A bit later, more than a little put off by this intrusion, Darrell walked to the edge of the property where Wright was living and yanked up a loose corner post with a NO TRESPASSING sign nailed to it. He carried the post back to the picnic spot and threw it on the fire. Not a bad move, you might think, except ten or fifteen minutes later Wright returned with a .45 semiautomatic pistol.

"There's a rifle in the brush on your heart right now," he said. "Make a move, me and my partner will drop you and everybody else here like flies."

Wright told Darrell to hand over his pistol, a .22 Ruger, and then he marched both Mease boys up the road, speculating aloud as to whether he should call the sheriff and have them charged with trespassing or just shoot them both on the spot and be done with it. If he was expecting Darrell and Larry to break down and plead for mercy, he obviously hadn't done his homework. Neither one gave any indication of being intimidated. Perhaps realizing he'd jumped the wrong crew, he eventually backed off and let them go. But Darrell was seething. He and Larry had just been kidnapped at gunpoint and the same guy who'd done the kidnapping had also threatened to kill their wives and kids. That evening he put in a call to the sheriff's department in Forsyth and lodged a complaint. It went against his grain, going the legal route rather than squaring matters with Wright on his own, but this was one time he couldn't see himself losing. A few weeks later there was a hearing on the affair at the courthouse in Forsyth but nothing came of it. Wright was never prosecuted for the kidnapping and Darrell was left wondering why he'd bothered going to the law in the first place.

But now it was two years later and Darrell was driving over to Rocky's house one evening in early June to pick up a package that was waiting for him and to rendezvous with Mary. He was excited about seeing Mary but a bit annoyed with himself for not having arranged to meet her elsewhere Rocky had been getting on his nerves lately—little things, nothing that jumped out at you, but add it all up and the guy had definitely become a full-time hassle. It was aggravating enough that he'd chintzed Darrell out of the profits on a couple of deals, but he'd also been getting in the way where Mary was concerned. Just a week or so earlier, for example, Darrell had been over by Cape Fair, selling fireworks for Rocky out of a tent. He'd been counting on Rocky picking him up around ten and driving him back to Reeds Spring for a date with Mary. He'd mentioned it three or four times, saying he didn't want to keep Mary waiting, and Rocky had assured him he'd be there. But he didn't show up and Darrell was forced to start walking home. He stopped off for a beer at a roadside tavern a couple of miles along and the barmaid drove him the rest of the way. But it was too late. Mary was gone, no doubt thinking she'd been stood up. And Rocky? He was probably off somewhere gloating.

So Darrell was driving down the dirt road off U.S. 160 toward Rocky's when a Bronco with a big guy in sunglasses behind the wheel, Rocky beside him, two other men in back, shot past going the other way. Darrell didn't like the looks of this but he drove on anyway, not wanting to be late for Mary. Around the last bend the road was blocked by half a dozen lawmen dressed in black. They pulled him over and found an unlicensed Smith & Wesson .38 Special under the seat and a thimble-sized bud of marijuana in his jacket pocket. They proceeded to cuff him and haul him off to the Taney County jail where he was thrown into a cell with Rocky.

Rocky said that his place was raided about an hour before Darrell came along and that the cops found a patch of marijuana he was growing in the milk barn out back. Darrell could tell that Rocky was upset but he had enough worries of his own right now. The weed-in-the-jacket bust he could live with, a mere misdemeanor, but carrying a concealed and un-licensed weapon was a felony offense. Not only that, but a couple of months back he'd hidden a sawed-off shotgun un-der a piece of folded carpet in Rocky's spare bedroom. If the cops found it he could be facing a stint of federal time—pro-viding, of course, he didn't let Rocky take the rap instead.

Sticky business, but Darrell actually came out of it in pretty good shape. The cops didn't find the sawed-off shot-gun and Taney County prosecutor Jim Justus let him off with a deferred prosecution on the misdemeanor possession charge. The felony weapon charge was dismissed on pay-ment of a $73 fine, not to mention a stern warning from Judge Joe Chowning against Darrell ever getting caught with a gun in Taney County again. He had to cough up a thousand dollars to his attorney, Steve Soutee, for pulling the right levers but, all things considered, it could have turned out a lot worse.

One evening in late fall Mary got snowed in at Darrell's house. She didn't make it home that night, or the two follow-ing nights. When she finally did get back to Branson, her mom delivered an ultimatum: *It's either him or me. You choose.* Mary packed some things and drove back to Dar-rell's with her two dogs—a pit bull named Slick and a little Benji-type dog named Gretchen Louise. She asked if he'd mind her and the dogs moving in with him full-time. *Mind it?* It was like asking a kid if he'd mind getting the Christ-mas present he'd been goggling in his dreams for months.

Darrell was badly smitten by this point but he still couldn't bring himself to say the magic words. He'd been holding back, fearful of looking foolish, and not wanting to expose himself to rejection. He worried that Mary was too good to be true. This sweetheart straight out of dreamland, so patient and tender: What was she doing with *him*? She'd floated into his world unexpectedly and there was no telling how long she'd stay around. Most things in his life, the things that truly counted, had ended in disaster. Was he set-ting himself up for another crash now? Within a couple of days of her moving in, his anxieties finally got the better of him and he tried running her off. It's no use, he cried, practically shoving her out the door. This thing can't work. Look at the age difference. Look at the financial situation. Look at—*everything*. He stood trembling inside the house, screaming silently over what he'd done, but twenty minutes later she was back, holding him in her arms and saying, "Baby, I couldn't stay away." The next night, lying in bed, he told her for the first time that he loved her. She said that she loved him, too.

As a couple Darrell and Mary still weren't drawing many rave reviews, but not everyone regarded them as hopelessly mismatched. Darrell's daughter, Melissa, remembers seeing them together for the first time at her grandparents' house and thinking that they were actually a pretty good fit. "It was right after they'd started living together. They came in, and my first impression was that they belonged together. Mary had curly blond hair and she was really young, just two years older than I was, but at the time the age thing didn't really hit me. She was wearing jeans and a T-shirt, very casual, and she seemed unconcerned about her appearance. I thought, 'Mary's exactly like my dad; she's another Darrell.' They both looked like they'd just flopped out of bed. I'm not saying they didn't have their problems, but I had a good feeling seeing them together that day."

They did indeed have their problems, none more nagging than Darrell's continued meth use. He hadn't slowed down since meeting Mary, even though she'd told him a number of times that she didn't like him cranking and wanted him to cut it out. One evening, disgusted with him for getting high yet again, she said, "I don't know why I fell in love with you. I could have married a lawyer or a doctor and kicked back."

On another evening, a few days after Mary moved in, Darrell was hanging out in Reeds Spring with Leonard Joe Graves. Leonard Joe suggested that they drive up to Spank's, a one-stop convenience store north of the junction, and grab a couple of pops. Spank's carried some off-brand soda that

Darrell really liked—not to mention the most delicious soft ice cream around. So off they went. Leonard Joe asked Darrell to wait outside with the car while he ran in for the pop. A few minutes later he came back out with Lloyd Lawrence. Lloyd had recently purchased a secluded farm off U.S. 160, not far from where Rocky was living. He was fixing it up, building a new cabin, laying down a road, making a weekend retreat out of the place. He told Darrell he'd put him to work on the property for four bucks an hour. Odd jobs mostly, Lloyd said, "Helping my guys out, handing them nails, tin, lumber, that sort of thing." Darrell bridled at the odd-jobs part, but he said fine, he'd take the job. He definitely needed the four bucks an hour and, besides, Lloyd wasn't a guy accustomed to taking no for an answer.

Darrell started the very next day and kept at it for a few weeks, clearing brush, thinning out trees with his chain saw, building chicken pens, helping Lloyd's guys install a tin roof on the cabin. Lloyd would stop by now and then to check up on things, but mostly to spend time with his grandson Willie. He had a soft spot for Willie, who was his oldest son, Buck's, boy. A good looking eighteen-year-old, Willie had been paralyzed from the waist down in a car wreck a couple of years earlier. He'd had several setbacks since then, once suffering burns to his wasted feet from the overheated muffler of an old jalopy he'd been cruising in with friends. In recent weeks he'd been coming to the farm quite often and buzzing around the property in an all-terrain vehicle. The four-wheeler gave him some mobility—a small measure of independence. Lloyd or Buck would secure him to the vehicle by tying the laces of his sneakers to the front rack, and then Willie would take off in a swirl of dust along the back roads.

Lloyd's wife, Frankie, was there most days, too. A big, eager-to-please woman, Frankie had married Lloyd in 1947, right after her seventeenth birthday. Over the years she'd gained a reputation, especially where her marriage was concerned, for patience and loyalty. Lloyd hadn't always been the most compliant or reliable of husbands, but no one could recall Frankie complaining, at least not in public. The farm, which was shaping up as a nice weekend getaway for the entire family, may have been a reward of sorts for her long endurance.

Darrell was happy for the work but he could have done without Lloyd's snide attitude. His gloating over hiring him on the cheap, never missing a chance to put him in his place, made Darrell bristle inside. One day Travis Clark, a guy Darrell liked and respected, came by. Lloyd brought him over to where Darrell was working on some chicken pens, chortling about how he was paying Darrell four bucks an hour, a buck less than Travis had paid him for a job a few months earlier, saying it just loud enough for Darrell to overhear.

At the end of the second week Lloyd dropped by Darrell's place uninvited and took a good look around. He liked what he saw: just one entry road, the shed out back, lots of privacy—the place definitely had possibilities.

"You want to make some money?" Lloyd said. "I'm talking big money, like you never even dreamed of."

Darrell pulled up a chair, having a pretty good idea of what was coming, and Lloyd laid out the deal. He'd set up a crank lab in the shed behind the house and the two of them would work it together. For the first little while Lloyd would take care of the actual cooking, but as soon as Darrell proved his mettle, Lloyd would teach him the tricks of the trade and Darrell could go into business for himself. And there was no limit to how much money he could be pulling in.

Darrell didn't need much convincing. He'd been broke or just barely scraping by for years now and lately he'd been feeling the pressure even more than usual. He was behind in his child support and Joyce, who'd recently moved back to the area and taken charge of their three kids, was threatening to turn up the legal heat. And then there was Mary. He knew that Mary wasn't accustomed, day after day, to running practically on empty. He wanted to fix her up with the kind of lifestyle she deserved.

Darrell wasn't kidding himself. He knew it was more

than just the money. He felt flattered that the big man had singled him out. He felt privileged—and grateful. Sure he'd had his problems with Lloyd, but that was all water under the bridge now. Everybody knew Lloyd was the golden goose. He could make you rich, and he could also do wonders for your self-esteem. To be chosen by Lloyd—it wasn't just the opportunity of a lifetime; it was a badge of outlaw distinction.

So Lloyd set up shop in the shed behind Darrell's house and the two of them went to work. Just a couple of weeks into the deal, however, it was starting to look like a serious mistake. Mary certainly thought so: she'd been opposed from the start to Darrell teaming with Lloyd and nothing she'd seen so far had caused her to change her mind. It was partly the drugs, the last thing she wanted Darrell getting involved with, but a lot of it was Lloyd himself. It wasn't anything in particular he'd said or done, but the guy somehow frightened her, unnerved her. He seemed to ooze lascivious menace. The way he looked at her when he came around, like he was staking his claim—*Later, baby, later, just wait and see.* The guy was obviously bad news. She told Darrell to break it off before he got in any deeper.

Darrell knew he shouldn't take Mary's concerns lightly. He'd heard the stories about Lloyd, his penchant for pretty young women, turning them into crank whores so they'd do his bidding. And now he remembered something else, rumors from long ago about Lloyd actually raping two of his own daughters. Like a lot of other people, he'd discounted the rumors at the time. But now Mary—his very own sweet Mary—was claiming to feel threatened by the guy. Chances were it wasn't just her imagination.

There was something else bothering Darrell, frustrating him no end. It was two weeks into the deal now, and Lloyd still hadn't given any indication of delivering on his promise. Teaching him the tricks of the trade? Turning him on to the recipe for crank so he could go freelance and start raking in the money himself? Forget about it. Two weeks in and he was still nothing more than a glorified gopher, helping Lloyd out, running errands for him, standing in as the butt of his putdowns. He'd tried bringing the subject up once or twice but Lloyd had just mumbled him off.

"I don't know if he's ever going to come through," Darrell told Mary. "It's like he just wants to keep the apple in front of my face."

There were additional tensions also, mostly of the you'd-have-to-be-there variety. Lloyd owned a beautiful Jack Russell terrier that he knew Darrell really liked. He offered the dog to Darrell as a gift but never quite got around to turning it over. It was always, "Not now, maybe later." Power tripping, Darrell thought, stringing him along, just another way of showing who was boss. Then one night, a week or so before Christmas, Darrell and Mary were awakened by the sounds of someone creeping around outside. They weren't able to pin it on him for sure, but they both assumed it had to be Lloyd. Lloyd the pervert—skulking about for cheap thrills.

But they kept at it, Darrell and Lloyd, two strong-headed outlaws not accustomed to budging an inch: Darrell stewing over whether he'd ever get his big break; Lloyd probably not caring one way or another.

PART
TWO

PART
TWO

FOUR

The day after Christmas of 1987, Lloyd dropped by Darrell's house with some meth, a special confection he said he'd cooked up for Darrell as a present. It was strange stuff, pink and gummy, and wickedly acrid. Darrell and Mary had never seen or smelled anything like it. After Lloyd left, Darrell dipped right in. It was too gummy to snort so he peeled off a big piece and stuck it inside his bottom lip next to his teeth. That way he knew it would work fast—get right into his system.

Darrell had already been up two straight nights cranking. He prided himself on having a high level of tolerance for meth, never showing the effects, never losing control. But this new stuff—it hit him in the chest like an iron fist. Before long he was pacing, back and forth, back and forth, *can't stop, can't stop now*, his heart thumping, fast and loud, fast, fast, fast and heavy, feeling like it was going to implode at any second and rip him to bits. Several hours of this, exhausted, feeling like he was dying, Darrell stretched out with his back on the floor and lay there the rest of the night, not moving, his eyes sealed shut, babbling, talking who-knows-what. Mary sat on the couch crying, scared and confused, with no idea what she was supposed to do. She tried prying his eyes open a few times but she couldn't bring him back. Darrell lay there moaning and jabbering, flickering in and out of reality. He heard Mary crying and he thought she might leave him. He was lying there weak and helpless. Mary didn't need this action. There was nothing stopping her from throwing her things together and going back home to her folks in Branson. He didn't want her to leave, he desperately hoped she wouldn't, but there was nothing stopping her. It might be the only good move she had left.

Sometime the next day Darrell opened his eyes and asked Mary to help him. "Please help me," he pleaded. "Please do something." She got him to his feet and took him outside and loaded him into her '80 Dodge. She considered taking him to the hospital in Branson but decided against it. It was too risky. It might spark an investigation into his dealings with Lloyd. She decided to take him to Lloyd's house near Shell Knob instead. She hated the thought of taking him down there and having to ask Lloyd for help, but she figured she had no choice. Surely Lloyd, of all people, would know how to deal with someone overdosing on bad crank.

They made it to Lloyd's just as he was leaving for the cockfights. He took them to a trailer out back and stood there by the door, looking at Darrell, looking at Mary, *really* looking at Mary, checking her out good. He told them to stay put. When he got home later, at two or three in the morning, he'd see how Darrell was doing and then drive with Mary to Darrell's house to pick up the crank that was waiting for him. "Does she know where it's hidden?" he asked Darrell, like Mary wasn't capable of speaking for herself. "Yeah, she knows," Darrell said.

Mary didn't like the looks of the situation. She'd never trusted Lloyd, she'd always expected the worst of him, and now she felt completely spooked with him standing there, so smug, so sure of himself, eyeballing her and Darrell. Darrell liked it even less. He was still sick, weak, and woozy, but he saw Lloyd dialing in on Mary and he knew they wouldn't be staying. There was no way they were going to stay and wait for Lloyd to finish off whatever he'd started.

Not long after Lloyd left, Mary put Darrell back into the Dodge and they headed for Reeds Spring. They talked about it along the way, driving east on Route 86 and up Route 13 past Lampe and Kimberling City. Now everything was taking shape. The bad meth, the tainted meth—whatever it was—hadn't been an accident. Lloyd was out to get Darrell. He wanted to hurt him, punish him, maybe even kill him. Both Mary and Darrell were certain of this. And Darrell was certain of something else besides: Lloyd was after Mary. He'd probably been after Mary since he first saw her. He was waiting for his chance—no, not just waiting, he was plotting it out, planning on getting her by herself so he could rape her, get her wired, turn her into his own little crank whore. And he could do it, too. No doubt about it—if they gave him half a chance, Lloyd could pull it off. In Stone County, Lloyd could get away with just about anything. In Stone County, Lloyd Lawrence was boss.

By the time they got back to Reeds Spring, Darrell and Mary had decided to break and run. If they stayed in Stone County, anywhere in the vicinity, they'd be sitting ducks. They loaded the car with clothes, guns, and traveling gear and put Mary's dogs in the back seat. Darrell went out to the shed and grabbed four pounds of powdered meth that Lloyd had lovingly wrapped in eight clear plastic bags. This was finished product, the stuff that Darrell had helped Lloyd cook the previous week or two. He reckoned it had to be worth at least fifty grand on the street—maybe twice that much. For good measure he grabbed two sixteen-ounce Pepsi and two sixteen-ounce Mountain Dew bottles containing P2P, the brown liquid substance that's used in the manufacture of meth. Somewhere down the line, maybe, he'd be able to sell this stuff and kiss the life of poverty goodbye. He shoved everything into a backpack and tossed it in the car.

Darrell was buzzing now, still disoriented but no longer feeling like he'd swallowed a live grenade. It was time to move. He didn't want to leave by his front road, in case Lloyd and some of his boys were keeping watch, so he had Mary drive the Dodge through the brush out back while he walked ahead clearing a path for it with his machete. Once they hit pavement they made their way over to Keystone

Ridge Road, the old fire tower road up by Reeds Spring Junction. They drove down it a short stretch, and then Darrell walked into the woods and hid the backpack with Lloyd's drugs in the crook of a tree. The stuff was too hot to handle. He'd come back for it later.

It was dark now. They were running but they still didn't know exactly where to. They only had fifty bucks in cash and the gas gauge was near empty. Needing someplace where they could cool off and get their bearings, maybe catch a little sleep, they made their way up U.S. 160 and over to Ponce de Leon, a crestfallen little town once famous locally for its medicinal springs. They spent the night in Ponce, the Dodge parked out of sight beside an old barn.

The next morning Mary couldn't believe it. Darrell had taken some of that bad gummy crank with him, and it looked like he'd been into it again. He was flying, sky-high. The damn stuff had almost killed him yet he couldn't keep his snout out of the trough. Crazy—just too crazy.

The next couple of days were nothing but crazy. Darrell was confused and manic. He had them running around in circles. He wanted to cross over into Arkansas but he picked a dirt road down by the state line south of Hollister that had gotten muddied by the early-winter rains. He had to jack the car up and push it forward a dozen times or more before they finally got back onto a paved road. Giving up on Arkansas, they headed north and west with the idea of hitting Kansas and then working their way across to Colorado. They hit Kansas but then Darrell insisted on turning around and going back to Missouri so he could deal with Lloyd. Why wait for Lloyd to come after them? he argued. This would just be playing into Lloyd's hands. Get the jump on him now and settle things once and for all.

Mary tried talking him out of it. It would be foolish going after Lloyd, she insisted. They had to forget about Lloyd right now and flee the area, try to get something positive started with their own life. Somewhere around Springfield she finally got through to him and they headed west again.

But Darrell, still sampling that bad crank, couldn't get

Lloyd out of his head. The more he played it through, the angrier he got. Lloyd had figured him for a patsy, a flunky, someone he could count on to hang around and take his crap and do his dirty work. But Lloyd had figured it wrong. Maybe Joe Dean and Leonard Joe and two dozen other local guys were content doing Lloyd's bidding, but not him, no way, not Darrell Mease. Darrell Mease wasn't anyone's patsy. He wouldn't be played for a fool, he wouldn't be intimidated—not by Lloyd, not by anyone. Lloyd had started this deal and no doubt thought he was going to finish it, too. Well, that remained to be seen. Darrell Mease would have something to say about that.

So back they went into Ozark country, so Darrell could take care of business with Lloyd. Mary, beside herself with frustration now, succeeded in talking him out of it yet again, and they swung west through Missouri one last time and stopped at a truck stop outside of Joplin where Darrell could grab a shower and maybe straighten himself out. By this time he knew he'd better straighten out. Mary hadn't given him an ultimatum, that wasn't her style, but the way she stood and looked at him in that truck stop left no room for doubt. She'd put up with enough nonsense.

Back in the Dodge, freshly showered, Darrell knew what he had to do. They edged into Kansas, close to the little border town of Galena, and he walked into some woods and buried the last of Lloyd's bad crank. One problem down, but there was still the matter of cash. After all the wasted motion of the past few days, Darrell had finally decided they should go to California, to a place called Palmdale on the edge of the San Gabriel Mountains north of Los Angeles where he had a couple of cousins they could hide out with. But they'd need money for gas and food and smokes. They'd already bitten into the biggest part of the fifty dollars they'd started out with.

They drove into Galena and stopped at a hardware store. Darrell had a nice chain saw he'd taken with them thinking he might be able to sell it somewhere down the road. His Aunt Margie had paid $325 for it and given it to him for his birthday. Darrell hadn't used it enough to hurt it any, so it was practically new. He took it into the store and told the manager he'd take a hundred dollars for it. The manager looked at Darrell and looked at the chain saw and said he wasn't in the habit of paying that kind of money for used tools, which peeved Darrell. He thought the guy recognized he was in dire straits and was trying to take advantage of him. "Yow, money's tight all over, ain't it?" he said, picking the chain saw up from the counter and starting for the door. A middle-aged guy who'd been listening in, a farmer probably, stopped Darrell at the door and peeled off five twenties in exchange for the saw. Down the street they found a pawnshop where they got another twenty-five dollars for a couple of Darrell's rings. Twenty minutes in town, a hundred and twenty-five bucks. Not a huge haul, but maybe enough to see them through to California.

From Galena they took I-44 and then I-40 straight down through Oklahoma and into Texas. Before they hit Tulsa, Darrell was gone to it all, crashed right out. He hadn't slept more than a few hours over the past five days, and now he was making up for it. He didn't wake up until Flagstaff, Arizona, when he felt the car juking and shimmying on the icy winter highway.

Karrell Graves was just settling in for the evening when the call came. It was his cousin Darrell, phoning from a gas station outside of town and asking directions to Karrell's house. Karrell had always liked Darrell but he'd lost touch with him over the years. They'd grown up together in Reeds Spring but then Karrell had gone off to California with his father, Herbert, as a teenager, and after getting married had stayed there, first in Lone Pine and then a hundred and fifty miles down the road in Palmdale. Karrell and his wife, Janie, had made a nice life for themselves in Palmdale. The town itself wasn't much, a suburban smudge north of Los Angeles, dead flat and charmless, but they had their kids and grandkids and a comfortable ranch house that was always open to visitors from back home.

Karrell told Darrell to stay put. He'd drive out and meet him and then lead him back to the house. When he got to the gas station he saw a brown Dodge Diplomat with red Missouri mud caked on the rear bumper and license plate. He walked over and said hi to Darrell and introduced himself to Mary. He told them he'd take it easy driving back so they wouldn't lose him.

At the house Mary refused to budge. Karrell invited her inside for a shower and something to eat but she insisted on staying in the car with her dogs. Darrell said that Mary's nerves were strung pretty tight and they should probably just leave her alone. A bit later, while Darrell was in the shower, Karrell came back out and gave her a sedative with a drink of water. This seemed to do the trick. When Darrell finished cleaning up, Mary was sitting at the kitchen table having a bite and exchanging a few words with Janie.

But this was as far as it went. Mary was uncomfortable with the situation and wouldn't stay the night. She was worried they might be intruding. Karrell and Janie seemed good and decent people but they were Darrell's relatives, after all, not hers. Karrell filled up some gallon jugs with water for them, and they drove off and found a place to sleep in the desert that night.

The next day, Darrell convinced Mary they should drop by and see Jack Graves, his other Palmdale cousin. Jack was Lexie's nephew, her brother Paul's son. He and Darrell had been good running buddies back in Reeds Spring before Jack moved out west, got married, and eventually settled down in Palmdale. Just about everyone who knew them thought Jack and his wife, Luana, were loads of fun. Jack himself was a real character. Handsome and animated, with a sparkling down-home wit, he was bursting at the seams with bright and funny stories of his childhood in southwest Missouri and his later years out west.

Jack arrived home from work and found Darrell sitting on his porch steps. The Dodge, with Mary and the dogs inside, was parked in front.

"What you doing, buddy? You on vacation?" Jack asked.

"I'm hot, Jack," Darrell said. "I'm looking for somewhere to hide out for a while."

Jack and Luana had a broken-down motor home parked beside the house, a big twenty-seven-footer. Jack said that Darrell and Mary could stay there as long as they wanted, which was too good a deal to pass up. The motor home afforded Darrell and Mary some privacy, and Jack and Luana gave them free run of the house for food and showers.

It was a good deal but they didn't take advantage of it for very long. After about a week camping out at Jack and Luana's, Darrell experienced what he would later call a "danger urge," a strong premonition that Lloyd was hot on their trail. They packed up and split in the middle of the night. Darrell left a note in the motor home saying, "I owe you big-time, Jack."

Years afterward, Jack and Luana were still having trouble making sense of it all. Why would Darrell and Mary run off in the wee hours without even saying goodbye? Darrell had taken Jack aside at one point and told him he'd run afoul of drug dealers back home, but why did he think they'd be able to track him and Mary down in Palmdale? And most perplexing of all, what were Darrell and Mary doing together in the first place?

"It just didn't click, them being together," Luana said. "They seemed a real odd couple. Darrell was a good ole country boy. Mary seemed more refined, very prim and pretty. She didn't seem his type. She was very reserved. She talked a bit but not a whole lot. She told me she loved George Strait. She went up and kissed him at a concert. I got the idea her family was wealthy. She showed me this expensive-looking ring she had, sapphire I think. My impression was she'd had a boring upbringing and was looking for excitement. Darrell was it. Darrell was the excitement."

"Mary acted well-educated, like she didn't come from the same class we came from," Jack said. "At first she wouldn't even come into the house. I told her, 'Get your ass in the house.' But I thought she was also trying to be an outlaw. When I first saw her—I'm stretching the memory a bit here—she was wearing combat boots, fatigues, and a M*A*S*H T-shirt, and she had a .25 automatic pistol in her pocket and another pistol in her purse. She seemed like she was a nice, good-looking gal trying to be Annie Oakley."

Darrell's idea, upon fleeing Palmdale, was to slip up to Lone Pine, a few hours' drive north. He was familiar with the area from visiting relatives over the years and he figured the remote and rugged countryside would be perfect for hiding out. He'd sold one of his guns to Karrell two or three days earlier, so they weren't traveling stone-broke.

Halfway up U.S. 395, a couple of hours past midnight, they had a close shave. Darrell saw something out of the corner of his eye just off the road. It was a highway patrol car, poaching for speeders. When he turned his head to check it out, Darrell bobbled the Dodge a little bit. The patrol car ducked in behind them and flashed its lights. Darrell pulled over. He didn't have a driver's license, and his .357 Magnum was lying on the front seat where he liked to keep it, near at hand. Just before the cop beamed his flashlight into the driver's window, Mary took the gun and put it on the floor under the dogs' water bowl. The cop asked Darrell if he'd been drinking. Darrell said no and explained why the car had bobbled. He asked for Darrell's driver's license. Darrell, playing it straight, said he didn't have one. He'd let his old license expire and they'd left Missouri before he'd had a chance to pick up his new one. The cop then walked around to Mary's window and asked if she'd put something on the floor. Mary flashed a sweet and innocent smile and pointed to the water bowl. She said she'd put it on the floor so it wouldn't spill. The cop stood there a minute sizing up the situation, this long-haired bearded dude with a pretty young woman up front and two dogs, one of them a pit bull, in back. He told Darrell and Mary to take it easy and walked back to his car.

They arrived in Lone Pine at daybreak. After a bite of breakfast they stopped by Darrell's cousin Connie's house. Darrell didn't get the impression Connie and her husband were thrilled to see him but he picked up a few more dollars for food and gas by selling them one of his rifles, a Winchester .375 H&H Magnum.

The village of Lone Pine sits in a valley with mountains ranging on either side. Drive fifteen miles west and you reach the beautiful high-meadow country of the Sierra Nevadas, where there's plenty of game, well-worn trails, and good tree cover. Winters can be severe in the Sierra Nevadas, however, and this winter the switchbacks leading in and out were almost impassable. Darrell figured they'd have better luck heading east toward Death Valley and hiding in the foothills of the Inyo Mountains. The Inyo region is pure desert: rugged range, isolated canyons, sagebrush, scrub piñon, and juniper. Tumbledown cabins are strewn throughout the area, many of them ghostly reminders of silver-, gold-, and lead-mining operations that bit the dust more than half a century ago. Once you hit higher elevations there are mule deer and bighorn sheep, but in the foothills game is sparse due to lack of rain. It's a harsh environment, but ideal for holing up and avoiding detection.

Darrell and Mary camped in the area for about a week, eventually making their way north to Independence, a little town strung out along Route 395 between Lone Pine and Big Pine. Broke and hungry, they went to a county dump just south of town in hopes of scrounging food or, who knows, maybe some scrap metal or lumber they could sell. They were picking through a mound of garbage when a small elderly gentleman, about five two, with silver hair and big jug ears, eased on over and asked if they'd mind if he foraged in the dump for copper. Darrell said hell no, go ahead, he had as much right foraging as they did.

The man's name was Truman Buff. He was a Paiute Indian and a fixture in the area. Everybody around Independence knew Truman. He'd worked for years as a water engineer for the town, and since retiring he'd kept the juices flowing playing trombone in a local band. He had a reputation for knowing everything there was to know about the surrounding desert. Darrell said he and Mary were looking for somewhere to stay—someplace cheap and out of the way.

Truman suggested they drive into the desert east of Independence and check out the old mining shacks. If cheap and out of the way was what they wanted, the shacks would be tough to beat.

They caught Mazourka Canyon Road on the edge of town and headed back into Inyo country. The pavement soon gave way to dirt and gravel and they wound their way deeper and deeper into the foothills, passing abandoned shafts clinging to jagged rock face and a couple of old shacks that looked undecided about sticking around another year.

Finally they came to a little tar-paper shack that was set back in a clearing behind a stand of runty junipers. It belonged to an old claim-staker named Bill Michaels who had mined silver and gold out in the desert for decades before packing it in and moving to town a few years earlier. Darrell and Mary had no idea who it belonged to. They'd never heard of Bill Michaels. They only knew this was the place for them. Far off the beaten path, eleven miles from town, the views from the clearing were immense and beautiful and barren. The solitude was staggering—no one for miles around, no sound but the desert wind. There was no way Lloyd could sneak up on them out here. If there was anywhere they'd be safe, this was it.

Mary was excited. She thought the old shack was romantic and she talked about fixing it up into a sweet little home for the two of them. She said they should find out who owned it and look into the possibility of buying it. Darrell was moved by this show of enthusiasm. The idea of Mary being so willing to rough it out in the desert for his sake and theirs, it was almost too good to be true. He couldn't imagine loving anyone more.

They asked around in town for Truman Buff's address and drove over to see him, thinking he could put them on to whoever owned the shack. Truman had other ideas. He was home when Darrell and Mary pulled up, but when he saw them he broke and ran. Just like that: not a word, nothing. He took off on foot like he'd seen a ghost.

Darrell didn't like the looks of this. He didn't know what

it meant, but it couldn't be anything good. Maybe the local police had been quizzing Truman about the newcomers in town with the Missouri plates. Or worse, maybe Lloyd himself had been nosing around. One thing was for sure: they'd have to forget about that little mining shack for now. It was time to move on.

There was a reason why Truman Buff took off when Darrell and Mary pulled up, but it had nothing to do with Lloyd Lawrence or the local police. Since running into them at the county dump, Truman had been thinking. Something about Darrell and Mary had made him uneasy. Here was this rough-looking, long-haired guy living in the desert and hanging out with a shy pretty girl a good fifteen or twenty years younger. Why was this familiar? Then it hit him. It wasn't so long ago that some other rough-looking, long-haired guy named Charles Manson came out of the same desert with a whole bevy of pretty young girls. Truman knew the story well. Manson had actually done jail time in Independence after being rousted from his lair near Death Valley. For all Truman knew, Darrell was a cat of a completely different color. But he wasn't taking any chances.

The next week Darrell and Mary had a pretty good time, considering they were scrounging for food out of dumps and sleeping in the car down nowhere roads where they figured they wouldn't be found. What the hell, they thought, they were in California. Why not check out some of the sights? They went up to the Mount Whitney Fish Hatchery north of Independence and spent an afternoon watching the trout swirling in circles, round and round, going nowhere. They picnicked in the shadow of two extinct volcanoes by Red Mountain on Tinemaha Creek, and they visited the old ghost town of Calico over by Barstow. They then swung down through Indio, close to the Salton Sea, and camped out a couple of nights in the foothills of the Santa Rosas, once or twice stealing into the tiny agricultural station of Oasis for fresh fruit and vegetables.

It was a good time but Darrell didn't want to push it too far. It was late January now. They'd been on the road a solid month, living down-and-dirty. He was concerned about Mary. She hadn't complained but he thought there might be a limit to her tolerance for this kind of lifestyle. Hell, he wasn't averse to a bit of an upgrade himself.

He phoned his mom and told her they were in California and could use some help. Lexie didn't have much money but she called in some favors, and came up with a cool twelve grand. Mary picked up two thousand dollars in cash at a Western Union near Palmdale and they cashed a check for the rest of it at a bank in Los Angeles. Twelve thousand dollars—just like that. Now they were rolling.

This was the first time Lexie had heard from Darrell in more than a month. A couple of days after Christmas she'd dropped by his house with his son Shane in tow, but Darrell and Mary were already gone. She didn't need anyone telling her they wouldn't be back soon. She'd known for some time that Darrell was "running in Satan's territory," and now, standing there inside the little house, soaking everything in, she could almost smell the danger. She closed her eyes and prayed, "God, please take care of Darrell and protect his life till he comes to himself and comes back to You." Almost at once she felt God answering her in her spirit: "Don't worry about Darrell; I'll take care of him."

For Lexie it really was that simple. As far as she was concerned, everything was now in God's hands. She was through worrying.

But not Barbara Epps. Down in Branson, Mary's mother was sick with worry. A week after Darrell and Mary dropped out of sight, Barbara phoned Lexie in hopes of finding out where they might have gone. Lexie said she didn't know.

"But wouldn't Darrell know you'd be worried and call to tell you where they were?" Barbara asked.

"I serve a God that's able to take care of them, and Darrell knows I'll pray instead of worrying," Lexie said.

Lloyd Lawrence wasn't worried. Lloyd was steaming mad. The day after Darrell and Mary's disappearance he went to Darrell's house to check up on business and found the place empty, his drugs cleaned right out. He'd been ripped off. Nobody ripped Lloyd off, least of all a mere lackey like Darrell.

Lloyd decided to call in some heavy artillery. He contacted a buddy of his, a hard case from Oak Grove, Arkansas, named Roger Dean Widner, and together they started scouring the area, stopping in at the local bars, asking around for information on Darrell's whereabouts.

When he wasn't on the road, a local truck driver named Ralph liked to relax evenings at Betty's Tavern, drinking a few beers, playing shuffleboard or an occasional game of pool. Betty's was a tough joint but nobody ever bothered Ralph. He could handle himself fine, even though he was small and past fifty, but the key to Ralph's survival in tough joints like Betty's was discretion. He didn't pry into other people's business, and he was always careful about where he sat and whom he talked to. Ralph didn't enjoy conflict; he'd made a habit of avoiding it. So he wasn't exactly pleased when Lloyd came storming in one night with "a pocketful of guns" and started jacking up the customers for information about Darrell. Eventually he worked his way over to Ralph's table and helped himself to a chair, Roger Widner standing behind him watching his back.

Ralph had seen quite a bit of Lloyd over the years, usually at the cockfights down in Blue Eye or over in Shell Knob. Lloyd had always struck him as "a real operator." Once Ralph had even thought of going into the cockfighting business himself ("even though I knew shit about chickens") and he'd talked with Lloyd about buying some birds to start out with. He'd also seen Darrell from time to time—here at Betty's, in town at the Nite Hawk, the usual spots—but he couldn't remember ever exchanging more than a few words with him.

So now Lloyd was sitting there asking about Darrell and Ralph wasn't comfortable with the conversation. There was obviously bad blood between the two men but it wasn't any of his business. Lloyd asked him two or three times if he'd seen or heard from Darrell. Then he asked him again for good measure. Ralph said he hadn't seen Darrell lately but he hadn't exactly been looking for him either. Lloyd told Ralph to keep his eyes open and let him know if anything turned up. He said he planned on killing Darrell but he had to find him first.

Ralph asked Lloyd if he was serious.

"Darrell Mease is alligator meat," Lloyd said.

Good old Lloyd, Ralph thought. Quite the charmer.

Having had their fill of California, Darrell and Mary drove deep into Arizona and dipped across the border into Nogales. They spent the afternoon walking hand in hand and taking in the sights. One thing in particular caught Darrell's eye. Just beyond the border crossing, at the portal of town, before Nogales gives way to its cobblestone streets, its arched sidewalks, hole-in-the-wall hotels, no-frill cantinas, and sun-scorched Coca-Cola signs, before the town turns distinctly Mexican, not just American with a Mexican twist, Darrell saw the street vendors with their handmade pottery and wood carvings and trinkets laid out on the sidewalk or displayed in streetside stalls.

He said to Mary, "Just look at all this stuff, monkey. I'd bet there's a lot of legitimate money to be made setting up shop and selling handmade stuff like this back home."

He filed the thought for future reference. Down the years he'd return to it often.

Now that they had some serious money in their pockets, Darrell and Mary were living it up a bit, taking the occasional meal in restaurants and camping in state parks. After leaving Nogales they decided they'd spend a couple of days at Lake Patagonia, a park twenty miles north of the border. The reception booth was closed for the night by the time they arrived so they spread their bedrolls out beside the little entry road and just lay there listening to the nighttime sounds. They heard wild burros bray, coyotes howl, and desert owls hoot. It put Darrell in mind of a line from an old Eagles song: "I want to sleep with you in the desert tonight."

The next morning a park ranger drove up and visited with

them for a while. He pointed to the mountains in the distance, the Santa Ritas to the north and the Huachucas to the east, and said that he had a pair of high-powered binoculars that would "draw 'em right up close." Because Darrell and Mary seemed like nice people, he said, he was going to let them visit a beautiful scenic spot on state trust land that was technically off limits to the public. Following his instructions, they parked their car by an old earthen dam on the lake and then followed Sonoita Creek past clumps of cottonwood and mesquite trees and down an arroyo until they reached a small pool with catfish visible beneath the clear surface. The ranger had told them to cross the pool by a narrow ledge along the far side, but halfway across they found the path blocked by a large boulder. Darrell tried lifting Mary's dogs up onto the boulder but they were scared and kept skidding back down. Seeing they weren't getting anywhere, Darrell and Mary backtracked to the creek and sat beside the bank.

While they were talking about how they might spend the rest of the day, Darrell was suddenly hit by "a strong feeling of terminal danger." He turned and saw the ranger hurrying down a trail toward them through the desert broom and cacti. Darrell had left his backpack, with a pistol inside, forty yards up the creek. He ran over and retrieved it, thinking this might be showdown time.

"Why the hell didn't you go to where I told you?" the ranger said, hostile, agitated.

Darrell explained that they hadn't been able to get the dogs across, though he suspected the ranger had been scoping them out all along with his binoculars and already knew as much.

Then, just like that, the ranger turned on a dime and became friendly again. He gave Darrell and Mary a lift back to their car in his pickup, the dogs riding in the bed, and wished them a nice stay at the park.

They didn't stick around much longer. Once again, it was time for moving on.

They took it slow and easy going up through Arizona,

camping here and there, but Darrell couldn't get the incident with the park ranger out of his mind. The more he mulled it over the more he became convinced that the ranger was a serial killer. The guy had the perfect black-and-white personality for the role, and he also had the perfect setup. Think about it: here was a trusted authority figure signing people into a park and then luring them to a remote area where he could kill them without anyone being the wiser for it. He'd selected Darrell and Mary as his next victims, but he knew he'd been busted when Darrell made the fast move for his backpack. That's why he'd been so hostile coming down the trail to confront them. He'd missed his chance to add to his tally. If the police could ever be persuaded to drag the bottom of Lake Patagonia over by the dam, Darrell believed they'd surely find some rusted-out vehicles. The remains of the people who'd once driven them were probably buried somewhere in the desert.

The encounter with the ranger also added to Darrell's sense of vulnerability. Here they were, Mary and he, out on the road, naked to the world, with Lloyd gunning for them and who knows how many other dangers lurking in the shadows. What's more, they were falling perilously short in the weaponry department. They'd sold most of their better guns since fleeing Missouri, leaving them with only a few pistols and knives. While they still had some money left, Darrell thought they'd better do what they could about restocking the arsenal.

On February 26 they pulled into Phoenix, as good a place for restocking as any other. For some time even before leaving Missouri, Darrell had wanted to pick up a Benelli Super 90, the fastest automatic shotgun on the market. They phoned around and found a place called Phoenix Arms, way up in a distant suburb, that had a Benelli available at a decent price.

Darrell waited outside in the car with the dogs while Mary went in to buy the gun. She was less likely to arouse suspicion, and she also had a valid driver's license as identification. Linda Cofone, who ran Phoenix Arms with her husband, Carl, at the time, remembers thinking that Mary seemed "very proper and conservative, a very nice young lady." Buying the Benelli was easier than checking out a library book. No mandatory background check—no mandatory anything. All Mary had to do was answer "no" to all the questions on the purchase form. "Have you been convicted in any court of a crime punishable by imprisonment for a term exceeding one year?" "Are you a fugitive from justice?" "Are you an alien illegally in the United States?" "Are you an unlawful user of, or addicted to, marijuana, or a depressant, stimulant, or narcotic drug?" "Have you ever been adjudicated mentally defective or have you ever been committed to a mental institution?" *No. No. No. No. And no again.* Mary paid $519.95 for the shotgun and she also picked up a sling, a shell holder, three boxes of buckshot, and another three boxes of slugs. She paid in cash, a total of $596.87, and signed the receipt Mary Epps of Reeds Spring, Missouri.

Back in Missouri, Rocky Redford was relaxing at home one late-January evening when Lloyd Lawrence and Roger Widner came busting through his front door with submachine guns. Lloyd knew that Rocky and Darrell sometimes ran together and he thought Darrell might be hiding out in Rocky's house. He certainly wasn't worried about hurting Rocky's feelings. If the guy was stupid enough, *crazy enough*, to be sheltering Darrell, he deserved to have his door busted down and a gun shoved in his face. Who the hell was Rocky anyway? Rocky was nobody.

Rocky pleaded innocence. He told Lloyd he didn't know where Darrell was. He hadn't seen Darrell since Christmas. He only knew Darrell had taken off somewhere with Mary. Lloyd had to believe him. No way would he lie to Lloyd. He'd have to be stupid or crazy to lie to Lloyd.

Lloyd seemed to believe him. He told Rocky to report to him immediately if he heard any news of Darrell's whereabouts. He said that Darrell had ripped him off big-time and he was anxious to settle the score.

Rocky wasn't stupid. The encounter with Lloyd hadn't been his idea of a good time but that didn't mean he couldn't play it to his personal advantage. He had an upcoming court date in connection with his recent drug bust and he'd already had a couple of conversations with the county prosecutor about working out a deal that would get him off the hook. Now he had a bargaining chip.

A few days later, at the Forsyth courthouse, Rocky met with prosecutor Jim Justus and criminal investigator Chip Mason. He told them about his exchange of pleasantries with Lloyd and Roger. He told them about the bad business between Darrell and Lloyd, and that Lloyd was threatening to kill Darrell and probably Mary, too. He told them he'd keep them posted.

One evening not long afterward, Rocky was sitting at his kitchen table, quite possibly feeling pleased with himself. He'd endeared himself to Lloyd, after all, and he'd also wriggled out of his drug rap. Things were looking bright again.

But perhaps not quite so bright after all. While Rocky was sitting there, a couple of bullets crashed through the kitchen window and punched holes in the far wall. Now this—even Rocky had to admit—this was not an encouraging development. Maybe Lloyd hadn't believed him after all.

Rocky packed up his things and drove back home to Kansas. He couldn't get out of Missouri fast enough.

On March 1, several days after buying the Benelli, Darrell and Mary drove into the cool highlands region of central Arizona and just before dusk entered the small city of Cottonwood. By this point they'd had enough of sleeping cramped up in the car or outside in their little two-man tent, so when they saw Camelot RV Park and Center on the main drag they decided to stop in and check out the merchandise. It didn't take them long to find something they wanted—a 1971 Starcraft pop-up camper, which set them back nearly a grand.

They still needed to get a trailer hitch put on the car, a job that would have to wait until the next day, so they took a room at the Little Daisy Motel just down the street. The motel manager caught a glimpse of Darrell sitting in the Dodge while Mary was checking in. He didn't feel right about the situation—this attractive young woman riding with such a tough-looking dude. Working up his nerve, he slipped outside and watched from the shadows beside the motel office while Darrell and Mary unloaded the car. He saw Darrell carrying the new shotgun into their room and, for the briefest moment, it seemed Darrell turned his head and saw him, too. Rattled, he retreated into the office, wondering whether he should call the police. He stewed over it for a few hours and then put in the call.

It didn't take long for the Cottonwood police to swing into action, largely because Mary's mom had finally taken some action of her own. A few weeks earlier, desperate for news about Mary and fearing for her safety, Barbara had gone to Forsyth and met with Chip Mason at the Taney County courthouse. Barbara had known Chip for years and considered him a friend. An unassuming, sandy-haired man in his mid-thirties, with pudgy cheeks and a laconic style, Chip had grown up in the Branson–Forsyth area and had been working as a criminal investigator out of the county prosecutor's office for almost a decade.

Barbara told Chip that Mary had disappeared with Darrell and that she was beside herself with worry. She didn't know much of anything about Darrell or if Mary was in danger. She asked if there was anything Chip could do.

Chip told Barbara about Lloyd and Roger busting into Rocky's place with submachine guns. He told her that Lloyd was making noise all over Stone and Taney Counties about killing Darrell and anyone Darrell happened to be with. Chip said there was one thing he could do straightaway. He'd send out a "missing and endangered person" Teletype to the National Crime Information Center (NCIC). That way any law enforcement officer in the country coming across Mary would know to make sure she was safe and advise her to call home.

Chip sent out the Teletype the same day. It included all of Mary's particulars (nineteen years old, five eight, 120 pounds, light brown hair, green eyes) and descriptions of Darrell, the dogs, and the Dodge (Missouri plate LGP688). It also included two photographs from Mary's senior yearbook, one an elegant headshot and the other the prank mug shot of her posing dimple-faced behind the Branson PD sign.

So the Cottonwood police, after hearing from the manager at the Little Daisy Motel, ran the Dodge's plate and got a positive hit. This looked like it could be nasty business. Mary was missing and possibly endangered, and the guy she was riding with was packing serious heat. They figured they'd better make a show of it.

At three in the morning Darrell and Mary were awakened by shouts of "Come out! Come out! Come out!" The room was bathed in spotlights. Darrell went to the window and drew back a corner of the flimsy curtain. Three or four police cars were parked outside with seven or eight cops, maybe more, crouched behind them, some with 12-gauge goose guns laid over the car roofs and pointed directly at the motel room. Darrell opened the door and stood in the threshold with his arms raised, and the cops came barging in. They were excited, pumped up, yelling and jostling. Finally, a smooth blond cop in his thirties ("a cool head," Darrell thought) took charge of the situation. He ordered everyone to lower their weapons and quiet down.

He asked Darrell why he had his shotgun leaning against the wall next to the bed. Darrell said someone had been spying on them from the shadows beside the motel office while they were unloading the car and he'd wanted to be prepared in the event of trouble. The blond cop asked Mary if Darrell was treating her okay. Of course, Mary said, Darrell was treating her just fine. He then told her she should call home. She'd been reported missing and endangered and her mom was worried about her. Mary said she'd phone home later in the day after they picked up their trailer. Okay, the cop said, but in the meantime he'd contact the Taney County Sheriff's

Department himself and tell them she'd been located in Arizona and seemed all right.

And that was it. The Cottonwood PD could do no more. Mary was legally an adult and couldn't be detained against her will. And what were they going to do with Darrell? Bust him for being mangy? He hadn't broken any laws and there were no warrants for his arrest. The cops left—a couple of them grousing on the way out about Darrell's shotgun being better than theirs. Their business here was finished.

Darrell wasn't so sure. Alone with Mary again, he knew he wouldn't be going back to sleep. His mind was racing with the possibilities. What if Lloyd had connections with the Cottonwood PD? There was a good chance he did. Lloyd had connections everywhere, traveling the country going to cockfights, buying and selling game birds. He even sometimes went to the cockfights near Phoenix. One phone call from Lloyd, that's all it would take, and those cops would be back with some trumped-up warrant, child support maybe, it didn't matter, anything it would take to land Darrell in jail in Stone County so Lloyd could get at him. Pour some gasoline into the jail cell through a window, set it on fire: that's the way it would probably play out. That would be Lloyd's style.

Oh man, forget it, Lloyd didn't even need connections with the Cottonwood PD to get at him. Didn't the blond-haired cop say he was going to get in touch with the authorities in Taney County and let them know where Mary was? That would do it. Lloyd was tight with plenty of people in Taney County. He'd probably already gotten wind of the incident and was setting the pieces in motion to have Mary and him eliminated.

Lloyd would know hard cases in Arizona who'd be happy to do it. Something was up—no sense waiting around to find out exactly what it was.

An hour after the cops left, Darrell and Mary packed up the car and headed for the interstate. The plan was for Mary to drop Darrell off across the state line, a good three or four hours' drive away, and then return to Cottonwood by herself and pick up the trailer. She'd be safer without him; riding with Darrell she stuck out like a daisy in a field of weeds. They drove east along Interstate 40 past Winslow and the Petrified Forest and into New Mexico. Just over the state line Darrell got out on a little dirt road and set up their tent in some scrub cedars.

Mary got back into Cottonwood around noon, bleary-eyed from the road. She dropped the car off at Camelot so they could install the hitch and then found a pay phone and called her mom.

Barbara asked if Darrell was treating her all right and Mary said he was. She said they'd left Missouri in a hurry because they were afraid of being killed by Lloyd. Barbara said they were right to be afraid. She said she'd talked to Chip Mason and learned that Lloyd and some of his cronies were looking for them with automatic weapons and with every intention of killing them. She said that Lloyd probably knew what kind of car they were driving. She told Mary to be careful and asked her to phone again the next day. Mary said she would.

The car and trailer were ready to go, but Mary was too tired to think of driving out to get Darrell right away. She needed to grab some sleep first.

She picked him up the next morning and they headed east along I-40 through New Mexico and into Texas, taking their time now, happy to be free of Arizona. (Mary never did get around to making that second phone call home.) On March 7 they stayed at Fort Griffin State Park north of Abilene, paying six bucks for a campsite, and then they took Interstate 20 across Texas and worked their way down Route 171 in Louisiana to the little resort town of Many.

After checking into Bird's Trailer Park just outside of town, they decided they'd better go looking for another top-drawer gun. There was no telling how close Lloyd was on their trail; they could use all the protection they could get. The pickings were slim at the pawnshop in Many and also at a gun shop in the nearby town of Zwolle, so the next day they drove over to Alexandria, the biggest city in north-central Louisiana, where they expected they'd have better luck.

It's a good thing Darrell and Mary weren't visiting Alexandria for the local color. The town is so drab and uneventful they could have been excused for thinking they'd wandered into the wrong state. They leafed through a local paper and hit on a business called Randy's Trading Post that was advertising guns for sale. Mary called and spoke with a guy named Randy Pias and arranged to stop by his office later in the day and pick up an H & K .308 assault rifle.

After lunch they drove over to Petron Oil Company at 727 McArthur Drive, a small complex of sheds, warehouses, and offices located next to a tangle of highway cloverleafs in a beat-down, shanty-shack-poor section of town. They parked outside a one-story cement-block building and then waited inside while a secretary fetched Randy Pias. Pias escorted them down a short corridor into a small rectangular office, windowless, wood-paneled, the desk stacked with files and papers. He opened a steel cabinet standing alongside the wall opposite the desk, took out four assault rifles, and gave them to Darrell for his inspection. Mary thought there was something strange about the whole deal. Here was this businessman, a perfectly ordinary-looking guy, medium build, straight brown hair, thin face, wearing glasses and a gray suit, selling high-powered weapons right out of his office. Darrell picked through the guns and found one he liked. Eight hundred dollars, Pias said, but he'd need to see a Louisiana driver's license before turning it over.

A nuisance, but nothing Darrell and Mary weren't prepared to deal with. A few days later, a brand-new Louisiana driver's license in hand, Mary returned to Pias's office and paid the eight hundred for the rifle.

The next two weeks they stayed at Indian Creek Recreation Area ten miles south of Alexandria, five dollars a night for a spot in the primitive zone. The first few days were as peaceful a time as they could have hoped for. They caught catfish in the creek and cooked them over an open fire. They bought groceries at the corner store in the tiny hamlet of Woodworth, and they stretched out on the grass and breathed in the lovely scents of loblolly pine, cypress, and sweetgum trees. The hours just melted away.

But then Darrell finally got around to asking Mary about her phone call home. It was an awkward topic and they'd been avoiding talking about it. Mary told him that her parents had been worried about her and wanted to know if she was okay. She also told him that Lloyd had been busting into places with automatic weapons looking for the two of them.

Darrell vividly remembers Mary telling him something else, too. He remembers her saying that Lloyd and another guy had actually gone down to her parents' place in Branson and threatened Barbara and Fred with submachine guns. It's possible that this really happened and Barbara mentioned it to Mary on the phone. Or perhaps Mary, in her fatigue, just imagined Barbara mentioning it. Or perhaps Darrell didn't hear Mary right. It's tough to say. The only thing that matters is that this is what Darrell believed he heard Mary telling him. And it seemed perfectly plausible. Lloyd loved the bold and brazen gesture. He believed himself invincible. Of course Lloyd would do something like this. Of course he would.

Darrell was mortified, and humiliated. He was enraged. He wasn't in good standing with Mary's folks to start with and now this. Lloyd threatening them was the last straw. He told Mary they'd have to change their plans. They'd spent all this time running and hiding from Lloyd. Well, they couldn't run and hide forever. They'd have to take matters into their own hands and go back and deal with Lloyd. Otherwise they'd never be safe. Right now Lloyd had the upper hand. They'd have to do something to change that. They'd have to go back and kill Lloyd before Lloyd had a chance to kill them.

Darrell had always suspected it might come down to this. He'd talked about it off and on with Mary since leaving Missouri but he'd never made a firm decision. Mary had always tried talking him out of it, saying she wanted them to buy a house in California or some other faraway place, get married, put the whole business with Lloyd behind them. But now his mind was made up. As he saw it, there was no other option.

On March 23 they went to Hickory Street in a seedy residential section of Alexandria and for two grand bought a blue '81 Oldsmobile station wagon from a guy named Michael Fritz. They'd seen the car advertised in the paper and they figured it was high time they got some new wheels. Riding around in the Dodge Diplomat was like giving Lloyd a free shot at them.

A week later they rented a twelve-by-twenty-foot unit at Inner Space Storage on Twin Bridges Road in the south end of Alexandria. Stow the Dodge here for now, they thought, and come back for it sometime later. It was still a good ride, just fifty thousand miles on the clock. Not only that, they had a lot of memories sunk into the Dodge. Give it a little time: they'd be back for it.

Lloyd was getting frustrated. So far his strong-arm tactics hadn't paid off. For more than two months now he'd been jacking people up for information about Darrell and no one had told him a damned thing.

This didn't mean Lloyd was giving up, which wasn't Lloyd's style. Someone had to know something. Darrell hadn't just fallen off the end of the earth. Someone had to know where he was.

Anyway, maybe he'd been approaching this whole thing wrong. He'd been spending too much of his own valuable time chasing Darrell down. There were plenty of people who'd be happy, with a little positive incentive, to do the job for him. Put out a contract on Darrell—ten thousand dollars, say—and let someone else dispose of the problem. For ten grand a lot of local boys would be fighting over the chance to be first in line for the assignment. Lloyd wasn't fussy. He didn't care who took Darrell out—so long as he was taken out.

Lloyd was right. Once news of the contract got around, Stone County bad guys were bumping into each other trying to stake their respective claims. The contract was hardly classified information. With his characteristic swagger, Lloyd wasn't shy about spreading the word. Nearly everyone with connections to the local underworld knew about it, and there was plenty of competitive bidding for the job.

The word around Stone County was that Joe Dean Davis, Darrell's very own cousin, was in on the action. Some people heard that Lloyd had offered Joe Dean ten grand to kill Darrell. Others heard that Lloyd had offered him the ten grand just to find out where Darrell was. Nobody heard anything about Joe Dean turning Lloyd down.

Years later, sitting in his house trailer on his raggedy property in Mease's Hollow, his hound dogs running loose outside and his fighting roosters crowing, Joe Dean would offer his own version of events.

Say what people might, Joe Dean said, he'd never actually agreed to take Lloyd's money in exchange for hunting his cousin down. He'd been in Blue Eye with Lloyd and some other people one day and Lloyd had taken him aside and offered him ten grand to do the job. But he hadn't agreed to do it. He'd told Lloyd this was something they should talk about again under less heated circumstances. But they never had the chance. This was the last time he saw Lloyd alive.

Now Joe Dean's a likeable guy. You want to give him the benefit of the doubt. He's a bit tongue-tied, with a lisp and a stammer that sometimes makes understanding him difficult, but he's witty and engaging and he looks you straight in the eye. He's not one for dodging tough questions. Even though they ran together for years, he'll tell you straight out that Lloyd was a bully who'd stop at nothing to get his own way. He'll even tell you about some of his own shortcomings. So you want to believe him when he says he didn't take Lloyd up on his offer.

You want to believe him—but there are one or two awkward facts that get in the way. Not too long after his chat with Lloyd in Blue Eye, Joe Dean dropped in to see R.J. and Lexie. He sat at their kitchen table and insisted they tell him where Darrell was.

"Joe, we don't know where Darrell is," Lexie said.

"Yes, you do," Joe Dean said. "Darrell was supposed to tell you and then you were supposed to tell me. That's the arrangement Darrell and me worked out before he left. He said he'd contact you and then I could come by and you'd tell me where he was. Darrell wants me to know."

Lexie knew Joe Dean pretty well. His mom, Ruby, was R.J.'s sister and one of Lexie's closest friends. She knew that Ruby thought the world of Joe Dean, and she'd always tried thinking well of him herself. But this was just too transparent. She knew that Joe Dean was trying to trick her.

"Joe, I don't know where he is," Lexie said, firmly now. "I would be the last one Darrell would want to know where he is because Darrell wouldn't want anyone to trouble me about this."

Lexie could tell that Joe Dean didn't believe her but she was through discussing the matter.

Darrell had made his hard decision but they didn't head back to Missouri right away. Perhaps stalling for time, hoping he'd change his mind, Mary said she wanted to drive down to the Louisiana coast and look around. Darrell agreed, saying he wouldn't mind doing a bit more exploring himself.

They took the Oldsmobile station wagon into the deepest part of the state, down Route 1 alongside Lafourche Bayou, past the docked shrimp boats and drawbridges and seafood restaurants. They came into Grand Isle at nightfall, the little seabound Cajun town decked out in all its dilapidated, glory-gone charm: the Creole-style houses with their shuttered windows, the lanes of oleander, the lush tropical smell of wild chamomile, the buildings crouching on stilts like they were poised for sudden escape. They went to the end of town, past a petroleum processing plant shimmering vast and spectral on the water's edge, and made a right-hand turn into the entrance drive for the state park. They paid a ten-dollar admission fee and drove right out onto the beach, backed the trailer up behind a clump of myrtlewax bushes, and fell asleep to the sound of the waves.

They spent five nights and four days in Grand Isle, their nicest stretch anywhere since leaving Missouri. A quarter mile down the beach, they found an old rickety pier stretching out into the water on wooden pilings for fifty or sixty yards before branching out into a T. Darrell stood there for hours every day, fishing for flounder, speckled trout, or bluefish, while Mary played in the water. She had never swum in salt water before; Darrell had a tough time convincing her to take a break. Sometimes they stood together on the pier and watched the shrimp boats trawling in the gulf, brown pelicans bopping and bumping in the surf, and the occasional dolphin venturing close to shore. They took the fish Darrell caught back to the campsite, where there were some open grills and a scattering of picnic tables, and cleaned and cooked them. Once or twice, for a change of pace, they went for a snack at one of the Cajun joints along Route 1.

Heading back north, late April now, they stayed a few days at Chicot State Park near Ville Platte in Evangeline Parish. Their money was running low again so Darrell bought two crayfish traps at a country store and set them up in a shallow swampy side of Lake Chicot. They got two meals a day out of those traps. Darrell also did some hunting on the sly in the park grounds. He killed a few squirrels with his pellet gun and he also bagged an armadillo. He found it kind of amusing: when he first met her, Mary was a vegetarian; now she was happily cooking and eating Louisiana mud bugs and anything else he brought back to their trailer.

Their second day at Lake Chicot, they saw a wild sow raiding some trash bins just across the lane from where they were camped out. A boar was with her but he seemed nervous and kept his distance, hanging back in the magnolias. Mary put out a saucer of red wine and the sow lapped it up and started staggering around. After a while she sobered up but then Mary put out some more wine and she got drunk again. Darrell and Mary got quite a kick out of watching her.

By the next day Darrell's mood had turned. He was tense now, zeroing in, consumed by thoughts of Lloyd. He felt like a balloon just waiting to pop. The spare tire to the station wagon was flat, and when Mary returned from running some errands in town without getting it fixed he yelled and screamed at her. He had never yelled at Mary before. Right across from them, a guy pulled up in an expensive camper and immediately started making a racket, cutting firewood with a chain saw and blasting music from a radio. This was nerve-wracking enough, but then the guy kept overthrowing his son while playing catch, the ball bouncing against Darrell and Mary's trailer. Darrell thought it was deliberate. He was convinced the guy was trying to provoke him. After the fifth or sixth overthrow, he stuck his head out the back of the trailer and cussed the guy's son out while he was retrieving the ball. The kid looked at Darrell, panic-stricken, and said, "It's not me; it's my dad." The guy stormed over to defend his son and flashed an auxiliary police badge with his name and picture on it. "You don't know who you're messing with," he said. Darrell wasn't impressed but decided against getting into it with the guy. He was trying to keep a low profile; he didn't need this kind of aggravation. He asked Mary to go to the entrance booth and report the guy for disturbing the peace. The rangers at the booth told Mary they'd take care of it. The guy might be an auxiliary cop, they said, but that didn't mean he was running the park.

On May 5, Lloyd flew to Phoenix with Travis and Bush Clark, and Travis's wife, Peggy. They rented a car at the airport and drove out to Ehrenberg near the California state line. Ehrenberg was the site of the Copperstate Game Club, the most prestigious cockfighting arena in the southwest. They spent the better part of four nights at the club, hanging out in the bleachers making side bets, kibitzing down by the drag pits, grabbing burgers and beers from the snack bar. For Lloyd it was a good time, a chance to catch up with some old acquaintances and temporarily forget his hassles back home. There was nothing quite like a good old-fashioned cockfighting derby for recharging the batteries. Nowhere did Lloyd feel more at home.

The foursome arrived back in Missouri on Monday, May 9.

On Thursday morning Lloyd dropped by Travis's house in Lampe so they could divvy up their winnings from the trip. After expenses they'd each come out ahead by seventeen hundred dollars. Lloyd had won almost a thousand dollars more for himself on top of this from side bets. Nobody knew cockfighting better than Lloyd.

Heading north on Route 7 in Arkansas from Russellville, Darrell and Mary could tell they were getting closer to home. The steep banks and zigzag bends of the highway; the tumble of trailer homes in the nooks and crannies of the rugged terrain; the hills unfolding in various shades of green and blue and brown; the broken-dream gift shops, weather-beaten and abandoned, sneaking up on them around the sharp corners: after more than four months on the road, they were back in the Ozarks, on the Arkansas side.

Just beyond the cozy village of Jasper, they made a left onto a dirt-and-gravel road and followed it for five and a half grueling miles to an isolated camping spot on the Buffalo River. It was a nice spot, with barbecue grills, picnic tables, wooden outhouses, and a drinking water depot. Better yet, they had it all to themselves; no one else was around.

They stayed here for four days—their final stop before Missouri. They were down to their case money now, just a few dollars left from the windfall of a few months ago, so they didn't even think of making the trek back to Jasper to pick up groceries or to grab a bite at the Dairy Diner or Sharon K's Café. Instead they stayed put, let the dogs run, and made do with the rock bass, sun perch, and slough perch that Darrell was able to catch out of the river.

Darrell was deep into it now, running various scenarios through his mind, trying to picture what he'd be up against when they got back to Missouri. One thing he was certain of: he wouldn't be tangling with just Lloyd. Lloyd would have people watching for him, looking for an opportunity to kill him. There'd be a bounty on his head by now. Lloyd would have seen to that. If he were going to get to Lloyd he'd have to go through some of Lloyd's henchmen first.

Roger Widner probably, maybe one or two other guys from Arkansas, some local Stone County talent: this was what he'd be up against. Oh yeah, and Marvin Yocum, don't forget about him—Marvin was sneaky-good with a pistol and a noted outlaw around Reeds Spring. Chances were Lloyd would have brought Marvin into this deal, too.

Just after dark, their fourth day on the Buffalo River, they made their way back to Route 7 and headed northeast toward Bull Shoals Lake on the Arkansas–Missouri border. This was it: no more stopovers, no more detours—they were going back into Missouri so Darrell could settle his long-overdue business with Lloyd. Mary was at the wheel, taking it slow and deliberate, caressing every curve of the highway, still hoping—still half believing—that Darrell wouldn't go through with it.

FIVE

They came back into Missouri through Protem, a tiny village a couple of miles north of the Arkansas line, and snaked their way up Route 125. An hour and a half of hard driving, all sharp curves and tall pines ghostlike in the moonlight, and they pulled into the Camp Ridge Recreation Area. Darrell wanted a secluded spot where they could lay low for a few days while he figured out his next move, and this seemed as good a bet as any.

Camp Ridge was a picturesque hundred acres of pine stands and picnic tables set back off Rural Route H in a remote corner of the Mark Twain National Forest. In daylight hours, the surrounding woods would be filled with the roar of trail bikes, but now, after midnight, everything was quiet and deserted. Half a mile away, up Route 125, was the broken-down hamlet of Chadwick, a scattering of trailer homes, abandoned frame buildings, a gas station and convenience store, a post office, an aluminum-clad elementary school, and, one short street off the main drag, a squat square building with white-painted bricks on the outside, and on the inside a cement floor, corrugated tin ceiling, green wooden shelves, and an old-fashioned wood stove. This was Harris Market, where Darrell and Mary would get most of their supplies over the next couple of days. Years later, ninety-two-year-old Audrey Harris, still minding the store, would remember the couple as "real polite but kinda quiet, like they was still finding their way."

Their first night back in Missouri, Darrell wasn't thinking about stocking up on groceries. He unhitched the camper and told Mary he wanted her to drive him over to the fire tower road, near the junction of U.S. 160 and Route 248, so he could retrieve the methamphetamine he'd left hidden in the woods five months ago. This wasn't what Mary wanted to hear. He'd promised her he was through with drugs. They'd been over this at least a dozen times, arguing, crying, the nastiness practically tearing them apart. She told him to forget the drugs, or else they'd never have a chance at a clean start. He said he wasn't interested in using the drugs himself. Once the business with Lloyd was done with, he'd sell them and put together a nice stake so they could get started on their future.

Mary knew she wasn't about to win this one. They drove without talking, watching the speed limit, shrinking back in their seats with every approaching headlight. They were going into Lloyd Lawrence territory now and they knew one false move, one unlucky break, and they could both be dead. They crept down the fire tower road a hundred yards or so and dimmed their lights. Darrell got out of the station wagon, easing his door shut, and moved quickly into the woods. Five minutes later he was back, carrying the knapsack with the stolen meth. Mary turned the car around and headed back to the campground, faster now, scared, wishing she was just about anywhere instead of in southwest Missouri.

After forty miles of silent, jittery driving, they pulled into the gravel entrance drive of Camp Ridge and nudged up alongside their pop-up camper. Mary got the camper ready for sleeping while Darrell transferred the drugs into a yellow plastic cooler—all but one plastic bag's worth, which he shoved into his jacket pocket, thinking he'd break it up later on and maybe sell it somewhere down the road. He decided to take a taste right now himself. *Just one taste, that's all, just to sample the stuff, one taste, no more, gotta be clearheaded for what's coming up*. He took a taste and then carried the cooler into the forest and buried it beside a large rock.

Mary spent the next two days feeling like a sleepwalker. She felt zonked-out, zombified. She'd been on the road so long, the days and weeks bleeding into one another, that time had stopped having any real meaning. She sat around smoking cigarettes, playing with her dogs, not talking too much with Darrell, the two of them going to Chadwick a few times for groceries and then coming back and making a fire. Groups of young guys, three or four at a time, would come into the campground, unload trail bikes from their pickups, and roar off into the woods. There was no running water on the grounds, just a wooden outhouse with separate doors for women and men. Groggy and grungy, Mary wished they had money to rent a motel room so she could shower and watch some TV. She thought about finding a phone and calling her mom, who was just thirty-five miles away in Branson, but what could she say? "How ya doin' Mom? I'm still with Darrell. We've come back to take care of Lloyd. Nothing to worry about"?

Late afternoon on the third day, Friday, May 13, Darrell said it was time. He knew what he had to do; there was no sense waiting any longer. They took the station wagon, with Mary driving, to U.S. 65 and then south twenty miles just across the Taney County line to Bear Creek Road, where Darrell told her to pull over.

He laid out the plan. Later on, after dark, Mary would drop him right here, on Bear Creek Road just off U.S. 65. He'd scuttle down to the creek and follow its curves behind a cover of trees for a couple of miles, then cut south across an open field and over a hill. From there he'd be in range of both Lloyd Lawrence's cabin and Rocky Redford's place, just half a mile apart. If Lloyd was around for the weekend, Darrell would take care of business. And if Rocky was also around, so much the better. He'd confront Rocky for trying to come between him and Mary—throw a good scare into the guy. Knock off two problems in one trip, then get the hell out of there. When the job was done, he'd come back the same way and tie an orange highway ribbon to a tree underneath the bridge that crosses Bear Creek on U.S. 65. Mary would check for the ribbon the next day, late afternoon, and if it wasn't there, the day after that. As soon as she saw it, she'd drive back north a mile or so and pick Darrell up at an old logging road that was cut into the forest off Route 176, a stone's throw from U.S. 65.

Driving back to the campground, Darrell went over the plan two or three more times, making certain Mary understood what she was supposed to do. She told him sure, sure, she got it, no need to keep going on about it.

Five hours later, almost midnight, the campground quiet now, with nobody else around, Darrell said it was time to move. He'd put on camouflage clothing and smeared his face with paint, stuffed his pockets with extra ammunition, and packed a knapsack with a bedroll, binoculars, and food. He was armed with a bowie knife, a Smith & Wesson .357 pistol, and the 12-gauge Benelli shotgun Mary had bought in Phoenix.

On the way back down to Bear Creek Road, a thin fog drifting out of the hills, Mary said maybe they should just forget about the whole thing. Turn back now before it was too late, pick up their camper, and clear right out of the area. Maybe they could go to California, change their names, try to find work. Darrell said there wasn't any point turning back now. They'd known for some time they'd have to deal with Lloyd, and this was what he meant to do.

What if Lloyd wasn't even at his cabin? Mary wanted to know. In that case, Darrell said, he'd maybe just burn the place down and then go over the next hill and pay Rocky a visit. But if Lloyd was there, he was going to have to kill him.

Darrell squeezed Mary's shoulder, told her he loved her, and slipped out of the car. He walked up the creek, no sign of life except for some farmhouses on his right, the glow from their kitchen windows lighting up the trees, and made his way to a hill overlooking Rocky's house. Since Mary had dropped him off, he'd been thinking of maybe settling things with Rocky first, then moving on to Lloyd, but the house was completely dark, no vehicles around, nothing doing. He found an abandoned barn nearby and decided to pack it in for the night. First thing in the morning, with a few hours' sleep under his belt, he'd assess the situation anew.

A few minutes before five on the evening of Friday, May 13, Jesse Lawrence decided to call it a day. He'd been working hard since early morning, trying to put the finishing touches on a gravel road he'd been building on his Uncle Lloyd's Taney County farm. He fished in the pockets of his jean jacket for his cigarettes, lit the last one, scrunched the empty pack in his fist, and tossed it into his Ford pickup. The new road was looking good. Another day or two, and the job should be done. Jesse was expecting Lloyd to come up from Shell Knob over the weekend to spend some time at the farm, probably bringing Frankie and Willie with him. No reason, he thought, for Lloyd not to be pleased with how the road was shaping up.

Lloyd was Jesse's favorite relative on his father, Howard's, side. As far back as he could remember he'd always liked Lloyd, always enjoyed being around him. Time spent with Lloyd was never dull. He always had some new scheme up his sleeve he'd be telling you about, or some recent adventure he'd dress up in colorful detail. Lloyd was a hustler, never at a loss for new angles, and he had personality to burn. He also had a generous side, which Jesse'd had occasion to see for himself. When times were tough, as they'd been since the breakup of Jesse's last marriage, Lloyd had always taken the trouble to throw some work his way. He'd given him this latest job laying the gravel road, a job down at Blue Eye fixing up his cockfighting arena, other pieces of work here and there. Actually, the arrangement worked out favorably for both men. Lloyd paid well, always in cash, and Jesse made sure he got his money's worth.

Jesse was nobody's fool. He liked Lloyd, respected him for his derring-do, but he also knew his uncle wasn't exactly in the running for a good citizenship award. He'd heard the rumors about methamphetamine, about Lloyd being an

Ozarks drug kingpin, and he strongly suspected the rumors were true. Nothing would have surprised him about Lloyd. He knew his uncle loved to live life on the edge, and that he'd have no aversion to operating outside of the law. As long as Jesse had known him, Lloyd had considered himself invincible. He took care of business the way he wanted, always assuming nothing could touch him. And who was going to argue with him? Lloyd was tough as nails, as fearless as the pitbulls he raised for fighting. Even now, in his sixties, slowed down and overweight, you wouldn't want to mess with Lloyd. Jesse remembered a few years ago, at the cockfights in Blue Eye, a big guy, drunk and obnoxious, started badmouthing Lloyd. The dude challenged Lloyd to a fight. Lloyd hammered him, knocked him ten rows back. The way Jesse saw it, Lloyd was into some nasty business but he was as likeable a guy as you'd ever meet. Just make sure you didn't cross him.

Jesse stamped out his cigarette, got into his cream-colored pickup, and drove out of the property, stopping to shut and lock the gate behind him. He figured on driving to Spank's on U.S. 160 for gas and cigarettes, then heading home to Kissee Mills the other side of Forsyth.

As Jesse was gassing up, Lloyd pulled up in his '74 black-and-gray Chevy Suburban, with his longtime sidekick Travis Clark in the passenger seat. Jesse had seen Travis around quite a bit over the years, mostly hanging out with Lloyd, and though he didn't know him too well, Travis had generally struck him as a pretty good guy. Slim, medium height, about Jesse's age, somewhere in his mid-forties, Travis was known locally as a smooth talker, always working the angles, never losing his cool. He was so smooth, Jesse'd heard, he could talk you into a scheme you didn't like faster and easier than just about anybody else could talk you into one you actually liked.

The three men stood outside Spank's for a while, thumbs hooked over their belt buckles, shooting the breeze. Lloyd said he and Travis had just come from their buddy Phil Church's car dealership south of Springfield, where they'd

spent the afternoon talking cockfighting. He gave Jesse a
hundred bucks toward what he owed him for the roadwork
and asked if Jesse'd mind spending the next day, Saturday,
finishing the job. That way, Lloyd said, he'd come by the
farm himself early in the morning and pay Jesse the rest of
what he owed him. Jesse liked the idea. He was just as eager
as Lloyd to see the job finished, though he wouldn't be holding his breath waiting for Lloyd to show up the next morning. His uncle wasn't known for his dependability. Anyway,
it didn't really matter whether he got paid the rest that was
coming him tomorrow. Lloyd would straighten him out
eventually; he always did. Jesse said that'd be fine. He'd
head home now and be back at work at about eight or nine in
the morning.

On Saturday morning, Darrell went outside and shook off
the straw that was still clinging to his clothes from his
night's sleep. He took a leak beside the barn, then gathered
up his gear and went down to Rocky's house to check out the
action. Still nothing doing, nobody home. Thinking he
might have to catch up with Rocky some other time, he went
back toward the barn, hid his knapsack in some bushes, and
made his way to a hill that gave him a partial view of the
Lawrence property, probably as good as he was going to get
without moving closer and risking being seen. He sat down
on the hillside and watched some cattle grazing on an adjoining property a couple of ridges over, coming close once
or twice to dozing off in the morning sun. About nine
o'clock, an old cream-colored Ford pickup, with a big guy
driving, too far away for Darrell to make out, came onto the
property and disappeared behind a stand of cedars by
Lloyd's cabin. Darrell thought he heard the door to the
pickup click open and slam shut, but that was it. Silence. The
guy must be a lookout, one of Lloyd's henchmen. Best wait
on the hillside and see if Lloyd himself showed up.

Darrell waited until late afternoon, getting hungry now,
annoyed with himself for leaving his pack with food and
binoculars way over on another ridge. About four o'clock,

deciding to go get the pack, he crept down the hill just as Lloyd barreled onto the property in a cloud of dust, his left elbow stuck out the open window of his Chevy Suburban. Darrell crouched in the brush beside the road and ten or twenty seconds later a second vehicle came along at a slower clip, a red-and-gray Chevy pickup, but it was too tough from his position in the brush to make out who was in it. He heard Lloyd talking with the big guy who'd come in earlier, then the sound of a door shutting, and the cream-colored pickup drove past him toward the gate. He began crawling out of the brush but some cranes nearby started kicking up a fuss, so he decided to stay put, just sit still for a while, before going over and getting his pack.

Later on, five or six hours later, after dark, Darrell left his pack in the brush by the road, and, shotgun in hand, stole up closer to Lloyd's cabin. He saw lights in the windows and heard country music playing on a radio; it sounded like a Waylon Jennings song. He edged closer, trying to get a clearer look inside, but once again some cranes started making a racket, hollering and beating their wings. Darrell froze. He heard Lloyd tell somebody to turn off the radio. Thinking Lloyd might send somebody outside to check on the noise, or if he had dogs with him at the cabin, turn them loose, Darrell retreated to the brush, all revved up, his breath coming in short, hard gasps. *Slow down*, he told himself. *Be cool. Get this thing under control.*

Darrell felt tired and spooked, too beat down from waiting and watching and worrying to try anything else right now. He found a little draw, a dry creek bed close to the road, shrouded in brush. He spread out his bedroll and lay down. A couple of hours later, still not sleeping but with his nerves settled, he felt ready for another try. He made it halfway to the cabin, saw a light inside, then thought, *No way, something's wrong here, too quiet, go back, go back now, get some sleep, wait till morning.*

Next morning, Sunday, May 15, Darrell decided he'd wait for Lloyd to come to him. He picked out a spot next to a big tree, right by the road leading from Lloyd's cabin, about twenty yards from where it forded a ten-yard-wide creek called West Fork. He cut some branches with his bowie knife and, throwing one on top of another, made a blind a little over six feet high, shaped in a semicircle. He hunkered down behind it, settling in for the wait.

Sometime later, a couple of minutes either side of noon, the day coming on hot and sticky, he heard the roar of a motor approaching from the direction of Lloyd's cabin, the sound muffled by the trees crowding both sides of the road. He stood up, shotgun poised, ready for action—*no more waiting, this was it*—and peered through an opening near the top of the blind.

The sound beat down on him fast until, five seconds, six seconds, no time at all, it was right on top of him.

Hold it. Hold it. Don't shoot. It's just the kid. Darrell lowered his gun. It was Lloyd's grandson Willie, the poor paralyzed kid in a T-shirt and sweatpants hammering past at forty or forty-five, his Yamaha four-wheeler jacked up full throttle. The laces of his white sneakers were tied to the front rack to keep his shriveled legs from falling off, and his back was arched and arms stretched to the limit so he could work the hand levers. The kid hurtled past, eyes dead-set on the road ahead. He shot through the creek, barely slowing down, picked up the road on the other side, and scorched around a bend.

Willie was gone, the roar from his engine trailing off into the woods, when Darrell heard the sound of a second four-wheeler coming his way, this one moving slow, forever slow. He raised the Benelli, waiting, then saw Lloyd and Frankie coming toward him, forty yards away, Lloyd driving, looking this way and that, Frankie sitting behind him holding onto his waist.

Thirty yards . . . twenty . . . *almost, almost . . . now*. Darrell stepped out from behind the blind and blasted Lloyd in the left side, crumpling him into the handlebars. He shot Frankie in the chest, exploding her heart and lungs, the force of the blast bending her backward and leaving her head and arms dangling in midair. He shot Lloyd again, in the right side this time, the slug ripping through his shoulder and out his chest, jerking him sideways and wrenching his head and upper torso out of the four-wheeler, facedown, like he was looking for something he'd dropped on the ground.

The blue four-wheeler drifted toward the creek. Darrell followed it ten or fifteen yards down the road and watched as it came to a stop in the shallow water.

Just then he heard a roar coming from the opposite direction. *It's Willie*, he thought. *The kid must have heard the shots.*

Darrell saw Willie come around the bend and bomb across the creek, headed straight for him. He shot him in the chest from fifteen feet. The impact lifted Willie out of his seat and sent him crashing headfirst into the ground. The four-wheeler, with Willie splayed upside down over the side, his feet still tied to the front rack, rolled backward down the creek bank and nudged up against Frankie and Lloyd's.

Darrell walked over and shot the kid in the head at point-blank range, spraying bits of brain over the creek bank and road. He turned the shotgun on Frankie and blew off the back of her head. Lloyd was next, a blast through the top of the forehead from four or five feet.

He slung the gun over his shoulder, reached across and took two gold rings, one of them diamond-studded, from Lloyd's left hand, and a gold Pulsar watch from his wrist. He reached into Lloyd's back jeans pocket and pulled out his wallet, a nice brown leather job, with two fighting cocks engraved on one side, and crossed spur gaffs on the other. He turned off the ignition of Frankie and Lloyd's four-wheeler, then Willie's, picked up some spent shell casings—*no time to look for them all*—and retrieved his pack and rifle from behind the blind. One last hurried look around—*move it, get outta here.*

Walking through the woods to Bear Creek, he paused to go through the wallet: six hundred dollars in tens, twenties, and fifties; a driver's license; telephone, insurance, and veteran's cards; a Missouri game breeder's card; a photograph of Lloyd's youngest daughter, Retha. He removed the cards and photograph—everything but the money—and hid them under a log. He started walking again, and then thought he'd better ditch the wallet too; just hang on to the money—the money, the rings, and the watch. He spotted another log, fifteen feet from the first one, and stuffed the wallet underneath.

He walked down the creek to the bridge on U.S. 65, tied the orange ribbon to the tree he'd pointed out to Mary, then crossed under and made his way to the little logging road up by the junction of U.S. 65 and Route 176.

Sunday afternoon at about two, Mary was sitting at Camp Ridge trying to figure out the best way of proceeding. She knew she'd have to leave soon for Bear Creek Road but she didn't want to get there too early, before Darrell had a chance to get away from Lloyd's farm and make his way to their rendezvous point. At the same time she didn't want to get there too late, leaving Darrell waiting in the woods, maybe wondering if she'd lost her nerve and wasn't going to show up at all. It was a question of timing, and she wasn't the least bit straight on how to get the timing right.

She'd gone down to Bear Creek the day before, on Saturday, but the ribbon wasn't there so she'd come right back. She'd considered checking again after dark but eventually thought better of it. The risk was too great. One of Lloyd's people might spot her, or someone might notice the station wagon with its out-of-state plates and then remember it later on for the police.

So she'd stuck it out here for the rest of the evening and all of today, trying to kill time. She'd given the dogs a good run, she'd listened to some music on the car radio, but mostly she'd worried. This whole business had left her a nervous wreck. It seemed to have just snuck up on her, scene by scene, like a plot in a movie she had no control over. That's what it sometimes felt like, a movie, like someone else was playing her, and someone was playing Darrell, and she was watching but couldn't change the direction of things. She was there, but she also wasn't there, and she was having trouble believing any of this was really happening.

Sure, they'd talked about it often enough, Darrell telling her how they needed to come back and deal with Lloyd, the two of them taking the trouble to buy the shotgun and the rifle, but she'd never really thought it would come to this. She'd expected, well, she wasn't exactly sure what she'd expected—she'd *hoped* that somewhere along the line things would have taken care of themselves. Lloyd would have grown tired of chasing them and called off the dogs. Or they would have slipped into new identities and started up a new life, free of worry, maybe somewhere in California.

Even over the past day or so she'd found herself hoping. Hoping that Lloyd wouldn't even be at his farm this weekend. Or if he was, that Darrell would just confront him and scare him into backing off—for good. Hoping, one way or another, that Darrell would get out of there safely so they could move on.

But now she had to think about going down there again and picking up Darrell—and hope she got the timing right. And there was something else. What should she do about the camper? Yesterday she'd left it at the campground, not wanting to risk maneuvering it around those back roads. But what if they needed to make a quick getaway? Once she got Darrell, they might not have time to come back for it. On the other hand, what if Darrell still wasn't ready to be picked up? She'd only make herself that much more conspicuous hauling the thing around. She decided to leave it where it was for the time being.

It was somewhere past four when Mary pulled off U.S. 65 onto Bear Creek Road. She saw the orange ribbon on the tree under the bridge, swung the car around, and drove to the designated pickup spot. *Where was he? Why couldn't she see him?* Mary hung on for a few minutes, once or twice thinking she saw some movement in the woods, then pulled back out onto U.S. 65 and headed north for the camper. It wasn't something she reasoned out, more like an instinct. Somehow she just knew that once she and Darrell hooked up, *if they hooked up*, they'd better be prepared to run.

It was almost dark when Mary returned, camper in tow.

She'd tuned the car radio to a local country station, hoping the music would calm her nerves. She sidled along Route 176, looking, looking, and there he was. Darrell came out of the woods and got in beside her. "Let's move," he said. "Let's go."

Just two minutes up U.S. 65, the music was interrupted for a news bulletin. Mary was too wrapped up in her driving to pay much attention, but she caught bits and pieces of it, more than enough to realize it had something to do with Darrell. *Three bodies found in a remote corner of Taney County . . . multiple gunshot wounds . . . a man, a woman, and their nineteen-year-old grandson . . . investigators on the scene . . .*

She said nothing for a while, not even looking at Darrell, giving it a chance to sink in.

"Who was it?" she finally asked. "Lloyd and Frankie?"

Darrell nodded.

"And the grandson?"

Darrell said it was Willie. "It's over with," he said. "It's finished."

They took the first Springfield exit off U.S. 65 and headed east along U.S. 60. They didn't have a particular destination in mind, no plan except getting as far away from Taney County as they could.

Thirty or forty miles outside the town of Cabool, Darrell showed Mary the watch and rings he'd taken from Lloyd. She looked at them with horror and disgust. She couldn't believe he'd taken these things and was showing them to her. She told him she wanted no part of them. Darrell rolled down his window, flung the watch into the night, and told her to forget it. He couldn't stand her being so upset.

He tucked the rings into his jacket pocket, thinking he'd pawn them or unload them at a truck stop somewhere down the line. Chances were they'd need the money.

They drove late into the night, tough going with the camper on the twisty two-laner, crossing into Illinois near Cairo. Working a road map, Darrell suggested they steer clear of the Interstate and head north on Route 127.

About fifty miles up Route 127 from the Illinois state line, not far from the village of Alto Pass, a huge cross constructed of marble and steel stands more than a hundred feet tall atop Bald Knob Mountain. The cross was built in 1963 as a monument to Christianity in America, and at nighttime, lit by powerful floodlights at its marble base, it can be seen for miles around.

Years later, thinking back on it, Darrell couldn't remember exactly how they came to spend that first night sleeping in the station wagon at the foot of Bald Knob Cross. Maybe they saw it shining in the nighttime sky from Route 127 and just gravitated toward it. Or maybe, finally giving in to fatigue, they just turned off onto the mountain road leading up to it not realizing what they'd find at the top.

SIX

For the first couple of hours after the bodies were found, there was some confusion over jurisdiction. No one knew for sure whether the murder site was in Taney County or Stone County. It was right near the border between the two, everyone was agreed on that, but it wasn't until maps were consulted and local residents queried that the jurisdictional issue was resolved. The killings, it was finally determined, had taken place in Taney County, less than a hundred yards from the Stone County line.

Deputy Jerry Dodd of the Stone County Sheriff's Department, who had been videotaping the crime scene, asked Taney County Sheriff Chuck Keithley if he had any plans for kick-starting the investigation.

"Same plan as always," Keithley said. "I'm going to put in a call to Tom and Jack."

Sergeants Tom Martin and Jack Merritt worked out of the Division of Drug and Crime Control at the Missouri Highway Patrol Troop D headquarters in Springfield. The DDCC had been established in 1983 as a statewide support agency for rural counties that didn't have adequate resources for investigating serious crimes such as homicide. As the mainstays of the Troop D unit, Tom and Jack had a tough beat: eighteen counties in southwest Missouri—most of them intractably rural, dirt poor, and drug infested. The two men were widely regarded in Missouri law enforcement circles as crack investigators, among the very best the state had to offer, but this didn't mean their services were always eagerly sought after. The fact is, Tom and Jack could investigate crimes in any given county only through the invitation of the local sheriff. The invitation was sometimes slow in coming; sometimes it didn't come at all. More than a few sheriffs were zealously territorial. Their counties were their fiefdoms; they didn't want hotshots from Springfield or anywhere else coming in and stirring things up, suggesting (by their very presence) that the local bossmen weren't fully in charge. Any investigating that needed doing, they'd take care of themselves.

Chuck Keithley was too good a sheriff to get caught up in petty issues of territoriality. Since being elected to office in 1972 he'd developed a close rapport with state and federal law enforcement agencies and over the past five years he'd routinely called Tom and Jack whenever a homicide struck close to home. He knew they were good at what they did, and he also appreciated that both men had worked the roads as state troopers before joining the Highway Patrol's crime unit. Chuck had a soft spot for state troopers. Just three years earlier, Trooper Jimmie Linegar had been gunned down by a baby-faced white supremacist from Idaho named David Tate during a routine traffic check south of Branson. Jimmie Linegar had been one of Chuck's closest friends. A devout Christian, he used to witness to Chuck while the two men played pool in the Keithley family home. Jimmie's death had a profound impact on Chuck. Just weeks afterward, almost by way of homage to the slain trooper, Chuck converted to Christianity.

Tom Martin drove down from Springfield as soon as he got the call. It was a Sunday and he'd been relaxing at home with his wife, Alice, but he knew this was a case that couldn't wait. A triple homicide was big enough; a triple homicide with Lloyd Lawrence as one of the victims just about broke the bank.

Tom knew a great deal about Lloyd; he'd been tracking

him for years but hadn't succeeded in pinning him down. He'd come close in August 1984 when a police task force busted a meth laboratory in a shed on Lloyd's family property down near Shell Knob. It was close—but not good enough. One of Lloyd's longtime associates, an Oklahoman named Richard Gerald Williamson, took the fall on this one and was eventually sentenced to a three-year term at a federal prison in Texas. Lloyd actually testified for the prosecution at Williamson's trial, saying he had rented the shed to the defendant but had no idea how it was being used.

A year and a half later, in March 1986, Tom discovered that Lloyd had recently purchased a truckload of chemicals and laboratory equipment from a firm in Tulsa. There was no question in Tom's mind what this stuff was meant for but he wasn't able to close the circle. All his trails went cold.

Things heated up again in February 1987 when a desperado named Glennon Paul Sweet murdered Trooper Russell Harper on U.S. 60 east of Springfield after the patrolman had stopped him for speeding. Sweet was closely connected to the outlaw drug culture of southwest Missouri, which meant of necessity that he was also connected to Lloyd. While heading up the investigation into the slaying, Tom obtained intelligence on the operation of at least a dozen clandestine meth labs within a seventy-mile radius of Springfield. Over the next couple of months, Tom and Jack and DEA agent Harley Sparks took down several major labs in Douglas and Webster Counties. They would have taken down even more if the people running them hadn't been tipped off. In every case it was the same story. There was plenty of evidence linking Lloyd to the labs but not quite enough to make any charges stick. Lloyd's influence was ubiquitous. Tom and Jack and Harley had even linked him to a doctor selling meth out of his office in Barry County.

For Tom the whole business had been maddening. It wasn't just the meth that disturbed him but the violence that went with it. During one recent stretch there had been almost a homicide a week on Lloyd's drug turf. And now this. At least one thing, apparently, had changed—it wasn't Lloyd's turf any longer.

Driving down U.S. 160 past Highlandville, entering Ozark country now, Tom couldn't help thinking of Harley Sparks. It was too bad Harley was back at his office in Kansas City. It would have been nice having him along. Harley was one of a kind. Most DEA agents wanted nothing to do with the Ozarks. It was a tough gig, stamping around in the backwoods, lying out in the brush for days and nights on end doing surveillance, sneaking up on meth labs at remote farmhouses and converted pig barns not knowing if they were booby-trapped with explosives. And the odor—that putrefying, death-and-urine stench that was the surest sign of meth being cooked. While other DEA agents were avoiding the job like the plague, Harley couldn't seem to get enough of it. For as long as Tom could remember, Harley had been working the Ozarks, spending nights in twelve-dollar motels, living out of a suitcase. Maybe it was the country boy in him (he'd been raised on a farm outside Konawa, Oklahoma), but Harley never complained about the rough going. Tom hated to think where they would have been without him. Practically every week, he and Jack could count on Harley making the drive down from Kansas City eager for another stint in the field. It was a comforting sight, tall and lanky Harley, even-tempered Harley, with glasses and thinning gray-brown hair, showing up at Troop D headquarters on a Monday morning with a fistful of case folders and a shoulder holster bulging with his 9 mm Sig Sauer. Maybe they weren't winning the meth war, Tom thought, but one thing was for sure: without Harley Sparks they'd have lost it a long time ago.

When Tom arrived, Jack was already on the scene gathering evidence: shell casings, cigarette butts, the usual stuff, flushing bits of brain out of the creek.

"It's a bad one, Tommy," he said.

Jack was in his early forties, tall and fit, and an accomplished investigator. He was born in the front room of a farmhouse in Christian County south of Springfield, and he'd been with the Highway Patrol in various capacities since 1970. A deeply religious man, a deacon in his Baptist church in Springfield, he didn't drink or smoke or gallivant (nor did Tom, for that matter), but he did have a devilish streak in him. Whereas Tom was all business, twelve hours a day, half an hour off for lunch, Jack was an irrepressible prankster. If you hung out with Jack, you'd want to be on your guard; you never knew when he was going to strike next. Just a few months earlier, Jack and Tom had been in Webster County investigating a multiple homicide. A dairy farmer named James Schnick had shot and killed seven family members, including his four young nephews. They were at the Schnick farmhouse in Elkland with Webster County sheriff Eugene Fraker the day after the killings looking for evidence. It was late, coming on midnight, and old Sheriff Fraker was worn slick from all the work and pressure. He lay back on a couch, thinking he'd just stretch out and relax for a couple of minutes, but he was soon fast asleep, snoring with his mouth wide open. Jack snapped a photo of Fraker in this indecorous pose and the next day had it blown up and kiddingly threatened to use it against the sheriff in his re-election campaign.

Tom was the supervisor of the Troop D crime unit, and in most respects a demanding boss, but he didn't seem to mind Jack's penchant for practical joking. For one thing, it helped ease the built-in pressures of the job. At the time of the Schnick killings, he and Jack had half a dozen other homicides in their active files. This was nothing unusual—just par for the course. If not for Jack's occasional pranks, the endless diet of tragedy may have been too tough to take.

Tom wasn't the kind of cop who stoked up his reputation with big talk and bravado. He didn't clamor to be noticed. He was also a country boy, raised on a farm in Pulaski County, the third of eight kids, and he'd spent fifteen years working the roads as a trooper before transferring to criminal investigations. He was going on fifty now but he wore the years well: six feet tall, weighing 180 pounds, with blue eyes and brown hair, ruddy complexion, and a country twang to his speech that nicely understated his sharpness of mind. Tom had made his mark in the DDCC through quiet persistence, cultivating informants, chasing down every imaginable lead, refusing to give up even on cases that weeks of intensive investigation hadn't made a dent in. He was at his best out in the field, interviewing people, digging up information. He could be ornery when the occasion called for it, but usually he took an easy-does-it, hands-in-the-pockets approach. He knew you generally didn't get very far trying to run over country people with a gun and a badge.

Tom told Jack he'd do some looking around and hook up with him later. He walked from the creek back to the road leading to Lloyd's cabin. By now there were almost as many newspeople as lawmen on the scene. Dennis Graves, the lead correspondent for KY3 TV, the NBC affiliate in Springfield, had arrived with his crew and was wrapping up an interview with Chuck Keithley. He caught Tom's eye. Tom liked Dennis, and admired his persistence and resourcefulness. He'd always thought Dennis would have made a terrific criminal investigator. Right now, however, he wasn't feeling up to facing the cameras. Tom corralled Chip Mason, who was also now on the scene, and they headed off for Rocky Redford's house at the dead end of County Road 160–10, just half a mile away. Maybe Rocky would be able to give them something solid.

But Rocky wasn't living there any longer. The new tenant, a man from Kimberling City named Donald Ousley, said he'd never laid eyes on the guy. He'd heard that Rocky had moved out in a big hurry some time ago.

Later on, back at the office, Tom and Jack compared notes. They both had Darrell pegged as a prime suspect, largely because of what Rocky had told Chip and Jim Justus a few months earlier. If Lloyd had been intent on killing Darrell, there was a good chance Darrell would have found out about it and decided to cut Lloyd off at the pass. Another strong possibility was Richard Gerald Williamson, whom Lloyd had ratted out in federal court back in 1984. They'd definitely want to track these guys down for questioning. But there was no sense at this stage zeroing in on just one or two individuals. Lloyd had moved in violent circles; the shooter could have been almost anyone.

First thing Tuesday morning Tom drove to Shell Knob. It wasn't something he was looking forward to, so soon after the killings, but he knew he had to touch base with Lloyd's children.

Buck and David Lawrence lived on farms just outside of town, a quarter mile apart. Buck, at forty, was the older of the two, and the oldest of Lloyd and Frankie's five children; he was also young Willie's dad. Tom interviewed the brothers separately but heard pretty much the same things from both. The Lawrence family got along well together—no major conflicts, no festering wounds. Many of them, Buck and David included, were active in the Jehovah's Witness church over in Cassville. They'd occasionally suspected their father of being involved in some kind of illegal activity, but he'd always denied it. If pressed, he'd insist that he made all his money cockfighting. And Darrell Mease? Well, a short while ago Lloyd had told them that Darrell had ripped him off for a substantial amount of money. He was clearly upset about it. It seemed he intended to kill Darrell, or have someone do it for him. He said that when he found him Darrell would be "alligator bait."

Tom met with Retha Lawrence, who had discovered the bodies two days before, and then with Retha's older sister Rita. Rita, thirty-two, lived with her husband on a farm near Lloyd and Frankie's place. She told Tom that her father had raped her when she was sixteen years old, and that he'd also raped her sister Rosemary, who was a year older. The two sisters had gone to Galena and signed a complaint against Lloyd. He was arrested and tried in Stone County court but wasn't convicted. Their mother left him when the rape allegations first came to light, but she soon came back and took his side. Since then, Rita said, she'd had only limited contact with her father. She did know, however, that he'd been involved for years with a woman from Crane, Missouri, named Dorothy Mangold. The affair had been an open secret: everyone in the family knew about it but had carried on as if they didn't.

Tom tracked Rosemary down in Bentonville, Arkansas, where she was living with her husband, Steven. Yes, it was true, Rosemary said. Their father had raped her and Rita when they were teenagers. She had left home immediately after the incident and hadn't spoken with him since.

"Do you think your father ever felt sorry for what he did to you?" Tom asked.

"As far as I can tell, he never felt sorry about anything he did."

"How did your mother feel about what happened?"

"Well, she stayed with him, didn't she?"

"Did you ever hear anything about your father being involved with illegal drug activity?"

"I can't say for sure, but I wouldn't be surprised if he was. Nothing would surprise me about him."

Back at the office, Tom puzzled it through. The Lawrences clearly weren't the best-adjusted bunch, but he seriously doubted the triple homicide was the work of a family member. It had all the earmarks of an execution-style slaying, which meant it was most likely tied in with local drug interests. Lloyd would have been the primary target; Frankie and Willie just happened to be in the wrong place at the wrong time. Darrell remained an obvious suspect but Tom was committed to keeping an open mind. There were plenty of other people he wanted interviewed. Who knew what might show up down the road?

Tom realized he and Jack had a lot of ground to cover in a short while, more than they could probably cover on their own, so he put in a call for assistance to the Highway Patrol's Troop G detachment in Willow Springs. Doug Loring and Carl Watson worked the crime unit in Troop G, and over the years they'd always been more than happy to lend a helping hand. Doug and Carl were big country boys, offensive-line size, and sharp investigators in their own right. They were also good and decent men, not an ounce of pretension between them. They were responsible for nine rough and scraggly counties in the southern Ozarks. Two of their counties had sheriffs who couldn't read; all of them were sprouting meth labs like wildflowers. Helping out from time to time on Tom and Jack's turf wasn't much of a stretch.

Doug and Carl started by interviewing Darrell's first wife, Joyce, who was now working at the Hillbilly One Stop service station on U.S. 160 at Highlandville. Joyce said she thought Darrell "was capable of doing the Lawrence killings" and recounted how he had once sprayed the hood of her car with bullets. She said that her husband, John, believed he'd seen Darrell recently in the Reeds Spring area driving a gray-and-blue Ford Grenada. She also said that she'd gone over to Galena recently and filed a complaint against Darrell for failure to pay child support. He had paid $375 in December but not a penny since. She said that the Stone County authorities had responded to her complaint by issuing a warrant for Darrell's arrest.

While Doug was at the courthouse in Galena checking on Joyce's story, Carl went to Crane and met with Dorothy Mangold in her trailer home. Was it true, Carl asked, that she'd been Lloyd's longtime lover? Yes, Dorothy said, she'd known Lloyd for thirty-two years, since she was nineteen.

"I was a secret. My family knew about Lloyd but Lloyd's wife and children didn't know about me."

She said that Lloyd would come to her place up to three times a week and they'd also make frequent trips to cockfights in Arizona, Oklahoma, and North Carolina. He'd spent the night with her on Friday, May 13, and had left about nine Saturday morning. This was the last time she saw Lloyd alive. She found out about his murder while watching television the next evening.

"Were you aware of Lloyd's drug dealing?" Carl asked.

"No, this is a complete surprise. But Lloyd never talked business with me."

"Do you know of anyone who might have wanted to kill him?"

"I can't imagine anyone wanting to hurt Lloyd," Dorothy

said. "He was very easygoing. I never heard of him having trouble with anyone."

Sure, Carl thought. Real believable.

The first week after the murders Tom and his team turned over every imaginable stone. Most of the local bad guys admitted hearing rumors of Lloyd's meth empire, but that was it: just grapevine stuff, nothing else.

"Sure, I heard things, but I wasn't involved. What do I know?"

"Hey, I had nothing against Lloyd. Why would I be interested in seeing him dead?"

"Come on, Tom, you know me. I wouldn't have anything to do with killing Lloyd. Anyway, I was out fishing when this deal went down. You don't believe me, I'll come in for a lie detector."

Some of his closest friends, including Travis Clark, insisted that Lloyd was a prince of a guy, a regular country gentleman, and that he'd been unfairly saddled with a bad reputation. No way was Lloyd involved in any illegal activity. This was just a smear campaign. To know Lloyd was to love him.

Tom and his team contacted Darrell's dad and younger brother. R.J. said he hadn't seen Darrell in five months and had no idea how to get in touch with him. It was his understanding Darrell had fled the state in order to avoid paying child support. Larry said he hadn't seen Darrell since Christmas and sometime before then he'd told him not to come around the house any longer. He didn't approve of the company Darrell was keeping. Larry knew Lloyd and his cronies; he knew they were dangerous men. If trouble arose between Darrell and Lloyd, he didn't want his wife and kids getting stuck in the middle of it.

John Prine, the new kid in the Troop D crime unit, tracked down Roger Widner in Oak Grove, Arkansas. Roger admitted that he and Lloyd had barged into Rocky Redford's house at gunpoint several months back. They'd thought Darrell might be hiding out with Rocky. He said he'd seen Lloyd at the coffee shop in Blue Eye a few days before he was mur-

dered. Lloyd was in good spirits. There was no telling who'd
want to kill Lloyd, he said.

On May 18, Jack Merritt and Chip Mason shot down to
Harrison, Arkansas, where a guy named George Shaw had
just been taken into custody. Shaw had gotten into a shootout
with the local police and wounded an officer after trying to
sell some jewelry at a pawnshop in town. This was potentially a case-breaking development. Jack and Chip knew that
some rings and a watch had been taken from Lloyd's body
after he was murdered. His children had insisted that he'd
always worn these items and they'd given a precise description of them to Tom. Maybe the shooter hadn't been Darrell
after all. As it turned out, the trip was a wasted afternoon.
The items that Shaw had been trying to hawk didn't fit the
description of Lloyd's missing jewelry and the shotgun he'd
used in wounding the Harrison cop didn't match with the
Taney County murder weapon.

Jack and Chip had better luck two days later when they
met with Rocky Redford off a side road north of Branson.
Chip had phoned Rocky at his father's house in Hutchinson,
Kansas, a day or two after the murders and told him he'd
better return to Missouri for a face-to-face conversation.

So now here they were, and Rocky seemed eager to
please. He said that Darrell had sometimes described how
he'd go about killing someone. He'd use a shotgun with
double-aught buckshot and slugs and then he'd destroy the
firing pin, cut the gun into pieces, and throw them in a lake.
He said that Darrell was an excellent shot and very knowl-
edgeable about guns and that he'd talked now and then about
wanting to acquire a Benelli. He said that Darrell and Mary
had fantasized about becoming a hit team.

Now that Rocky was warmed up, there was no shutting
him down. He speculated that Travis and Bush Clark had put
Darrell up to stealing drugs from Lloyd and, perhaps, killing
him. He said that Darrell would have come onto the
Lawrence property by foot off Bear Creek Road. He suggested that the Clark brothers might be hiding Darrell down
in Arkansas at Roger's place.

Jack and Chip knew better than to take all this at face value. They knew that snitches tended to overplay their hands. Rocky was trying to impress them, make himself look important. Some of the things he was telling them simply didn't add up. Darrell hiding out at Roger Widner's? Not likely, Rocky, not likely at all.

Nevertheless, there were certain things they couldn't ignore. Double-aught buckshot and slugs had been used in the killings, for example, and the murder weapon might very well have been a Benelli. What's more, they had canvassed the area around Lloyd's property, talked to all the neighbors, and no one had seen a strange vehicle coming or going the day of the murders. Chances were the shooter had in fact come down Bear Creek Road by foot.

For Chip this just about cinched it. He'd strongly suspected Darrell from the start; now he was almost certain.

"It doesn't look good for Darrell," he said to Jack after they'd sent Rocky on his way.

"You might say that," Jack agreed.

At the courthouse in Forsyth, Chip briefed county prosecutor Jim Justus on the rendezvous with Rocky. The two men agreed they'd definitely want to locate Darrell and pick him up for questioning. The problem was finding a way to do so. They couldn't very well go to a judge and expect, on the strength of Rocky's blabbering, to get a warrant issued for Darrell's arrest. Rocky was a mere informant—and not a terribly reliable one at that. This left them a little short in the probable cause department. Anyway, it was still early. Who could tell? Maybe they'd get lucky and Darrell would turn up somewhere in Missouri. Maybe Darrell and Mary would turn up together and one or both of them would be ready to talk.

SEVEN

But Darrell and Mary weren't about to turn up somewhere in Missouri. They were already long gone. After spending that first night at the foot of Bald Knob Cross, they cut north through Illinois and then went west along Interstate 80 all the way to Nevada, finally stopping in Elko. Along the way they picked up fake IDs at a truck stop and Darrell cut his hair and shaved his beard. By the time they hit Nevada they were passing themselves off as Kyle and Mary Hamlin.

They hadn't planned on sticking around Elko. They were driving through, looking for something to eat, when Darrell saw a construction site on the edge of town. A couple of Mormon contractors from Utah were building an extension on the Red Lion Casino. Darrell found out who was in charge and said he wanted a job as a carpenter. The Mormons said they'd take him on as a laborer and see how things worked out.

The promise of some steady money: maybe this was the fresh start they'd been hoping for. Elko was a town that seemed built for fresh starts. A neon oasis in the barren lands of northern Nevada, it had long been a hangout for gamblers, roughnecks, and desperadoes. Idaho Street, the main drag, was a glittering parade of all-night coffee shops, whiskey joints, and quick-jump motels. In the older section of town, along Railroad and up and down Fifth, you could take your chances at the Stumble Inn, Stray Dog, or Poker Slots Bar, or maybe test your luck at Stockmen's Casino. Everywhere you went there was a sense of new possibility, surprises sneaking up on you, sudden prospects lurking around dark corners.

About a mile south of town Darrell and Mary turned onto a dirt road off Lamoille Highway and wound their way into the hills. At road's end, on a high ledge studded with clumps of sagebrush, they parked the station wagon and got the camper ready for the night. It was an enchanting location. To the north were the dusk-drenched lights of Elko and miles beyond the rolling foothills of the Adobes. The Ruby Mountains sprang up in the distance to the south, and immediately below their hilltop perch—too late now to be clearly visible—there was an archery range and a small dirt racetrack.

Darrell was pleased. They could make their home here indefinitely, he thought. It was private and out of the way; there was a good chance nobody would bother them.

For most of the next two months they camped out in the same spot, cooking supper over an open fire, falling asleep to the rustle of the desert wind. Nobody bothered them; nobody seemed concerned whether they were up there or not. Most mornings Mary would cook breakfast and then Darrell would go off to his construction job at the casino. At lunchtime they'd usually meet for burgers and ice cream at the Dairy Queen on Idaho. Sometimes after work or on weekends they'd go down by the railroad station off Twelfth Street and sit on the bank of the Humboldt River drinking beer. Darrell and Mary didn't realize it at the time, but over the years this area by the river had served as a vagrants' camp, with hoboes and busted-out gamblers putting up tents and shanties and the local police periodically coming and clearing everything away.

Darrell had been a big fan of Louis L'Amour Westerns growing up, so it wasn't surprising that the high desert country around Elko held a special romance for him. He enjoyed visiting the original Pony Express cabin that sat on the front lawn of the Northeastern Nevada Museum on Idaho. The cabin had been erected in the Ruby Mountains in 1860 and relocated to Elko a century later.

Darrell had read about the Rubys and was eager to check them out in person. One long weekend he and Mary decided to do just that. They drove down scenic Route 228, all sagebrush and open sky, hardly a building in sight. After a stop for lunch in Jiggs, a tiny frontier outpost twenty-seven miles south of Elko, they took a treacherous rutted road twelve miles deep into the mountains. Two miles beyond Harrison Pass, right by a steep bend and dip in the road, they came to an abandoned mine tucked into the crevice of a canyon. It was the old Star Tungsten Mine, lost and forgotten, six dilapidated shacks, some still bearing traces of their original white and pink and yellow paint, a collapsed shaft and storage shed, and a small wooden building, probably the old mining office, standing beside a crackling mountain stream. The rusted-out hulk of a 1940s pickup truck and the skeletons of two other ancient vehicles lay in the rabbit brush near the front gate.

Darrell and Mary liked the haunted feel of the place—the prehistoric boulders and gnarled junipers perched on the surrounding cliffs, the hushed solitude, time at a standstill. They decided they'd bed down here for the night and see what the morning might bring.

The next morning Mary poked her head out the door of their camper and gasped in astonishment. They were snowed in. It was the middle of July and the Rubys were blanketed. Stranded, they survived the rest of the weekend on potatoes, the only food they'd brought with them. At one point a mule deer ran straight through their camp, but Darrell was caught off guard and didn't have a gun close at hand. He also saw some partridge, which he later found out were Himalayan snow cocks, but they came and went before he could make a move.

Darrell had taken a small quantity of meth with him when they fled Missouri after the killings. It was part of the batch he'd retrieved from the fire tower road and then buried at the campground near Chadwick. He'd been carrying it around in the station wagon, dipping into it occasionally behind Mary's back (though he suspected she knew exactly what he was up to). Now the two of them, stranded and bored, decided to dip into it together. It wasn't a good idea. Before long, Mary was complaining of feeling sick and disoriented. She said she hated taking meth and she also hated Darrell having anything to do with it. She insisted he swear off the stuff for good. Darrell agreed, saying that was it, never again. This time, more than ever before, he truly meant it.

The snow melted and they got back to Elko in time for Darrell to make it to work. He would have hated missing a day. Things were going well on the job. The Mormons were treating him decently and seemed to value his contributions. A few weeks earlier one of their carpenters hadn't shown up and they'd asked Darrell to fill in for the day. He'd quickly proven himself more skilled than the regular guy and ever since they'd been piling more responsibility on him. They also liked Darrell personally and Darrell and Mary as a couple. They'd given them access to private showers in the casino and offered them free weekend use of a Winnebago that was parked at the construction site. Darrell and Mary happily made use of the showers but politely declined the offer of the Winnebago. They were content enough sleeping up in the hills.

Toward the end of July the construction job at the casino came to a close. The Mormons didn't want to lose Darrell. They asked him to join them in Provo, Utah, where they had another job scheduled. Darrell turned them down. He was grateful for the invitation but was anxious to move on. His fake ID was shoddily made and he was concerned it might catch up to him if he stayed with any one outfit too long. Besides, he had already promised Mary a trip to Colorado.

Their last night in Elko they splurged on a steak dinner at a restaurant across the street from the Red Lion Casino and then took forty dollars apiece over to the slot machines. In no time Mary had lost all her money and talked Darrell out of half of his. Soon they were both tapped out. They had another six hundred, saved from Darrell's job, which they'd agreed they wouldn't touch. They were counting on it for gas and food. Mary searched the station wagon for loose change and found a dime buried behind the front seat. She held it up triumphantly and went back inside for one last crack at the slots. Darrell was impressed. Mary loved to gamble but she'd been able to shut it off without siphoning into their travel funds.

The next day, Colorado-bound, they stopped for a breather at Cherry Creek, a map-speck five miles off U.S. 93. They didn't find evidence of an actual creek, just a few beat-up shacks and a dirt road that petered off into the desert. Not to mention a rattlesnake that appeared out of nowhere and sent Mary and her dogs scurrying for cover. After the snake had gone its way, with no harm done, Darrell left Mary at the camper while he took a little walkabout.

When he returned, he found her balled up in the station wagon with her hands covering her face. He'd never seen her so distraught. He tried sweet-talking her but she didn't respond. He realized the pressure she'd been under, carrying the terrible burden of their recent past, and he wondered how much further she could go.

They sat together in the front seat, brooding, the two of them buried in their own private thoughts. Then they saw it, the red, purple, and yellow glow of the desert sunset, hauntingly beautiful. They'd never seen anything quite like it. Mary took their camera from the glove box and tried to capture it forever.

By mid-June Jim Justus and Chip Mason had given up on Darrell surfacing in the Ozarks. If (as seemed likely) he had committed the murders, he had probably fled the area soon afterward. Tom Martin and his team had looked everywhere, followed every lead, but Darrell was nowhere to be found.

The best way of tracking him down would be through an arrest warrant. Get Darrell into the NCIC computer system and he'd eventually be pulled over and taken into custody. Every cop in the country would be on the lookout for him. The problem was, they still didn't have probable cause to get a warrant issued for his arrest on the Lawrence homicides. It had occurred to them, however, that they might have another card to play. The previous June, after Darrell had been caught with a concealed weapon and a small stash of marijuana up by Rocky's place, Justus had placed him on deferred prosecution for the marijuana. The deal was that Taney County would dismiss the charge after two years, providing Darrell abided by certain conditions. One of these was his notifying the county within forty-eight hours of any change in his residence. This, apparently, he had failed to do.

On June 15, Jim and Chip met with Judge Joe Chowning at the Taney County Courthouse and requested a warrant for Darrell's arrest on the grounds that he had violated the terms of the deferred prosecution. Chowning gave them what they wanted; the warrant was issued the very next day. Somewhere along the line, however, there must have been an administrative screwup. The arrest warrant was issued on the wrong charge: not the misdemeanor marijuana charge but rather the felony weapons charge that had been wiped clean when Darrell paid a $73 fine in Judge Chowning's courtroom the previous June. The weapons charge was dead and gone; there was no just cause for resurrecting it. Nevertheless, Jim and Chip had their arrest warrant, though technically an invalid one. Now they were in business. Somewhere, sooner or later, Darrell would be picked up and held for questioning. It was simply a matter of waiting.

While waiting for Mary outside the Kettle Restaurant in Glenwood Springs, Colorado, Darrell was starting to feel a little drowsy. He rolled down the front windows of the station wagon but not even the crisp mountain air succeeded in perking him up. It was still just nine-thirty. Mary's shift wouldn't finish for another half hour. Might as well climb into the back of the wagon and grab some sleep.

He woke with Mary shaking him and saying, "Darrell, what happened to Louie?"

The little blond-haired dog was covered in soot and reeking of hickory smoke. It didn't take them long to realize what had happened. Darrell had parked right next to an open barbecue pit in the lot across the street from the Kettle Restaurant. He'd tied Slick up before going to sleep but hadn't bothered with Gretchen Louise. The little dog had jumped out the window and gotten into the pit and then come back while Darrell was still dozing. Mary didn't say another word about it but she was obviously annoyed. It would take quite a bit of scrubbing to get the dog back to normal.

The scrubbing would have to wait until the next day. For now they had to find a place to spend the night. Since arriving in Glenwood Springs in late July, they'd been improvising, sleeping here one night, there another, never sticking around very long in any one place for fear of drawing attention to themselves. They'd camped out at roadside parks and along creek banks in the hills, sometimes venturing as far as Basalt, Aspen, and New Castle in their quest for privacy, *invisibility*.

Only once had they actually paid for a place to sleep. Their first night in Colorado they'd spent fifteen bucks for a trailer hookup at the Hideout, an old campground three miles from downtown Glenwood Springs. They hadn't regretted it. The Hideout was a comfortably offbeat place, with a clear burbling creek and a clutch of rustic rental cabins. Back in the Roaring Twenties the oldest of the cabins had served as bordellos for railroad workers. If Darrell and Mary hadn't been running low on funds they would have enjoyed sticking around longer.

A day or two afterward Mary had landed the waitressing job at the Kettle Restaurant. For more than a month now, this had been their only source of income. It wasn't much but it had kept them going. Mary's tips were generally pretty good and she usually managed to salvage some leftovers from the kitchen at closing time.

Mary had sandwiches with her now, which they ate in silence driving east along the interstate. Feeling beat, they decided to crash for the night at a roadside picnic spot not far from Glenwood Springs.

The next morning Darrell suggested they go hiking up a

steep, mile-long trail in Glenwood Canyon. Halfway up
Mary said she'd had enough. She said she'd go back and
wait in the car with the dogs. Darrell expressed surprise.
Hadn't she always told him that she hated quitters? He set
out again on his own but before long Mary caught up with
him. She said she'd changed her mind about giving up and
wanted them to finish climbing the trail together. It was
worth the effort. At the top they found a beautiful, crystal-
clear pond with a small waterfall. The pond was known locally as Hanging Lake. They stood beside it, arm in arm,
losing themselves in the scenery.

Darrell was pleased that the hike turned out well, that he
and Mary were able to enjoy a moment of closeness by
Hanging Lake. The truth was, moments of this sort had
grown scarce in recent months. Since their latest flight from
Missouri a certain tension had developed between them.
Mary had become wary and distant. Sometimes Darrell
sensed that she was afraid of him. But he couldn't be sure:
talking had never been Mary's strong suit, at least not in her
relationship with him. Since they'd gotten together he'd
grown accustomed to searching for meaning in her every
solitary word and gesture. But now he couldn't seem to read
her at all. He had lost the key to her moods.

It didn't help that Darrell himself had fallen into a deep
funk. He had thought, an eternity ago, that disposing of
Lloyd would constitute a new lease on life. It hadn't worked
out that way. Most days he woke up depressed and confused,
unsure of who he was or where he was headed. It was a gigantic effort simply washing and getting something to eat.
And then there was the silent fuming, the anger he felt toward himself for not being able to find a job since the Mormons in Nevada, the anger he still felt toward Joyce and
Donna and a dozen other people back home. It was always
one or the other, the depression knocking him down or the
anger eating him up—never a day at peace.

There was something else, too, another cloud hanging
over the two of them. They were experiencing sexual troubles: Darrell wasn't able to perform as consistently as he

was accustomed to. It had been a periodic problem since Missouri and it had him flummoxed. Here he was, with the woman of his dreams, and things weren't always going according to program. Maybe all the stress he was under was canceling him out. Or perhaps it was payback for the drug and alcohol abuse. Making matters worse, they'd recently been forced to part with the pop-up camper. Needing money for food one weekend, they'd sold it to a woman at a gas station for a measly forty bucks. Now they didn't even have a place to stretch out in private and give things a chance to come together naturally. It was frustrating, *damn frustrating*.

With several hours yet to kill before Mary started work they drove into town and made their way to Veltus Park. Over the past month or so this had been their regular afternoon hangout. It was a pretty spot, a splash of green against Roaring Fork River, oak and pine trees, a covered picnic area, a playground, and standing right in the middle of it all, an old defunct one-room jailhouse. If the weather was cooperative, they'd spread their bedrolls on the grass and catch some sleep. Sometimes Mary would wash her uniform in the river and hang it on a tree to dry.

There were times they wished they could have saved themselves a trip out of town after Mary got off work and crashed right here, or maybe at Twin Rivers Park less than a mile away. No chance of that though. Glenwood Springs was a spic-and-span tourist enclave and the local authorities were determined to keep it that way. The parks were off limits after nightfall and anyone caught trying to sleep in them was either arrested or hustled out of town. Transients (at least those without cars) were generally forced to spend nights by the train tracks along the Colorado River east of town, where they'd hunker down in a cave and wash up in one of the hot springs for which the area was famous. Come September or October they'd hop a southbound freighter for warmer climates.

Darrell and Mary napped a bit and then made the short drive over to the Kettle Restaurant. Darrell said he'd pick her up later on. With time on his hands, he popped into a coffee shop and leafed through a newspaper thinking this might be the day he finally found a job. Nothing doing: not even a whisper of something he could take on.

After Mary cashed out they dropped by Doc Holliday's, a bar on Main Street near the bridge. They'd been here once or twice before. Doc Holliday had died in Glenwood Springs and some of his original letters were preserved under glass on the wall by the phone. In one of them Doc describes how he and Wyatt Earp once dry-gulched a couple of guys up in Glenwood Canyon: shot them to death in their bedrolls as they slept.

Over beers Mary said she'd met somebody interesting that evening, a middle-aged man who sat in the restaurant drinking coffee for three or four hours straight, talking with her every chance he got. He told Mary that he was a missionary for a new religious group and that the group's leader ("a great prophet") was holding a meeting at a motel in town the next day. He invited her to come along. Now she wanted to know if Darrell would go with her. Darrell didn't like the setup but he couldn't see turning Mary down. He knew that she'd been grasping for meaning these past few months, desperately seeking some kind of personal salvation. She'd been reading the Book of Revelation from a Bible she'd picked up at a secondhand bookstore and she'd occasionally dropped hints about wanting to make a commitment to some higher purpose. Okay, he said, he'd go. But she shouldn't be disappointed if he wasn't swept off his feet.

When Darrell and Mary arrived the next day, about fifteen seekers were huddled in the motel room, some sitting on metal folding chairs, others on the floor against the walls. The Prophet, a gaunt white-haired man of about sixty with a long gleaming face, was sitting with his legs crossed on the edge of the single bed. He hurried to his feet when he saw Mary and directed her to a chair in front that he'd apparently been saving in the event she showed up. (The missionary, slouched in a corner, must have told him about the delectable prospect he'd encountered at the restaurant the night before.) Darrell sat next to an attractive woman in a blue dress who gave no sign of even noticing him. She and the man beside her were leaning forward, hands clenched between their knees, faces frosty with anticipation, looking for all the world like they were ready to be raptured to heaven that very afternoon.

The Prophet smiled beatifically, held out his hands in welcome, and spoke in a voice deep and aching with concern, a voice for the ages.

Brothers and sisters, this is truly a blessing. I have come to give you guidance and you are here to receive it. Most of you are new. One or two of you have already learned what it means to walk in my shadow and lie down in the cold nights of despair with my heavenly burden.

Still smiling, he cocked his head and looked coyly at the woman in blue. Darrell stole a sidelong glance. She was gushing with pleasure, appearing almost on the verge of fluttering away.

You're here to receive my message but the forces of evil don't want you to. They're massing against me, spreading ugly rumors, trying to destroy me. But not just me: they're out to destroy all of us here today and everything we stand to accomplish. There's nothing surprising about this. The righteous have always been persecuted. This is the way of the world. In coming here today you've shown that you're unhappy with the way of the world. You're willing to risk a higher meaning, a greater truth . . .

Yow, this guy's too much, Darrell thought. Look at him making eye contact, checking out the prospects, lingering on Mary, taking his time with it.

. . . Brothers and sisters, our enemies, the enemies of truth—they want you to believe that I am soiled goods, a common sex criminal. But let me tell you, I didn't even fight the charges that were brought against me, false and blasphemous as they were. I knew I had to walk the path of suffering that had been laid out for me. I knew this was also the path of salvation . . .

Going right after Mary now. Not even bothering to disguise it. Going right after her with that voice of worn velvet, that patent-medicine smile. Trying to cut her out of the herd, Darrell thought.

. . . I would stand out in the yard of that prison and look up at the four guard towers not realizing at first what they symbolized . . .

Darrell was zoning out, the message coming at him in disconnected fragments. He felt a hand brushing against his knee. It was the woman in blue, reading the handwriting on the wall, maybe, going for a consolation prize.

. . . they were divine emissaries, these four Indians I met in prison. They had never told anyone else about their discovery: a clay tablet covered with sacred writing. They knew who I was even before I knew . . .

Now she was whispering something. Darrell shifted in his chair, his body language saying, uh-uh, not interested. The guy beside her was still leaning forward in rapt attention. The missionary got up and maneuvered his way into the bathroom.

. . . a corner of the tablet was missing. It had broken off. According to ancient prophecy, someone would eventually come into possession of the missing corner. That person would be Jesus Christ the Messiah . . .

Let me guess, Darrell said to himself. I wonder who just happens to have that missing piece.

. . . and so I was led, after my release, to a secret hiding place. And there it was. Brothers and sisters, there is no other way of putting it . . .

Pausing now, waiting for the toilet to finish flushing.

. . . there is no other way of putting it, brothers and sisters. I am the Messiah.

The next meeting, a few days later, Mary asked Darrell if he'd mind waiting outside with the dogs. She wanted to give it a go on her own. Darrell said okay but he advised her to be careful. He told her he'd read an article recently that said religious cults preyed on young people who were under stress and estranged from their families. She told him not to worry; she had the situation under control.

This second meeting was Mary's last. She didn't discuss

it with Darrell afterward and he didn't ask her about it. She simply let him know that she'd seen enough. In any event, they both knew that their days in Colorado were numbered. It was getting far too cold for sleeping outside. Arizona was beckoning again. This time, though, they planned on steering clear of Cottonwood.

Even Tom Martin, who wasn't in the habit of taking anything for granted, was convinced by now that Darrell was his man. He'd run down all the local outlaws, checked their stories, and one by one eliminated them as possibilities. Only Darrell was left standing. There was something, however, that didn't quite add up. If Darrell had been intent on killing Lloyd, why had he also killed Frankie and Willie? Why the three of them? Why not just the main guy?

Tom wasn't the only person in local law enforcement perplexed by the sheer extravagance of the crime. Just that morning a veteran patrolman had popped into his basement office at Troop D headquarters for a chat. The two men talked about the deer-hunting season just starting up and then the patrolman switched to the Lawrence homicides. He said he'd heard that Darrell was at the top of the suspect list.

Tom shrugged, noncommittal.

"The thing I can't figure out, Tommy, is the wife and the grandkid. Why take them out, too? This has got a lot of us scratching our heads. If Darrell just does Lloyd, maybe it's not such a big deal. Maybe there's people lining up to pin a medal on him."

Tom let the remark pass. He'd heard others exactly like it in recent weeks. At any rate, he'd been too busy of late trying to clean up the mess Lloyd had left behind to think of pinning a medal on anyone.

It was quite a mess, with more blasted-out lives than Tom cared to think about. Just a few weeks earlier he and Chip Mason had spent several hours in Taney County interviewing Billie Marlene MaCrae, one of the many walking wounded in the region's drug wars. Forty years old with brown hair and brown eyes, good looks faded by hard mileage, MaCrae first met Lloyd in 1985 through her then boyfriend Bill Gold, a tough and raunchy guy who rode with the Galloping Goose motorcycle gang out of Kansas City. Lloyd, looking to step up production, taught MaCrae and Gold how to cook meth and helped set them up in labs at two locations in Douglas County. In late 1986 MaCrae fled the county after Gold beat her to a pulp and burned her car. Lloyd, bless his heart, put her up at a motel in Cape Fair for a stretch and then she moved in with Kendall Schwyhart in Lampe. She was visiting relatives in Oklahoma when Gold, in March of 1987, confronted Schwyhart at his home and stabbed him in the side, leaving him to bleed to death in his living room. Lloyd Lawrence, Kendall Schwyhart, and Bill Gold: three of the leading outlaws in southwest Missouri—two of them now dead, the third awaiting trial on murder charges. MaCrae told Tom and Chip that she was trying to put her life back together.

Over in Reynolds County, not long after Tom and Chip's meeting with Billie MaCrae, Carl Watson and Doug Loring helped bust a meth lab that was being run out of a trailer belonging to Billie Dahms, a hard case known locally for his prowess at bare-knuckle boxing. The day before the bust, during an otherwise quiet evening at home, Dahms had shot his wife, Brenda, in the head. At the county courthouse in Centerville, he told investigators that he'd gotten into the crank business in 1986 when Lloyd approached him at the cockfights in Blue Eye and made him an offer he couldn't refuse. He said that he'd never been to the Lawrence farm property over in Taney County and that he'd last seen Lloyd alive in January 1988. He also said that he knew Darrell Mease but hadn't heard from him in quite some time. He had no idea where Darrell could be found.

"We're going to have to do something about Slick," Darrell said, climbing into the station wagon and slamming the door. He'd left Slick outside, tied to a tree.

Mary started to cry.

"Go ahead and shoot him," she said.

Shooting the bulldog had never even crossed Darrell's mind. Whipping him, sure, maybe even abandoning him, but certainly not shooting him. But now that Mary had mentioned it, shooting him didn't seem like such a bad idea. It had been one thing after another with Slick in recent weeks: growling at Mary, bullying Gretchen Louise, once or twice trying to attack kids in the park in Glenwood Springs. The dog had become a menace.

Slick certainly hadn't helped his cause just now. He'd been at his defiant worst. They'd been getting ready to move on after spending the night at a creek near Rifle, Colorado. When Mary tried loading him into the car he snarled at her and held his ground. Sweet-talking didn't work; nothing worked—he wouldn't budge. Darrell attached his leash and secured him to the tree but when he stepped back the dog came up on him fast with a murderous look in his eye.

So maybe shooting him wasn't such a bad idea after all. Maybe at this point they didn't have any other option.

Darrell asked Mary if she was sure. She nodded and said she wanted his collar and lead rope to remember him by.

Darrell drove down Route 6 a quarter of a mile and left Mary and Louie by the side of the road. He then backtracked, pulled up beside Slick, and shot him from the car. He buried the dog at the base of a large pink granite boulder.

Afterward, headed south toward Grand Junction, Mary sat motionless in the passenger seat, looking straight ahead, muffling sobs. Darrell didn't know what to say so he decided against saying anything. It hadn't been his idea, shooting Slick, though he was convinced it had been the right thing to do. He hoped it wouldn't drive a wedge between them.

Early afternoon, sitting in a parking lot near downtown Grand Junction, down to their last dollar, trying to figure out their next move, they were approached by a bag lady pushing a shopping cart. After chatting with her a bit, Mary, who'd dabbled in witchcraft back in high school, sensed that the old woman might possess psychic powers.

"Will we be rich someday?" she asked.

"Yes, you will," the bag lady answered.

An upbeat forecast, but Darrell wasn't able to muster much enthusiasm. Not when their immediate challenge was simply scraping together a few bucks so they could get back on the road. He knew Mary wouldn't like it but he decided he'd try to sell some of the meth he'd been carrying with him since Missouri.

They left the car near a park across from the Greyhound station and walked down to the pedestrian mall on Main Street, a six-block stretch of Western-wear shops, bookstores, and smart-looking bistros. There was plenty of life on the mall, transients hanging out on benches, office workers chasing after a quick sandwich and beer, but for Darrell's purposes the place might as well have been deserted. Never mind actually selling the meth: it would have been a score simply giving some of it away. He was uncomfortable approaching people and whenever he worked up the nerve the results were pretty much the same. He was rebuffed, stared off, ignored. He couldn't understand it: back home people would have been climbing over one another trying to get a taste. Adding insult to injury, the last guy he approached before packing it in for the day gave him a religious tract.

"Look at this," he said, showing it to Mary. "I'm out here trying to make a sale and this clown's trying to save me."

He wanted to throw the tract away but Mary said she'd prefer hanging on to it.

Later on, looking for somewhere to sleep, they turned onto a dirt cutaway just south of town near the intersection of U.S. 50 and 32 Road and parked behind a mound of alkali. They were awakened in the morning by the sound of bullets whizzing over the station wagon. Without realizing it, they'd spent the night on the firing range of the Orchard Mesa Gun Club. They considered themselves lucky just escaping in one piece.

No sense pushing it too far though. The stopover in Grand Junction obviously wasn't working out. They decided they'd hit pawnshop row on Colorado Avenue, pick up some cash, and clear out of town as fast as possible. They got two hundred dollars at Credit Jewelry & Loans for the assault rifle they'd bought in Louisiana six months earlier and another twenty dollars at a pawnshop around the corner for some binoculars. It was more than enough to give them a chance for a fresh start somewhere in Arizona.

In October investigators back in Missouri caught a break when Mary's Dodge Diplomat was located at Inner Space Storage in Alexandria, Louisiana. The manager of Inner Space, wondering why he hadn't been receiving rent money from Mary, opened the shed in which the car was stored and then called the Rapides Parish Sheriff's Department. After running the plate and scoring a hit, detectives with the department contacted Chip Mason in Taney County.

Chip flew down the next day with Tom Martin. A search of the Dodge turned up nothing, but it was by no means a wasted trip. Checking with the local Motor Vehicles office, Chip and Tom learned that Mary had purchased a blue Oldsmobile station wagon (Louisiana plate 195E178) in Alexandria on March 23. At least now they had updated information for the NCIC database.

The Triple T Truck Stop sits right off exit 268 on Interstate 10, a few miles east of Tucson on the way to El Paso. It's one of the busiest truck stops in the Southwest, tractor trailers pulling in and out twenty-four hours a day, usually a hundred or more big rigs jamming the parking lots out back and along the side. Inside there are rest rooms and showers, a trucker's store and gift shop, a video-game station, a barbershop, and, the main attraction, Omar's Hiway Chef Restaurant.

Outside there are fuel pumps, a truck scale and truck wash, an oil-and-grease depot, a CB shop, and a chiropractor's trailer. There's also the sign, perched fifty feet above the grease-stained pavement out front: three blood-red T's emblazoned on a white oval background, the T in the middle slightly larger than the two flanking it so that from the highway at night they resemble the three crosses of Calvary.

The restaurant is where most of the action takes place, a

perpetual clutter and clatter, two big rooms, one with a horseshoe-shaped counter and a display case filled with thick-cut pies. Show up at three or four in the morning, almost any time at all, and you'll find truckers hunched over coffee or digging into bacon and eggs. Triple T is a regular stop for many of these guys, and they're on a first-name kidding basis with the waitresses in black pants, white shirts, and maroon aprons serving the counter and waiting on tables. Just beyond the restaurant's inside door, at the edge of a small lounge area, there's a metal stand containing neat stacks of dust-coated pamphlets with titles such as *What Must I Do to Become Saved?* and *Repentance: The Battle for Your Soul.*

Darrell breezed right by the pamphlets on his way in. He'd been coming to the truck stop quite often of late and he always breezed right by. Repentance and salvation weren't uppermost on his mind these days. He grabbed a spot at the counter and ordered a Pepsi, but soon caught himself eyeing the pies. He made a mental note not to sit so close to the display case next time. No sense tempting himself with something he couldn't afford. He barely had enough change in his pocket to cover the cost of the Pepsi. But who could tell? Maybe Roamin' Joe would show up and his luck would change. Maybe tomorrow he'd be able to treat Mary to a full-course meal, dessert included, all the pie they could eat.

Heaven knows, he was due a change of luck. This was the eighth or ninth time he'd dropped by Triple T since they'd arrived in Tucson a month ago and so far he'd been shooting blanks. At first the place had seemed a sure thing. The biggest and busiest truck stop in the area: if he couldn't unload some crank here, there was no telling where he could unload it. Everyone knew truckers used meth to stay awake during those long midnight hauls. But no way: with the exception of Roamin' Joe, everyone he'd approached so far had turned him down. Either they were born-again and had gone off drugs altogether or they'd switched from meth to something else. It was unbelievable. After so many times coming out, only one person had shown even the slightest interest. Somehow or other, he had to make a sale. He was worn to the bone by their constant money problems. And he knew Mary was, too.

Their first couple of weeks in Tucson had been the worst, scrounging around, living off handouts, selling newspapers in the street. This couldn't have been the kind of life Mary had envisioned for herself. There were times Darrell thought he might lose her. Then she'd gotten a job at the Arby's on 6th Avenue near Veteran's Boulevard and their circumstances had improved a bit. At least now they had money for some necessities: groceries, rent, gas, an occasional all-you-can-eat buffet. Those buffets had been a godsend. After their long months on the road, they'd learned to milk them for all they were worth. They'd eat their fill and when they couldn't eat anything more Mary would coolly slip some food into her bag for later on.

Their circumstances were improved, sure, but still not nearly good enough. Even with Mary working, each day was a struggle just getting by. Darrell hadn't been able to find a steady job, the story of his life, and he'd grown increasingly miserable knowing he hadn't been pulling his weight. So he'd started coming out to Triple T in the hope of making a quick sale. But this was it: if something didn't go down today, he was calling it quits. He wouldn't be coming here again.

Two nights earlier he'd gone out behind the truck stop where there was a small circular dirt area rimmed by flat-topped rocks and cactus plants. Truckers sometimes congregated back here after dark, sharing a bottle and shooting the breeze. A young guy with shoulder-length hair and tattooed arms sauntered up and said, "What's up?"

"I'm trying to sell." Just like that. Straight to the point.

They ducked into the shadows so the young guy could give it a sample.

"Not bad," he said. "Listen, everybody calls me Roamin' Joe. I'll tell you what, come back in a couple hours and I'll have your rent money. Any luck, I'll have your rent for next week, too."

Darrell came back in a couple of hours and then twice again the next day. He lurked around out back, he patrolled the parking lots, he cooled his heels in the restaurant. No sign of the guy. He thought of asking around for him but decided against it. Why risk complicating matters?

So he'd returned today for one last shot and still no sign of him. He sat at the counter for an hour or so, nursing his Pepsi, and then he took one final swing through the truck stop, checking everywhere. Forget about it, he muttered to himself. It was a hopeless cause. No way was he going to sell any of those drugs.

Five or six hours later, sitting with Mary in their tiny rental trailer, Darrell still couldn't get over his run of bad luck out at Triple T. *I must be the least successful drug dealer in the world*, he thought.

He was sick of being broke and jobless, sick of being in the doldrums. Come to think of it, he was sick of the rental trailer, too. They'd only been living there several weeks but both he and Mary were already dreaming of greener pastures. The trailer itself wasn't so bad, a sawed-off number tucked into a funky semicircle of a trailer park in South Tucson, almost directly behind the Paradise Motor Inn on 6th Avenue. Rather it was the surrounding neighborhood that was getting them down: Sixth Avenue this side of town was a grungy stretch of tire-repair shops, check-cashing joints, discount food and clothing outlets, bummer bars, last-ditch apartment rentals, and vacant lots. It was sometimes a challenge simply navigating the sidewalk without stumbling over the discarded needles and empty Night Train and T-Bird bottles. No sense kidding themselves: Darrell and Mary knew they weren't cut out for this particular brand of urban living. The trailer afforded them a semblance of domesticity but most nights they probably would have preferred camping under the stars.

Added to this, Mary was growing increasingly homesick. It was December now, Christmas was coming, and she'd already told Darrell that she wanted to spend the holidays with her folks back in Branson. *Branson! As in Taney County!*

Just about the last place on earth Darrell wanted to be seen right now. Nevertheless, he'd assured her that they'd try to work something out.

The next day they didn't get up until past noon. This had been their pattern of late, sleeping ten or twelve hours at a stretch and always feeling it wasn't enough, always tired. They'd talked about it a few days earlier, their chronic over-sleeping, and Mary had volunteered, "You know, I think it's because we're depressed."

"I know," Darrell said.

They might have stayed in bed even longer just now if it weren't for Harold dropping by. They'd met him when they first moved in, a thin sour alcoholic in his late fifties with an endless repertoire of sad stories, shattered hopes, big plans gone badly awry. He was living in the trailer across the way and Mary had bummed a pack of smokes off him. A couple of weeks later he was evicted for not paying his rent but he still liked coming by every few days to chat. Normally they didn't mind him visiting but today they weren't in the mood. After sitting there a half hour listening to Harold going on about his ex-wives and bitter divorces and his two-year stint in a state prison for busting up a billiards parlor, Darrell said that he and Mary had plans for the day and they'd have to cut the visit short.

"All right," Harold said. Then, looking right at Mary, he added: "You know, you can't do thirty years. You can't handle it."

They were flabbergasted. Where had this remark come from? Harold knew nothing about their past. They'd been exceedingly careful not to reveal anything he might be tempted to use against them. So what was this? A premonition? Or just a shot in the dark? Either way, it was damn unsettling.

"I can't do thirty years in prison," Mary said after he left.

"Don't worry," Darrell said. "You won't have to."

They really didn't have plans for the day, beyond scrounging something to eat. They drove two miles to Reid Park, a large attractive greensward off 22nd Street with playgrounds, snack bars, and a small zoo. They'd been coming here three or four times a week, foraging for food in trash bins by the zoo. The pickings were usually pretty good. School kids on day trips would sometimes discard entire lunches: unwrapped sandwiches, apples, pieces of cake. The trick was being alert and retrieving the stuff before it had a chance to spoil.

Sitting on a bench finishing off his share of the day's haul, Darrell saw those black ducks again. There were plenty of ducks in the park but it was those beautiful black ones, Cayugas, native to upstate New York, which always caught his eye. If he could only find some way to steal a couple of them, a male and a female, he thought, he could start breeding them and maybe make some money putting them up for sale. Running the possibilities through his mind, he was suddenly struck by the absurdity of it. Here he was, a guy with all the trouble in the world, banking everything on a couple of ducks.

Back at the trailer Darrell and Mary decided to break into their supply of meth. The meth again: their comfort, their torment, their near-constant companion. Meth had helped bring them together and then done its best to pull them apart. It had strung them along, plunged them into disaster, and vandalized their hopes. It had been there almost every step of the way, alternately grinning and grimacing, never shy about asserting its mastery.

Once, just a couple of weeks earlier, it had even stopped them from getting married.

They'd seriously discussed getting married a few times since hitting the road the previous December. The first time was in California. Mary was all for it but Darrell talked her into waiting. He was a bit gun-shy after Joyce and Donna, and, besides, he still wasn't legally a free man. The divorce from Donna hadn't yet come through. Nevertheless, he'd signaled his intentions by taking some of the money Lexie had sent them and buying Mary a gold ring inlaid with three diamond chips. In the ten months since then she'd worn the ring every day, except for their first week in Tucson when they'd been forced to pawn it for grocery money. After they'd gotten the ring out of hock, she'd started talking about marriage again and then two weeks ago they'd made their decision. Forget about waiting any longer—waiting for the divorce to be finalized, waiting for some elusive upturn in their fortunes. They'd drive over to Tombstone and find a justice of the peace and get married right on Boot Hill. Boot Hill, the fabled graveyard of the Old West, final resting place of gunslingers and desperadoes and no-account bad men: this was where she wanted it done. Darrell didn't argue. He knew that graveyards held a certain romance for her. She'd grown up next to one in Branson and had played in it as a child on warm summer evenings. He remembered her telling him, not long after they first met, that she'd actually thought of becoming a mortician. *Boot Hill.* After all they'd been through, there was something almost poetic about it. So late one night they headed out for Tombstone and pulled off on a side road halfway there. This was the plan: catch some sleep in the car and then arrive at Boot Hill early the next day and round up a justice of the peace. Except Darrell wasn't in the mood for sleeping. He sat in the front passenger seat watching Mary drop off and then he stayed up all night cranking. Once he'd started in, there was no turning it off. When Mary awoke she took one look at him and knew that he'd had his snout in the trough again. After promising her—swearing up and down—promising that he was through with the stuff, he'd been going at it all night long. She didn't say a word. She simply pulled the car off the side road, made a left-hand turn, and headed back to Tucson. So much for the Boot Hill wedding.

So here they were, back at the trailer after their excursion to Reid Park, and still upset over being blindsided by Harold earlier in the day. Getting high was the only avenue of relief they could think of. It didn't work out any better now, however, than it had at the old Star Tungsten Mine in Nevada several months ago. Once again Mary complained of feeling sick and later on, lying in bed, she started to cry and told Darrell that she was afraid of him.

Darrell was devastated. He'd suspected as much from

time to time but hearing her actually say it was more than he could bear. He put one of their guns in her hand and told her that he loved her and that he'd sooner die than see any harm come to her. If she didn't believe him, he said, he wanted her to shoot him right now. Shoot him in the head and throw his body somewhere out in the desert.

At daybreak he placed all the drugs they had left on the counter, two plastic bags each containing roughly an ounce of crank. He snipped off the ends with a pair of scissors and flushed the stuff down the toilet. Mary waited a few days to make sure he wasn't holding anything back. When she finally saw he meant business she said, "Darrell, I love you."

One evening the next week Darrell was killing time over by Santa Rita Park off 22nd Street near 5th Avenue. He was waiting for Mary to get ready so they could go to a little carnival that had set up in a vacant lot nearby. A young Mexican woman with two small children and a shopping cart full of groceries approached him and asked if he'd mind escorting her to the other side of the park. A big tough-looking guy with long hair was lurking in the shadows halfway across and she feared for her safety. Darrell had seen the guy walking into the park from the street a few moments earlier and he felt she had every reason to be afraid. He escorted her across, his cold-steel combat knife under his jacket, and smiled at the guy as they passed.

He told Mary about the incident when he picked her up at the trailer. "You really are a good man," she said, sounding like she meant it.

At the carnival they stopped by a booth and watched as one guy after another tried unsuccessfully to knock down three pins with a dart gun. Mary asked Darrell to give it a go. She wanted him to win the prize for her: a miniature teddy bear. On the first string, three shots for a buck, he ciphered it out. The gun shot about six inches high and five or six inches to the left. On the second string he nailed the pins and won the teddy bear. You would have thought he'd bagged a grizzly: it was one of his proudest moments.

Going out the door of their trailer the next morning Mary said, "I want to spend eternity with you."

"You will," Darrell answered, though in truth he hadn't a clue how this could happen. The only eternity he could imagine for himself was something very different from what Mary must have had in mind. In his view he was a sinner beyond reprieve, bound for no place but hell.

PART
THREE

EIGHT

Skid Row, Phoenix: not quite hell, Darrell thought, but it couldn't be far removed. He hadn't wanted to return to Phoenix, it was too big and intimidating, but toughing it out in Tucson had proven a losing proposition. He hadn't come close to finding work and just before Christmas Mary had lost her job at Arby's. They'd been forced to eat Christmas dinner at a shelter that Harold had turned them on to. So much for Mary's dreams of making it home for the holidays.

"I can't go on much longer like this," she had said one afternoon in late December.

So they had packed their things and moved here. Why not? It was worth a shot. So far, however, it hadn't been a winning move. They were still jobless and, what's more, Phoenix had them spooked. After dark, with the downtown office workers safely ensconced in their suburban homes, the city center was like an open morgue, a prowling ground for zonked-out addicts and prostitutes. Out on Van Buren, a seamy east-west thoroughfare not far from where they were staying, you'd be hard-pressed most evenings finding somewhere to buy coffee and a sandwich. Everything was locked up, bolted down, a sinister feeling in the air.

For the past week they'd been paying ten bucks a night for a room in a flophouse on the western edge of downtown. From the street the place possessed a certain lubricious charm: ancient neon sign, tall unwashed windows, a fringe of palms around the corner. Inside, however, the charm rapidly gave way to gloom and decay, the paint in the fetid lobby cracked and peeling, the furniture and drapes in the upstairs rooms carrying the long-gathered stench of bitterness and despair. Back in the 1940s it might have been a decent, moderately priced hotel; now it was a haunting place for the broken-down and dispirited. On some level Darrell and Mary must have known they were near the end of the line. The fight had been knocked out of them. Staying here was almost a gesture of defeat.

At the moment all Darrell was hoping for was some peace and quiet. They were lying in bed trying to watch a movie on the old TV set by the window but the neighbors weren't cooperating. There was shouting and cursing from the adjoining rooms and loud vomiting from the bathroom down the hall. Every few minutes someone pounded on their door, probably a hooker or a john checking on the room's availability.

Despite the distractions, Darrell found himself really getting into the movie. It was an old Vincent Price flick, *The Baron of Arizona*, about a middle-aged guy in 1870s Arizona who manufactured a huge land fraud giving him and his much younger wife control of the entire territory. He was eventually found out and narrowly escaped being hanged. Sentenced to prison, he told his wife that he'd only been interested in acquiring land and money so he could treat her right. She replied that money meant nothing to her provided she had him by her side. The movie ended with the guy walking out of prison and getting picked up by his young wife in a buggy.

The next morning, braving the stink of puke and urine and disinfectant, Darrell broke a piece of clear glass into tiny fragments and spread them on the floor of the shared bathroom down the hall. He'd already decided they wouldn't be staying here another night and this was his way of getting even for the constant disturbances of the past week.

Late afternoon, sitting over coffee and a newspaper in a

small café, they saw an advertisement for jobs at a warehouse not far from downtown. Darrell phoned and the guy in charge said the two of them could start the next day. Mary wanted to celebrate this stroke of luck by renting a motel room for the night but Darrell said they should conserve their money. They'd pawned the Benelli for a C-note at a place on North Central a few days earlier and they only had about thirty dollars left. He said they should drive out to the desert and spend the night in the car.

After dark they drove up through Cave Creek and down Pima Road. They found an isolated spot off Shea near 142nd Street a little bit east of Scottsdale. They backed the station wagon off the road and went to sleep, Camelback Mountain behind them to the south, the McDowell Mountains invisible in the night sky to the north. Parked out there in the desert, with the plastic suburbs of Scottsdale close at hand—their fancy shopping malls dressed up in pretty desert frills, red tile roofs, stucco façades, but otherwise no different from the shopping malls you'd see in Los Angeles or Boston or Chicago—Darrell was about as far away from the Ozarks backwoods as he could possibly be.

Twenty-seven, slight of build, brown-eyed, and boyishly handsome, Deputy Gary D'Agostino, a two-year veteran of the Maricopa County Sheriff's Office, was working the graveyard shift in the boondocks. At that time the sheriff's office ran a satellite station out of a trailer near Fountain Hills, and D'Agostino was one of two deputies assigned to it overnight. It was two in the morning, not much happening, so he thought he'd swing by his favorite stakeout spot, a little cutoff by Shea near 142nd Street. He'd had success in the past catching speeders going down a knoll here on their way to Scottsdale. Pulling onto the cutoff now, his headlights splashed against an Olds station wagon backed into the desert. He was surprised—he'd never seen anyone parked out here before—and more than a little annoyed that someone was on his turf.

D'Agostino walked over to the Olds, flashlight in hand,

and tapped on the driver's window. Darrell and Mary were
jolted awake. They sat up, blinking, groggy from sleep.
D'Agostino asked them if they were all right. *Uh-huh*, they
said. He asked them to get out of the car and give him their
names. Mary, hugging a blanket, gave her real name. Darrell
said his was Kyle Hamlin. They said that they were sleeping
out in the desert because they didn't have enough money for
a room.

D'Agostino asked for Darrell's Social Security number.
Darrell knew by heart the bogus number he'd been using as
Kyle Hamlin. Standing out there in the January chill, he
could actually visualize it, all nine digits, almost as if it were
printed on a screen before his eyes. The problem was, he
could visualize his real number just as readily, and in his
state of disorientation, he gave D'Agostino the real one.

The Social Security gaffe probably didn't matter much
anyway. D'Agostino returned to his unit and radioed in the
rear plate of the Olds. He got back information that the vehicle had been flagged with a possible occupant ("Caution:
Armed and Dangerous") matching Darrell's description. He
was also advised that the same subject ("Darrell Jay Mease
of Missouri") was wanted on two felony warrants: child support and carrying a concealed weapon.

By this time D'Agostino's backup, Mike McGhee, fresh
out of the academy, had arrived on the scene. "How do we
know for sure it's him?" McGhee asked.

"Let me try something," D'Agostino said.

"Hey, Darrell," he called out, standing behind the open
door of his unit.

"Yeah," Darrell answered. Just like it was dinnertime.

"Why didn't you give me your real name the first time?"
D'Agostino asked.

"I've had some problems with police before."

"There's warrants out on you, one of them for something
big."

Darrell just stood there, saying nothing.

The two deputies cuffed him and placed him under arrest.
A brisk search of the station wagon turned up two revolvers

and a machete. They decided they'd put the weapons into the property department at the Fountain Hills trailer station before taking Darrell to Mesa for booking. Mary followed them in the Olds and told the deputies outside the trailer that she was broke and had no place to stay. D'Agostino gave her the address of a shelter on West Madison in downtown Phoenix.

Driving to Mesa, D'Agostino tried engaging Darrell in small talk, but nothing doing. Maybe Darrell was busy contemplating the irony of the situation. He'd just been arrested in the desert outside Phoenix, no more than a ten-minute drive from where he and Mary had purchased the Benelli the previous March. Thousands of rollicking miles across the vast American countryside, and this, of all places, was where the journey had ended.

When D'Agostino pulled into the sally port of the station in Mesa, five detention officers were waiting to meet him.

"Radio wants you to call," they told him.

He called up and the dispatcher said, "Gary, are you all right? This guy's wanted for a triple homicide back in Missouri."

"You're kidding me," he said.

Just before his shift ended, homicide detectives from the sheriff's office contacted him wanting to know where Mary was.

"You might want to check the shelter on West Madison," he said.

Mary wasn't at the shelter. After Darrell had been hauled off, remembering that she still had twenty-nine dollars left, she drove back into Phoenix and looked for a motel. She settled on the Desert Inn, the last of a string of cut-rate motels along Van Buren leading west out of downtown. The last and the sorriest. The coffee shop in front was boarded up, the blue-painted doors along the side were battered and bruised, and the swimming pool by the parking lot looked like it hadn't seen clean water for a decade or more. She checked in at the bulletproof window of an office facing 10th Avenue and went up to her room with Gretchen Louise. Grimy beige carpet, brown dust-streaked drapes, tiny bathroom with pink floor tiles, and a dirt-encrusted window crisscrossed with iron bars: the shelter mightn't have been such a bad idea after all.

At nine that evening homicide detectives found Mary at the motel and told her she was under arrest.

She asked what for.

Hindering prosecution, they said. A fresh warrant out of Taney County, Missouri.

Darrell and Mary were arrested on Wednesday, January 11, 1989. Chip Mason and Jack Merritt flew to Phoenix the same day and at eight-forty Thursday morning they visited Mary. She was in a holding tank with a dozen other women on the ground floor of the Madison Street Jail, a twelve-story concrete facility located directly across from the Central Court Building. She recognized Chip right away and seemed relieved to see him, a familiar and friendly face from back home. Any doubt she may have had about the purpose of the visit was immediately dispelled when she noticed that Chip was carrying a folder clearly marked "Lawrence Homicides." Chip chatted with her for a while, talked about her parents and how worried they were. Jack stood back, giving it time, Mary striking him as "a scared kid in a bad situation." The two men then advised her of her rights and Mary signed a waiver consenting to be interviewed without benefit of a lawyer present.

The interview was conducted in a private conference room in the main offices of the sheriff's department across the street. Speaking softly and slowly, occasionally punctuating her answers with a nervous laugh, not always straight on the precise chronology of events, Mary told Jack and Chip everything they needed to know. She recounted her and Darrell's conflicts with Lloyd ("He was so evil," she said), their initial flight from Missouri, their fateful return in May, and their subsequent wanderings as fugitives. Jack and Chip pressed her on certain details—the weapons Darrell was carrying when she dropped him off at Bear Creek Road, the jewelry he took from Lloyd, the pawnshop where they disposed of the Benelli—and then they plugged in a tape recorder and walked her through the entire story again. Mary signed a "consent to search" for the Olds station wagon and Chip told her that someone would be down from Missouri in a day or two to bring her home.

Back at the jail Mary phoned her mom. She said that she'd spoken with Chip and was scared and hungry. Barbara told her not to talk to anyone else until she got home.

Jack and Chip rummaged through the station wagon, which was still parked at the Desert Inn Motel: an assortment of knives, a jar of ammunition, a poncho, and two camouflage head covers. They retrieved the Benelli from Central Pawnbrokers in north Phoenix and, after lunch, Chip phoned Jim Justus back in Forsyth with a progress report. At one-thirty they returned to the Madison Street jail and checked on Darrell.

Darrell wasn't in the friendliest of moods. He was worried about Mary and also immensely frustrated about being in jail. His mood didn't improve much when Chip told him that he'd been arrested for the weapons violation up by Rocky's place a year and a half ago. The weapons violation? The .38 Special under the seat? But this made no sense. He'd paid a fine on that rinky-dink deal at the courthouse in Forsyth the very next day. As far as he knew, that should have spelled the end of it. So what was going on here? There had to be more to this business than met the eye. It didn't take much straining to imagine what it might be.

"No way," he said to Chip, fighting back anger. "That deal was done with when I anted up the seventy-three bucks. You've got nothing on me there."

"No sense arguing about it," Jack cut in. "We're here to question you about the Lawrence homicides."

Yeah. Out in the open now. This wasn't about a penny-ante weapons rap. It was about Lloyd and Frankie and Willie. The arrest warrant had just been an excuse for trapping him. Darrell had already guessed as much but he was determined not to lose his cool. Better than even money they didn't have anything solid linking him to the Lawrence killings. He invoked his right to an attorney, refusing to answer any questions, but agreed to sign a waiver of extradition. If Chip and Jack wanted to bring him back to Missouri on the old weapons charge, they were welcome to it. The two lawmen said they'd pick him up the next day. While they were getting ready to leave, Darrell asked if they had any word on Mary. Chip said that she'd been arrested and would be transported home before the end of the week.

They flew out of Phoenix early Friday and switched planes in Dallas. On the second leg of the trip Darrell sat beside the window, Chip right next to him, and Jack immediately across the aisle. Jack spent the greater part of the flight writing case notes on a yellow legal pad. At one point he crossed his legs with the pad resting on his knee and Darrell was able to make out some of the writing. He caught references to "two diamond rings" and "ten-by-ten plastic bags filled with crank."

Darrell didn't know whether Jack had put the notes in his view inadvertently, or whether he'd done it on purpose and was trying to rattle him. It didn't matter. Right then there was one thing he did know for sure: Mary had talked. No one else could have given Jack and Chip that information. Chances were she had broken down and told them everything.

Just thinking about it now was churning him up. Imagine the interrogation she must have been subjected to. And imagine her emotional state. For Mary to talk, and talk so soon after she'd been arrested—she was probably on the verge of a complete meltdown. Darrell thought back to all her tough times on the road the past year: the constant pressure, the squalor, the gnawing desperation. The whole business must have finally caught up with her.

Once again, he asked Jack and Chip about Mary, how she seemed to be doing when they saw her at the jail in Phoenix.

Chip looked over and noticed that Darrell's eyes were brimming with tears. He said that Mary seemed to be doing okay.

Darrell would later claim that Jack added something at

Darrell Mease. (*Reeds Spring High School yearbook photo*)

DARRELL MEASE
Football 4; Basketball 4;
Track 3, 4; Lettered 3, 4;
Hi-Lights Staff 4; Letter-
mens Club 4.

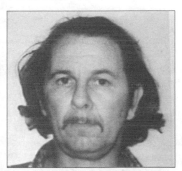

Mug shot of Darrell Mease. (*Photo courtesy of the Division of Drug and Crime Control of the Missouri State Highway Patrol*)

LEFT: Darrell Mease. (*Reeds Spring High School yearbook photo*)

A typical meth lab in the Ozarks of southwest Missouri. (*Photo courtesy of KY3 News, Springfield, Missouri*)

LEFT: Emergency workers at the crime scene in rural Missouri. (*Photo courtesy of KY3 News, Springfield, Missouri*)

BOTTOM: Willie Lawrence is discovered at the crime scene, with the laces of his sneakers tied to the front rack of his all-terrain vehicle. (*Photo courtesy of the Division of Drug and Crime Control of the Missouri State Highway Patrol*)

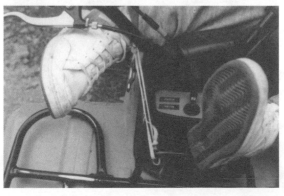

The crime scene, more hours after the triple homicide. (*Photo courtesy of the Division of Drug and Crime Control of the Missouri State Highway Patrol*)

ABOVE: Taney County sheriff Chuck Keithley. (*Photo courtesy of KY3 News, Springfield, Missouri*)

Sergeants Tom Martin (*left*) and Jack Merritt (*right*) of the Missouri State Highway Patrol's Division of Drug and Crime Control. (*Photo courtesy of Tom Martin*)

Patrolmen Wayne Murphy (*left*) and Lee Stephens (*right*) at the Springfield airport, waiting to transport Darrell Mease to the Taney County courthouse for his arraignment. (*Photo courtesy of KY3 News, Springfield, Missouri*)

LEFT: Darrell Mease, exiting an American Eagle aircraft in Springfield following his arrest in Arizona. (*Photo courtesy of KY3 News, Springfield, Missouri*)

BOTTOM: Darrell Mease, escorted by patrolmen Wayne Murphy (*left*) and Lee Stephens (*right*) through the airport in Springfield, Missouri. (*Photo courtesy of KY3 News, Springfield, Missouri*)

ABOVE: Darrell Mease confesses on videotape to Sergeant Jack Merritt. (*Photo courtesy of the Division of Drug and Crime Control of the Missouri State Highway Patrol*)

LEFT: Jim Justus, prosecuting attorney of Taney County, Missouri. (*Photo courtesy of KY3 News, Springfield, Missouri*)

LEFT: Bill Wendt, Mease's trial attorney, addressing the media at the Greene County courthouse after the guilty verdict. (*Photo courtesy of KY3 News, Springfield, Missouri*)

Mary Epps, leaving the courtroom in Springfield following the penalty phase of the trial. (*Photo courtesy of KY3 News, Springfield, Missouri*)

Mary Epps is escorted to the Taney County courthouse for her arraignment. (*Photo courtesy of KY3 News, Springfield, Missouri*)

Darrell Mease is escorted into the Greene County courthouse for his criminal trial. (*Photo courtesy of KY3 News, Springfield, Missouri*)

Willie Lawrence's mother, Anita, consoles Lexie Mease after the guilty verdict in Darrell Mease's criminal trial. (*Photo courtesy of KY3 News, Springfield, Missouri*)

Lexie Mease addressing the media after the death verdict is reached in her son's criminal trial. (*Photo courtesy of KY3 News, Springfield, Missouri*)

On the occasion of his historic visit to St. Louis, Pope John Paul II chats with President Bill Clinton (*left*) and Archbishop Justin Rigali (*second from right*). (*Photo by Dave Preston*)

this point, something he'd been hinting at off and on since Phoenix.

"Your life is probably over in this world, Darrell, but Mary is young and she can go on."

This is what Darrell would claim Jack said.

Jack would deny ever making the comment.

The arrest was big news back in Springfield. When the American Eagle flight landed, reporters and camera crews were lying in wait. Darrell, wearing a faded plaid shirt and brown corduroy pants, his hands shackled in front of him, couldn't believe it. Going through the terminal, he felt like a sideshow freak on public display. People were snapping pictures, jockeying for position, trying to provoke him into a reaction. He hated to think of Mary having to run the same gauntlet when she returned home.

Outside the terminal, while he was being escorted to a waiting patrol car, some guy strode up and stuck a camera right in his face. Darrell was so enraged by now that he tried to step on the guy's foot. He had visions of walking up his leg and torso, all the way onto his head. He missed. The guy jumped away. *Dang, how'd I miss?* Darrell said to himself.

Patrolmen Wayne Murphy and Lee Stephens had been given the assignment of transporting Darrell to the courthouse in Forsyth for his arraignment. Stephens sat in back with Darrell, lighting cigarettes for him, while Murphy drove at a good clip, sixty-five most of the way. It was as pleasant a trip as anybody could have hoped for, under the circumstances. Darrell had always held the Highway Patrol in high regard. He had two cousins who were state troopers, and riding with Murphy and Stephens, good ole country boys in their own right, seemed to put him at ease. Every few miles he'd tearfully bring Mary up, talk about how much he loved her and how he regretted getting her involved with this mess. But then he'd brighten for a bit and tell amusing stories about his experiences in the local hill country. A few times he had the troopers almost in stitches. He told them how he once took a pistol and shot a deer behind the Holiday Inn down in Branson. And how once, over by Reeds Spring, a couple of guys who knew him only by reputation asked for his help sighting in a .357 they'd recently picked up second-hand. He threw a rock into the air, busted it with one shot, and handed the .357 back to them, saying, "It shoots about a half inch high and an eighth of an inch to the left." "That's just what we thought," one of the guys said.

Darrell and Stephens hit it off especially well. Sitting there in the back seat, they were like long-lost buddies, swapping tales about their bad marriages and congratulating each other on having finally struck gold with a good woman. Stephens would later recall that he found Darrell "a real witty individual" and "enjoyed talking to him."

At one point he asked Darrell if he'd hired an attorney.

"No, but I guess I'll have to get one," Darrell said.

"Have you given a statement?" Stephens asked.

"No, I'm going to sleep on it, then I may."

At four in the afternoon Darrell was arraigned before Judge Joe Chowning in Forsyth on three counts of murder and three counts of armed criminal action. Twenty minutes later he was back on the road with Murphy and Stephens. Sheriff Chuck Keithley had already reserved a cell for Mary in the Taney County jail and he'd decided ("for security reasons") that he didn't want the two of them housed in the same facility. So he'd asked the troopers to return Darrell to Springfield and deposit him for the time being in the county jail there.

On the drive back the three men chatted just as amiably as they had on the way down. Half an hour into the trip Murphy and Stephens received instructions over the radio to bring Darrell by Troop D headquarters on Kearney Street in Springfield for processing. A bit later Darrell asked if there was anything Stephens could do "to help keep Mary out of this." Stephens said he didn't think so: that was something Darrell would have to take up with the appropriate authorities in Taney County.

Waiting for the stoplight on the Kearney exit ramp off U.S. 65, Darrell said to Stephens: "The only thing I hate about this is Willie."

"Why Willie?"

"Willie would have recognized me. I had to do him, too."

"Would you like to make a statement, Darrell?" Stephens asked.

"I will to you and Jack Merritt but not to anyone from Stone or Taney County."

Jack and Chip had gone directly to Troop D headquarters from the airport. They were still there when the two troopers showed up with Darrell. After being briefed by Stephens on the conversation at the stoplight, they took Darrell into Tom Martin's basement office and pulled up some chairs. Chip advised Darrell of his rights but that was as far as he got. Darrell asked him to leave and to send in Lee Stephens instead. He thought he'd made himself clear: he'd talk to the Highway Patrol and to no one else. The county boys weren't to be trusted.

Jack and Lee spent more than an hour with Darrell in Tom's office. Stephens mostly watched and listened while Merritt prodded and Darrell talked. At first Darrell was all over the place, riffing about this and that, the logistics of crank production, local blood feuds, local outlaws, but always coming back to Mary, agonizing over Mary, insisting she had done nothing wrong. After a while Jack managed to steer the conversation to the Lawrence homicides and Darrell agreed to give a videotaped confession.

By this point, apparently, Darrell was under the impression that if he gave himself up and confessed to everything, all charges against Mary would be dropped. She'd be set free at once with nothing more than a "slap on the wrist." This is what he believed Jack had promised him in Tom's office. Afterward Jack would deny promising Darrell anything. He hadn't cut any deals, offered any inducements. All he'd done was point the conversation in the right direction. Darrell had taken care of the rest.

The videotaping was carried out in a large basement room that normally doubled as conference and recreational space for the Troop D platoon. Tom, who'd been keeping a low profile, letting his partner handle the interviewing, set up the camera while Jack and Lee positioned themselves on either side of Darrell at a table by the front wall.

Jack got things started by once again advising Darrell of his rights and asking him about his relationship with Lloyd. Darrell, bleary-eyed and unshaven, answered in his no-hurry Missouri drawl, thick and lazy, sometimes pausing for a drag on a cigarette, occasionally coughing into a bunched fist.

Ten minutes into the confession, Darrell reached the point where he and Mary returned to Missouri from their first road trip and Mary dropped him off at Bear Creek Road.

"What was your original intention and what was her thought of what you were going to do when you went down there?" Jack asked.

"Well, like I told Lee, I'm not real straight on that except that she'd try to talk me out of it and going and deal with Lloyd. I led her to believe that I was gonna burn his cabin and go over the hill and deal with Rocky and I may have told her or not, but the fact is that she didn't believe it. You know how if you get mad and fly off the handle and say you're gonna kill somebody, everybody's done it sometime, but she really didn't believe it. And after it was over, she kinda went into shock and she was watching me like I was somebody strange or something. She just—she couldn't believe it and she was real different, paranoid."

"Okay."

"She didn't want me to do none of that."

Jack pushed on, asking Darrell about the actual shootings.

"Lloyd came through just real slow, creeping, looking both sides of the road. He knew I liked Willie, but I was determined that nothing was going to stop me, because once, once I got started, I, you know, I didn't—it was all the way or nothing. I thought if I didn't get Lloyd, he would get Mary, do something bad to her. In fact, I'm sure of it."

"So, when Lloyd came by, what happened?"

"Well, I shot him and then I shot Frankie and then, uh, I shot Willie."

And then the getaway, Jack still pushing, Darrell stumbling a bit over the exact sequence of events.

"Now after you left the shooting scene, where did you go?"

"I walked down the creek until I got to Highway 65 and crossed under the bridge and went up to the top of the hill to that junction."

"And what occurred at the junction?"

"Mary had heard it on the radio. We've talked about it since then. She said it was just like she was in a dream and she functioned automatically and she just come and picked me up."

Wrapping up, Jack asked Darrell why he had finally decided to confess.

"For Mary's sake, because she tried to talk me out of this and, uh, she didn't—she didn't want no part of it. But she loved me and she was probably intimidated by me or something."

"For your sake, do you have any remorse or regrets on what has occurred?"

"Not for Lloyd. I believe I had to do that. I do for Willie and Frankie."

Jack asked Darrell if he had anything to say in closing.

"Yes, I do. The reason I'm doing this is for Mary because she didn't want any part of it and I dragged her into it. She's the finest person I know and I'll do anything to get her out of it and she was just kinda in shock at the time."

Saturday morning Tom, Jack, and Lee picked Darrell up at the Greene County jail and drove down to Bear Creek Road where they met Chip Mason and Chuck Keithley. Darrell directed the men to where he'd hidden Lloyd's wallet and papers eight months earlier and then they drove over to the campground near Chadwick and unearthed the plastic cooler containing Lloyd's stolen drugs. Perhaps there was something else Darrell could have done to help cinch the case against him. Tough imagining, however, what it might have been.

• • •

Mary arrived back in Springfield late Friday, two or three hours after Darrell's confession at Troop D headquarters. Chuck Keithley had sent veteran deputy and onetime U.S. marshal Doug Van Allen to Phoenix to collect her, and since a female prisoner couldn't be transported in the company of a man alone, he'd deputized Van Allen's wife, Scotty, and sent her along, too.

The Van Allens picked Mary up at the Durango jail, a low-slung, brown-brick, barbed-wire facility, where she'd spent the night after being transferred from the main jail on Madison. She was quiet and sullen on the way back, her wrists cuffed in front of her, her clothes giving off a detectable jailhouse odor. Scotty tried talking with her but after a while decided there was no sense pushing it. All she was getting in response were terse yes-or-no answers. The threesome drove to Forsyth from the Springfield airport and Mary phoned her mom from the Taney County jail. She wanted to know when Barbara and Fred would be coming over to get her.

The next morning, wearing an orange county-issue jumpsuit, her hair matted and her eyes puffy, Mary was escorted the short distance from the jail to the courthouse for her arraignment. Judge Chowning set her bail at $100,000 cash or $200,000 property. Later the same day she was back home.

NINE

The Taney County jail sits right next to the courthouse in downtown Forsyth. It holds thirty men and eight women and is usually booked to capacity. At the rear of the jail, along a short corridor, there's a small maximum-security unit: three identical eight-by-eleven cells with twelve-foot-high ceilings and cement-block walls. Each cell in the unit has a set of bunk beds, a stainless-steel toilet, a sink with hot and cold running water, and a tiny molded-plastic table with attached stools. Outside the cells, on the opposite side of the corridor, three window slots afford a dim view of a do-it-yourself car wash and a hunting-and-fishing store across the street.

Darrell was transferred from Springfield to the maximum-security unit in Forsyth two days after Mary was set free on bond. As a celebrity prisoner, he was assigned a cell to himself. One of his new neighbors in the unit asked him what he was in for.

"Homo-cide," Darrell answered.

"Do you mean homicide?"

"Yow, that's it."

His first afternoon he called Mary's number in Branson from the jailhouse phone and got Barbara Epps on the line. Screwing up his nerve he told her who he was and asked for Mary. Barbara said she wouldn't allow him to talk with

Mary. She asked him if it was true: Was it really he who had killed the three Lawrences?

"Yeah," Darrell said, "I killed them."

Barbara started crying. She hadn't wanted to believe it; she'd been holding out hope it wasn't true. When she first heard about the Lawrence homicides and Chip told her Darrell and Mary might be involved, she'd been defiant in her disbelief. No way, she'd said. No way could her daughter have had anything to do with such a thing. Even over the past few days she'd refused to concede the obvious. But now she had no choice: the last shred of protective doubt had been stripped away.

"Why'd you get Mary involved in a mess like that?" she asked.

Darrell had no easy answer. He said he was sorry. He hadn't meant Mary any harm. He loved her and thought she was the best person he'd ever known.

"Are there any more hoodlums in Stone or Taney Counties that could harm my daughter?" Barbara asked.

"No," Darrell answered.

The conversation with Barbara Epps didn't improve Darrell's appetite. Since getting arrested he hadn't eaten a thing; he'd been too depressed and torn up even to think of food. He'd been surviving on water, unfiltered Pall Malls, and Skoal chewing tobacco. He certainly wasn't up to eating anything now. He felt lost and helpless. He wanted to do something for Mary but he hadn't a clue what it might be. Then it dawned on him: he'd try praying for her, asking God to give her strength and courage and peace of mind.

Back in his cell he lay down on the bottom bunk and closed his eyes. Hesitantly, feeling his way, *awkward, awkward, so awkward*, he tried finding the right words, the right frame of mind. It had been so long. He couldn't help thinking back to when he was a boy and praying had come as naturally as breathing. But after all those years running with Satan, the pores of his spirit had contracted. His heart had congealed with fear and hate.

During the past months on the road with Mary the most

he'd been able to muster was an occasional plea before falling asleep, not so much a prayer as a groan from the gut: "Please, God, if I die tonight I don't want to go to hell." *Hell*—he'd never stopped believing in hell. It was one of the few teachings from his Pentecostal boyhood he'd never lost sight of. And he'd known, those windswept nights in the hills outside Elko, those crying times in Tucson—he'd known, as surely as he knew anything, that if he died right then, there was no other place he'd be going.

So he lay there on his bunk trying to find the right words, his face glistening with sweat and tears, not knowing if the words would be heard even if he found them to say. *Please, God, help Mary.* Then again, and again. *Please, God, help Mary.* A jailhouse mantra. He didn't dare pray for himself. He couldn't begin to imagine God helping someone who'd done what he had done. He couldn't imagine prayers on his own behalf making any difference. His was a lost cause; his damnation was sealed. But Mary was another story: maybe, *please God,* his prayers could help turn the tide in her favor.

All that day and the next Darrell kept at it. *Please, God, help Mary.* He still wasn't eating and his emotional pain was so intense that it sometimes felt as if his internal organs were trying to claw their way out of his body. By the third day, Wednesday, he began to note a change. The praying was coming easier now and he felt himself growing softer and more alive, like a chrysalis thawing out after a long dark winter. It was worth a shot now, he thought. Besides praying for Mary, he'd try praying for himself.

At first it was a chore. He was long out of practice and still not in the least sure his prayers would be heeded. He asked God to forgive him and to save him. He said that he was sorry for his sins. He knew that he'd been saved once before, when he was just a boy, but for more than twenty years he'd been stuck on the path of rebellion. All he wanted now was to get right with God.

Darrell kept at it all day long, struggling for the right words, wiping away the tears with his sleeve. By evening he felt his appetite returning but he decided against eating. He'd gone this far—might as well take it all the way. He'd keep praying and fasting, praying and fasting, hoping against hope that God would see fit to forgive him and save him.

Late that same Wednesday, Chuck Keithley's older brother, Roscoe, was sitting in his living room wondering what in the world was going on. It was almost midnight and for two hours he'd been trying to read his Bible. So far, however, it had been a colossal waste of time. From one line to another he couldn't keep track of what he'd just read. It was a hopeless muddle. Nothing of this sort had ever happened to him before. For years he'd done a little Scripture reading before tucking in for the night and it had always come as easily to him as the bluegrass tunes he still enjoyed picking on his vintage Martin flattop. But not tonight: so far tonight had been a total loss.

But there was something else troubling him, something beyond his maddening inability to concentrate. For the past half hour he'd been hearing a voice—soft at first but then louder and more persistent. *You've got to go visit Darrell Mease*. This was what the voice was saying, the same message, over and over. Roscoe had tried ignoring it at first, he'd tried putting it out of his mind, but there it was again. *You've got to go visit Darrell Mease*. Try as he might, he simply couldn't escape it.

And why Darrell Mease? Of course Roscoe had heard of Darrell: the past few days you couldn't pick up a local newspaper without coming across his name. Perhaps, too, he'd heard something about Darrell from his wife, Wanetta, who'd once worked with Lexie Mease at a Christian summer camp just outside of Branson. Or from his younger brother, Chuck, who was the sheriff of Taney County. But that was as far as it went. Roscoe had never laid eyes on the man and until tonight he'd never given him more than a passing thought.

So where was the message coming from? As far as Roscoe was concerned, there were only two possibilities. Best deal with them one at a time, he thought. Pressing his Bible against his chest, he spoke quietly but firmly: "Satan, in the name of Jesus, I rebuke you. In the name of Jesus, depart from my life." Then, lowering his head and closing his eyes, he prayed: "Jesus, if this message truly is from You and not from Satan, give me a sign. Make these Scriptures clear to me."

Almost at once, as he would recall years later, Roscoe was filled with "a sense of peace and resolve." He returned to his Bible and the Scriptures were suddenly as plain as day. Convinced that the message he'd been hearing was "truly from God," he stayed up reading until three in the morning, all the while "feeling a powerful infusion of the Holy Spirit" compelling him to visit Darrell.

Over breakfast Roscoe told Wanetta and their thirty-nine-year-old daughter that he'd be visiting Darrell Mease in the county jail later that morning. They pleaded with him to reconsider.

"Dad, don't go there. You don't have to do this," his daughter said.

"Remember Folsom," Wanetta said. "After Folsom you promised you'd never go into a prison again."

It wasn't likely Roscoe would ever forget Folsom. In 1968 he and Wanetta were living in Sacramento where Roscoe was working in mining manufacturing and playing bluegrass on the side. He'd always loved bluegrass, long before it was even called bluegrass. He'd developed a passion for its sweet clean sounds while growing up in the hill country outside Forsyth and he'd bought his first guitar for thirty-three dollars at a music store in Springfield when he was thirteen. Since moving to Sacramento he'd started up his own group and he'd also kept some impressive company emceeing fiddle contests and country music festivals throughout the region. Bill Monroe, Merle Haggard, Earl Scruggs, Lester Flatt, Bob Wills: at one time or another Roscoe had rubbed shoulders and traded riffs with just about all the big-time players.

So it was 1968 and Roscoe and his group had been invited to give a gospel concert in the chapel of the maximum-security unit at Folsom State Prison. They'd just gotten through their second number when a riot broke out. At the height of the action a prisoner was killed with a homemade shiv. This was the same prisoner who'd chatted with Roscoe just prior to the concert and insisted on plugging in his Fender Stratocaster for him. The guy responsible for the stabbing then tried to herd Roscoe and his group into a little room off the chapel. "Get in there, punk," he said to Roscoe.

When the smoke had cleared, Roscoe swore he'd never go into a prison again. "That's it for prisons," he said.

But now, more than twenty years later, he'd had a change of heart.

"I remember Folsom," he told Wanetta. "But I've got a burden from God to go see Darrell in jail."

After breakfast he phoned Chuck and said that he was heading over to visit Darrell. Chuck said that he'd be in Springfield on business most of the day and that Roscoe should check in with the jailer, Kenny Hicks.

At the jail Kenny told Roscoe that he couldn't see Darrell. "I'm sorry, Roscoe," he said, "but your name isn't on the authorized visiting list."

"I've got to see him, Kenny. Jesus told me to go visit Darrell Mease."

"All right, come with me and we'll see what we can do."

Roscoe had assumed he'd talk to Darrell through the bars of his cell but Kenny set them up for a private chat at a small table in the jail's kitchen. Darrell had no idea who Roscoe was, this gangly old-timer in boots and jeans with a friendly weather-beaten face. Just about everybody who'd visited him so far, family members mainly, had come into the jail with their features frozen tight, somber, whispering, mourners-in-waiting. But here was Roscoe, somebody Darrell had never met, traipsing in like it was the first day of spring, big smile, happy to be there.

"Darrell," he said, "I was up past two this morning waiting on the Lord and I've got a burden to talk to you."

Darrell suddenly felt self-conscious about his long, unkempt hair and two-week growth of beard, wishing he were more presentable. He apologized to Roscoe for his appearance.

"You don't need to be concerned about that," Roscoe said. "God doesn't care how long your hair is."

Roscoe then said an impromptu prayer—a good strong prayer, Darrell thought. They chatted for a while, so casual and unforced they could have been old hunting buddies.

Finally Roscoe came to the point.

"I've got a message for you, Darrell," he said. "You have nothing to worry about. You've got the best lawyer in the world."

I wonder if F. Lee Bailey's taken me on, Darrell thought, still not exactly sure what to make of this unexpected visitor.

"Listen to me, Darrell," Roscoe went on. "You have absolutely nothing to worry about. God is your lawyer and God can't be beat. This is the message I was called to bring you."

Darrell looked at Roscoe, looked right into his big open face, no trace of irony, all warmth and sincerity, a face telling no lies. *God is your lawyer*. Darrell didn't know whether to take this literally—it sounded too far-fetched to be true—but there was one thing he did know for sure: Roscoe was no ordinary visitor. He'd been especially chosen to deliver this message.

Darrell broke down crying.

"You know, Roscoe," he said. "I was called to be a preacher when I was fourteen years old, before I started running with Satan and his bunch. The past couple of days I've been praying for God to take me back."

"Keep praying," Roscoe said. "And remember what I've been telling you. God is your lawyer. You've got nothing to worry about."

The next two days Darrell did little else but pray. Pray and fast and chain-smoke. And write Mary. He'd been writing Mary daily since first arriving in the Taney County jail. He still hadn't heard back from her but in his present circumstances a one-way contact was better than no contact at all.

Late evening the second day, January 19, he felt his world

turn. Lying in his bunk, his face pressed against the cement-block wall, he pleaded with God to forgive him and take him back. Suddenly, he knew it had happened. Twenty-plus years of wandering, he'd returned home. He'd been restored to God. As he would tell his mom the next morning, he went from "intense agony and despair to total joy in a split second." Lying there in his bunk, he experienced a "soft velvety feeling" washing over his entire being. His fears and hatreds, his longstanding resentments, they had been broken into tiny bits and cast into the ether, vanished, gone. In their place was an "unspeakable sense of peace and happiness and spiritual fullness." It was as if he had never sinned, never gone astray. His slate was clean. He was convinced, utterly convinced, that there was now nothing standing between him and God.

It took a while longer for Roscoe's message to sink in. *God is your lawyer.* Several days after his conversion Darrell still wasn't entirely sure what this meant. One evening, praying in his cell, he whispered: "You know what I want, God. I want to be freed from prison and married to Mary. If you truly are my lawyer, I know you can make this happen. But whatever you decide, I'm with you all the way. I'm absolutely through with Satan."

A week or so later it struck him. Nothing dramatic—no bells or whistles, no voices from on high. He just knew. One second he didn't know, the next he did. As simple as that: a gift of faith. He knew that Roscoe was right. He had nothing to worry about. He knew, strange and baffling as it might sound—that God was on his case. He had never been more certain of anything in his life.

Early afternoon, February 11, Michelle Beth Katzenell dropped by the Taney County jail in hopes of finagling an interview with Darrell Mease. As a regional reporter for the *Springfield News-Leader*, Michelle was always nosing around the jails and courthouses of the so-called Tri-Lakes area, keeping tabs on local murders, drug busts, and political scandals. The death-and-destruction beat of southwest Missouri: that's what she half jokingly called it. She'd started at the *News-Leader* just a few months earlier, after graduating from Northwestern with a bachelor's in journalism. It was her first reporting job, her first *real* job of any kind, and she'd taken to it with gusto, chasing down stories in the Ozarks like she'd been working the area with a pencil and notepad all her life.

Some of Michelle's more veteran colleagues at the *News-Leader* enjoyed kidding her about her early successes as a reporter. At five four and barely a hundred pounds, with long brown hair and matching brown eyes, she looked so sweet and innocent, they'd say, that she generally caught folks off guard. She'd have her story in the bag before anyone even realized she was after a story.

Michelle knew there was more to it than this, of course, but right now she certainly appeared to have caught the Taney County jailer off guard.

"Could I talk with Darrell Mease?" she asked Kenny Hicks.

"All right," Kenny said, and a few moments later, just like that, she found herself seated in a tiny visitation booth with Darrell facing her behind a partition of bulletproof glass.

Ever since the media crush at the airport in Springfield, Darrell had made no secret of his distaste for reporters. He'd refused all requests for interviews and he'd even enlisted the help of his jailers in keeping the press at bay. Michelle hadn't really expected to get in to see him just now but here they were, facing each other through the glass, and Darrell seemed to know exactly who she was.

"You're a reporter," he said, casual, no edge to it.

"Yes."

"And a born-again Christian, too, aren't you?"

Michelle was taken aback. She tried putting on her best poker face, not wanting to lose control of the interview, but it was tough not giving away some of her surprise. It was true. She'd been raised Jewish in New Jersey and had converted to Christianity at the start of her senior year in college. How in the world had he suspected this? It wasn't something she was in the habit of talking about—not even with colleagues at the newspaper.

Don't let this thing get sidetracked, she thought. After all, she was here to find out about Darrell, not the other way around. She knew that with a preliminary hearing scheduled for March 6, he still didn't have a lawyer. The public defender's office in Springfield had bailed out on him, pleading inadequate resources for handling a first-degree murder case, and his prospects of landing a half-decent private attorney seemed grim at best.

"Your hearing's coming up, Darrell, and so far no one's stepped up to bat for you," she said.

This was all the opening Darrell needed.

"I'm not worried about getting a lawyer," he said. "I'm not putting my faith in man."

Michelle waited, already happy she'd taken the trouble to drop by.

"God is my lawyer," Darrell went on. "He's the best lawyer in the world. Whatever God wants, it will be. God can do anything."

He then talked about the crucial events of the past few weeks: the fasting and praying, the unexpected visitor with the strange message, the conversion, and the conviction of salvation.

"I turned to God in desperation in trying to help my best friend," he said. "I wanted God to take care of her. I ended up saving myself."

He showed Michelle several religious booklets that he'd been reading for spiritual sustenance.

"People who talk to me act like it's doomsday," he said, "but I'm in better shape now than I've ever been in my life."

Michelle tried nudging the conversation toward more mundane matters. She asked about his onetime friendship with Lloyd ("Lloyd didn't have any friends," he said) and the relative ease with which the murder weapon had been recovered ("This was all part of God's plan. I'm not that stupid"). But that was as far as it went. Darrell obviously had his own agenda for the interview and he wasn't about to be budged.

After fifteen minutes a detention officer told Michelle that her time was up. Darrell thanked her for coming by.

Michelle was impressed. Darrell had been exceedingly pleasant throughout the entire exchange, not artificially chummy but pleasant and polite, simply laying it out for her. Pleasant and polite and tranquil—unbelievably tranquil, she thought, for someone in his circumstances. It wasn't a judgment she'd want to make as a journalist, but as a woman she believed he was perfectly sincere. His conversion wasn't a front; it was genuine.

She went to her car, furiously scribbled everything down in a notebook, then found a phone and called her editor. The editor was excited. An interview with Darrell Mease—quite the scoop: How in the world had Michelle pulled it off?

The next day the story appeared in the *News-Leader*, under the banner headline MAN IN MURDER CASE SAYS, "GOD IS MY LAWYER."

Darrell's mom phoned the newsroom and told Michelle that both she and Darrell loved the article. They were convinced that Michelle had been called by God to help spread the message.

TEN

People in law enforcement are understandably cynical about jailhouse conversions. Criminal investigators, detention officers, county prosecutors: they see it happen all the time. The murderer, the rapist, once arrested and thrust behind bars, his wild times brought crashingly to a halt, as often as not becomes an entirely new man. Deprived of fresh opportunities for violence and mayhem, he is reborn as a sweetly innocent child of God. Betrayed by the flesh, incarcerated in the flesh, he finds his victory and his true identity in the spiritual realm. Listen to his testimony and he'll tell you: he isn't merely reformed but utterly transformed, with only an accidental biological relationship to his previous self, the old dead self that rampaged and grimaced its way to imprisonment.

People in law enforcement are mostly unimpressed. So many convicts suddenly finding God, so many convicts experiencing last-ditch transformations of the heart and the spirit. It seems somehow too convenient, somehow too tidily packaged. Why now? Why all this converting and spiritual awakening after the throats have already been slashed, the bullets dug out of the bodies? It would have been nice, law enforcement people say, if some of these guys had seen the light a bit earlier. Prior to their hurting sprees perhaps, or at least prior to their arrest and imprisonment. A religious conversion after the damage is done, when there is possibly nothing left to do but convert—this seems less a genuine change of heart than a gesture of expediency, a culturally scripted maneuver calculated to assuage guilt and enhance survival prospects down the line.

On the face of it, then, Darrell's conversion was hardly exceptional. In southwest Missouri, no less than elsewhere across the country, outlaws were always finding religion after landing in prison. Sometimes they'd lose it just as rapidly if they were lucky enough to get released and then find it again during a subsequent stint behind bars. Among detention officers at the Taney County jail, clanging-door salvation of this sort was something of a standing joke. "Most of us never took it too seriously," one officer recently said. "We had a judge say to us once, 'God must be working right in your jail because there sure are a lot of people getting converted in there.' But don't ever think we were fooled about how long these conversions usually lasted."

More than a few people in local law enforcement, however, saw Darrell's conversion in a rather different light. Like Michelle Beth Katzenell, they believed that it was authentic—or at least gave every appearance of being so. One day Jack Merritt, in the vicinity anyway, decided he'd stop by the jailhouse and check up on Darrell's spiritual condition. Jack was not necessarily averse to doing a little religious witnessing on the side.

"Darrell, your life's not looking very good right now," Jack said. "You're probably going to get convicted on this and there's a good chance you're going to get the death penalty. Now I've always been taught, and I've always believed, that God is merciful and loving and that if you truly repent, truly ask God for forgiveness, then God will forgive you, even for a triple murder."

Darrell sat on his bunk quietly for a few minutes, looking straight at Jack.

"I know this to be true, Jack," he finally said. "I know you're right. I've already done it. I've already begged forgiveness of God and I know that God has forgiven me."

Years later, Jack was still able to recall the scene in vivid detail.

"Now there's lots of jailhouse conversions and I'm generally suspicious of them," he said during a conversation at his church one evening. "But Darrell spoke with such amazing peace and tranquility and confidence that I honestly believed he had it in him to repent and seek God's forgiveness. Had he truly done it? I can't say for sure but I wouldn't be surprised. It was really amazing. It left an impression on me."

For Lexie there was no doubt whatsoever: she knew that Darrell was saved and she also knew that God was his lawyer. Her prayers had been answered. Her first-born son, her golden boy, the son she'd believed would one day become a preacher—he'd finally come home. After twenty years of running lost and wild, Darrell had come back to God. She'd always known God would take care of him, this is what she'd prayed for, and now, after more than twenty years, her prayers had been answered.

God is your lawyer. Lexie believed Roscoe's message every bit as much as Darrell did but this didn't mean she was content simply sitting back and watching events unfold. The way she saw it, pull out all the stops, do everything possible—let God take care of the rest. She had a distant relative who was an attorney in Oklahoma City and she found out from him that the best criminal defense lawyer in the Springfield area was Bill Wendt. She then contacted some friends and family members who'd had personal dealings with Wendt and they vouched for him also. Finally she met with Wendt in person and he agreed to take on the case for a fee of twenty-five thousand dollars. Lexie and R.J. had to reach deep but they succeeded in coming up with a substantial retainer. For someone of Wendt's stature it really wasn't an exorbitant price.

Bill Wendt certainly wasn't God, but in southwest Missouri—insofar as lawyers were concerned—he was widely regarded as the next best thing. He was a local legend, the most celebrated criminal defense attorney of his generation.

In more than thirty years of practice he had represented close to a hundred people accused of murder or manslaughter. He hadn't always won but he'd never gone down without putting on a good show. He had a reputation as a courtroom gunslinger, feisty and fearless, but as often as not it was his folksy charm, which he could call up with a wink and a smile, that won juries over to his side. Wendt prided himself on knowing juries, their prejudices and vulnerabilities, how far he could risk pushing a point, dissecting a witness, without losing their attention or confidence. He also prided himself on maintaining good community relations: after more than thirty years thrashing it out in court, he was still handshaking friendly with just about every judge in southwest Missouri, and most prosecutors as well. But the thing that made him proudest? Fifteen death-penalty cases under his belt to this point, and so far an unblemished record. Fifteen lives hanging in the balance, and not a single execution.

To those who knew him, it made a certain sense that Wendt should take Darrell as a client. He'd always been attracted to the big draw, the high-profile case, and in recent years especially, with retirement looming on the horizon, he'd found it increasingly difficult settling for anything less. He enjoyed a tough challenge, and Darrell's case, given the strength of the state's evidence, looked like it could be one of his toughest to date.

Wendt met with Darrell at the Taney County jail a few days after Michelle Beth Katzenell's visit. He didn't bother asking Darrell if he'd actually killed the Lawrences. In his long career he'd never asked clients if they were guilty of the crimes with which they'd been charged. "A waste of time," he'd inform anyone curious about his approach. Darrell told Wendt he was grateful for his help but that he was still counting on God to see him through. Afterward Wendt told the *News-Leader*, "He has done a great deal of soul searching and I'm very pleased with that."

Darrell was indeed grateful but he was also supremely confident that victory was already in the bag. With God as his lawyer, as Roscoe had assured him, he had nothing to worry about. Having Bill Wendt on board was simply an added bonus, someone to help keep track of the paperwork.

What Darrell was most concerned about these days wasn't his case, but rather his maddening inability to make contact with Mary. After being rebuffed by Barbara Epps the first time he'd tried phoning, he'd called again weekly but with no better luck. He kept getting Barbara on the line and no amount of pleading or cajoling would convince her to turn the phone over to her daughter.

"I love Mary and I only want to help her," he told Barbara at one point.

"Well, there's nothing you've done to help Mary," she said.

"I confessed to get her just a slap on the wrist."

"Your confession hasn't done nothing for Mary."

Barbara had a point. Mary was still facing a charge of hindering prosecution and she was also under a fair bit of emotional distress. Her first month or so after coming home from jail, she'd seemed almost shell-shocked to Barbara and Fred. They'd set her up for counseling at a clinic in Hollister and she'd also been prescribed antidepressants by a psychiatrist in Springfield. She was confused, conflicted. She felt intense love for Darrell but she was also afraid of him. Try as she might, there was no way she could simply wash away their bittersweet times together.

On the legal end Barbara and Fred had enlisted the help of local attorney Peter Rea. They'd known Rea for years. He was a colorful guy, funny, voluble, opinionated, the kind of guy Ozarkers usually referred to as a "character." He had a large repertoire of offbeat stories, some of which may actually have been true. Years earlier, for example, when he was working out of the local prosecutor's office, an older colleague apparently showed up one morning and said, "Son, I've got bad news. I just learned there's a contract out on you." "That's terrible," Rea said, genuinely concerned. "Wait a minute," the older colleague said. "It's worse than you think. I found out the contract was only for fifty bucks. I felt so embarrassed for you, son, I threw in another ten bucks of my own."

Right off the top Rea had strictly forbidden any communication between Mary and Darrell. No phone calls, no correspondence, no jailhouse visits. He confiscated the first nine of Darrell's letters and deposited them, unopened, in his office. Darrell suspected something might be up when he didn't hear back from Mary but he continued writing at a furious rate, most often to Mary, occasionally to Barbara, too. Concerned that his correspondence was somehow being intercepted, he would sometimes—much to the chagrin of Barbara and Fred—have his mother or his sister, Rita, hand-deliver letters to the Eppses' household. Barbara had never seen such a torrent of letters. Inside of a month she had accumulated enough to fill a grocery sack. Darrell pouring his heart out on the written page: professing his undying love for Mary, crying for forgiveness, pleading for understanding—there seemed no end to it.

In mid-February, about a week after Darrell's initial meeting with Bill Wendt, Peter Rea unaccountably eased up on the communication embargo. He said that Mary could read Darrell's letters so long as she didn't write back and that she could even speak with him occasionally on the phone.

Their first couple of conversations were a bit of a letdown for Darrell. He was thrilled to get Mary on the line at last, but she seemed distant and wary, frightened, perhaps, of her own feelings for him. He suspected that her parents might be hovering in the background, dampening the spirit of things, so one evening he called quite late, hoping to catch her after Barbara and Fred had already gone to bed. For Darrell it was thirty minutes of pure bliss. Mary seemed warmer, more relaxed. He thought they were almost back to where they'd once been. He breathed in every word she said, holding it, holding it, not wanting to exhale, trying to absorb everything to its fullest. He told her about his conversion and asked if she'd seen the article in the *News-Leader*. She laughed and admitted that when she first read it, Darrell going on about God being his lawyer, she thought he'd gone crazy.

The next week Darrell phoned late again and it was more of the same. For twenty minutes he thought they were on a really good vibe, but then Barbara took the receiver and cut the conversation short, saying, "That's it—no more phone calls." She told him that she was afraid of him and that she hadn't wanted him calling Mary to start with. But now with his preliminary hearing and depositions coming up, Mary's talking to him anymore was absolutely out of the question.

So that was it: the communication lines were shut down again—tighter, apparently, than even before. Darrell saw no point in fighting it. For the time being he resigned himself to making do with whatever tiny glimpses of Mary might come his way. The glimpses weren't many, but he milked them for all they were worth. One time she dropped off some new underwear for him at the front desk of the jail—jockey shorts, the kind she'd always encouraged him to wear when they were on the road. Another time she sent him a store-bought card engraved with a verse of Scripture (Acts 20:32) that he'd talked about in one of his letters. She sent him a short note with some biblical passages condemning fornication and, sometime later, an envelope containing three blurred photographs. These were the shots Mary had taken, six months earlier, of the gorgeous sunset in Cherry Creek, Nevada. They hadn't turned out very well, maybe because it had taken her so long to get the film developed. The quality of the photographs, however, was hardly the point. On the back of each one Mary had printed a single word, spelling out, in heartrending ambiguity, the message, "DON'T EVER FORGET." Three words, each of which for Darrell might just as well have been an endless volume.

One day in late spring a highway patrolman named Vernon Cole was escorting Darrell through the courthouse. Cole had been transporting Darrell quite a bit to and from hearings and whatnot, and the two men had gotten to know and like one another. Darrell appreciated Cole's courtesy and kindness ("Anything you need, just let me know," the patrolman had once told him), and Cole knew he could always count on Darrell for a good old country quip or two. (Darrell might have found religion again but that didn't mean he'd lost his sense of humor.) On their way down the main corridor, Darrell spotted Mary through the window of a door leading into a small courtroom. She may have been there for a hearing herself; it was tough to tell. Cole stopped and waited while Darrell pressed his face up against the glass, hoping to get her attention. When Mary looked over, he grinned and mouthed, "Baby, I love you." From where he was standing, it appeared that she mouthed the same thing back to him and then started crying. Seeing this, he raised his cuffed wrists and, still grinning, gave her the thumbs-up sign. Someone snapped his picture while he was stuck in this pose, and, sure enough, in the next edition of the *Taney County Times* there was Darrell in all his grinning glory, thumbs brandished, looking for all the world like he couldn't be happier in his jail-issue jumpsuit and handcuffs.

In early July Darrell's jailhouse celebrity shrank somewhat when Marty Strange was booked into the last cell down the corridor of the maximum-security unit. The Lawrence killings were grisly enough but Strange had considerably upped the ante in local horror, inexplicably slashing his wife, Melanie's, throat and strangling their two young sons after the family returned home from a July 4 outing on Bull Shoals Lake. A couple of Darrell's mates in the unit had been planning a welcoming party for Strange, thinking they'd lay a whipping on him, but nothing came of it. Strange seemed so utterly mortified by what he'd done, and so genuinely bewildered, that they decided to leave him alone.

Not long afterward Darrell was driven to Springfield by two deputies for psychological testing. Along the way the men were talking about local outlaws and the conversation eventually shifted to Marty Strange. The deputies had been hit hard by the murders. They had known Melanie Strange; they had kidded around with the two young boys. They were still horrified by what had happened.

"I can't see how he can live with his conscience after what he's done," Darrell interjected.

That ended it, right there. Nobody said another word. They drove the rest of the way in silence.

ELEVEN

Maybe he didn't need it, maybe it was redundant, but Jim Justus wasn't taking any chances. He already had Darrell's confession, he already had the murder weapon, and he already had the statement Mary had given Jack and Chip in Arizona. But there was one more thing he wanted. He wanted Mary's trial testimony. With her testimony the case would be a mortal cinch—no way in the world could it slip away.

The case looked like a cinch anyway, but you never could tell. You've got what looks like a sure thing on your hands but then some sharp defense lawyer starts chipping away and, before you know it, you've lost the confession, you've lost who knows what else, and the sure thing isn't so sure anymore. It's suddenly up for grabs, anybody's game. It had happened to him before; it had happened to every prosecutor he knew. There was no guarantee it wouldn't happen here. Especially now that Bill Wendt was involved. Wendt was a guy who knew his way around the law, knew how to take charge of a county courtroom. Wendt wouldn't be content just sitting back, waiting for the prosecution to play its hand. He'd be going on the attack, dealing out some cards of his own. And that's why Jim wanted Mary's testimony. Make a deal with Peter Rea; immunity for Mary in return for her taking the stand against Darrell. Not even Bill Wendt would have an answer for that.

For now the deal could wait. Jim knew that he had plenty of leverage when the time was right. Hindering prosecution was one thing, but Peter Rea surely realized Mary could be facing additional and more serious charges if she didn't cooperate. There was no need to spell it out. Rea wasn't stupid. Accessory to first-degree murder: Jim had been dropping hints in this direction and he'd continue dropping them until he got what he wanted.

Jim Justus was the kind of guy who took people by surprise. A local product, born and raised in Branson, he'd first been elected prosecuting attorney of Taney County in 1977, when he was just twenty-six and fresh out of law school. Even now, twelve years later, he still had a boyish, wide-eyed look about him. Check him out, slight of build, soft-spoken and earnest, you'd figure him for a college intern in the prosecutor's office maybe, certainly not the guy who actually called the shots. Even the beard he'd taken to wearing in recent years accentuated his youthful appearance, making him seem a young guy in a big job trying to come across as older than he really was. But this was where he'd catch you by surprise. Jim was tough—and experienced. In his twelve years on the job, he'd prosecuted close to forty murders and gone to trial in twenty. He'd also won a grueling battle with testicular cancer during his early thirties and then sealed the victory by impregnating his wife with their third child. Peel away the boyish wrapping, here was a guy that definitely bore close watching.

Peter Rea, Mary's attorney, knew better than to take Jim Justus lightly. What Rea didn't know was that Jim really had no intention of bringing more serious charges against Mary. He'd been dropping hints about accessory to first-degree murder because he wanted to coax Rea into doing a deal. There wasn't much chance, however, of Jim actually following through. He didn't want Mary; he had no interest in digging up any more dirt on her. If anything, he regarded her as a victim in the whole affair. He was convinced that Darrell had manipulated and controlled her. "I didn't want Mary. I didn't care what she did," he would recall years later. "I wanted Darrell—just Darrell."

There was another, more personal reason why Jim wasn't interested in pursuing more serious charges against Mary. Living in Branson, he knew Barbara and Fred Epps pretty well and as a parent his heart went out to them. Jim's oldest daughter was close to Mary in age, and she'd recently been going through some rough, rebellious times of her own. She hadn't gone so far as to run off with a local outlaw but maybe this was because she hadn't yet met an outlaw as charming as Darrell.

Jim wanted Darrell, and he wanted him all the way. Not long after the arraignment he'd decided to shoot for the death penalty in the case. As the elected prosecuting attorney of Taney County, he had considerable discretion in such matters. Support for capital punishment ran strong and deep in the Ozarks, but Jim wasn't known for playing to the crowd. Only once before in his career had he gone for the ultimate penalty. This had been in the David Tate case. Tate was the white supremacist who'd killed Trooper Jimmie Linegar during a traffic check south of Branson in 1985. Jim hadn't gotten what he wanted on this one; Tate was sentenced to life without parole. Jim was determined this time around not to fall short.

A cynic might argue that Jim's motivation in seeking the death penalty for Darrell wasn't as pure as the driven snow. He was coming up for reelection the following year, and a fresh notch on his belt certainly wouldn't hurt his chances. Jim was insistent, however, self-interest had nothing to do with it. If ever there was a case that cried out for the death penalty, he believed, this was surely it. Indeed, Missouri's revised Capital Murder Law, in effect since 1977, seemed to have been written with precisely a case of this sort in mind. The law spelled out fourteen aggravating circumstances, any one of which qualified an offense as a potential death-penalty case. Jim hoped to prove at trial that Darrell's offense included at least two of these aggravating circumstances. Darrell had committed *three* homicides, not just one, and then he had demonstrated "depravity of mind" and rendered the offense "outrageously and wantonly vile" by blowing his victims' heads off.

Blowing their heads off . . . For most people this was the shuddering perplexity of the case. Why had Darrell gone so far? Why the overkill? To those who knew him—friends, family members, even people in law enforcement—there seemed no easy answer. This wasn't Darrell, they'd say. Darrell at his very worst was utterly incapable of such a thing. Jim Justus believed he had the answer. It had been a drug hit, he claimed—pure and simple. Darrell had been intent on taking over Lloyd's crank empire. Killing the main man wasn't enough. Darrell had wanted to deliver a message, make a dramatic point. *There's a new boss in the hills and if you don't believe it, just check this out.*

An interesting thesis, but anyone who'd had contact with Darrell in the months leading up to the killings would not likely have been convinced. Simply getting through the day in one piece had been challenge enough for him and Mary. Setting himself up as the new drug kingpin of the Missouri Ozarks? This hadn't been Darrell's ambition; it wasn't even a distant fantasy. His one and only ambition at the time was surviving.

Bill Wendt wasn't catching many breaks. In early spring he found out that Greene County Circuit Judge Tom McGuire had been assigned to the trial. Judge McGuire could never be accused of trying to blend in with the woodwork. Off the job he was known for big-time partying, world-class drinking, and a fondness for guns. (Several years after Darrell's trial, in fact, he would get into trouble for allegedly going on a drunken shooting spree.) On the job he kept a billy club and a loaded pistol under the bench—not always, apparently, completely hidden from view. He had a well-deserved reputation as a prosecutor's judge. In close calls, having to do, say, with the admissibility of evidence, he'd generally give attorneys for the state the benefit of the doubt, letting them push their cases to the limit. Wendt knew he wouldn't be getting many favors from Judge McGuire.

One thing Judge McGuire did early on—though it could hardly be termed a favor—was to uphold Wendt's request for a change of venue, moving the case from Taney County to the Circuit Court of Greene County in Springfield. Wendt had been hoping for a more neutral location than Springfield, where the case had already kicked up a sandstorm of publicity, none of it favorable to Darrell. They probably would have been no worse off staying put in Forsyth.

Wendt didn't fare any better at an evidentiary hearing held in Judge McGuire's courtroom on September 6. The hearing had been called in response to a motion Wendt had filed with the court to suppress Darrell's confession and admissions of guilt. Wendt's principal argument was that Darrell hadn't confessed voluntarily; rather he'd been tricked, manipulated, and coerced into doing so. After he had invoked his right to an attorney in Arizona, Jack and Chip had allegedly subjected him to implicit interrogation, in clear violation of the Supreme Court's *Innis* ruling of 1980. The investigators had permitted him to steal a glance at their notes, and they'd traded on his concerns for Mary, even to the point of promising that if Darrell gave himself up Mary would "walk away with just a slap on the wrist."

The hearing went pretty much as Wendt had anticipated. He knew coming in that trial judges were disinclined to sustain motions of this sort, and that Judge McGuire was even more disinclined than most. Darrell testified that the investigators had been on him "like vultures on a dying animal," ripping his natural defenses to shreds, tearing the confession out of him. Jack and Chip insisted that they'd played it by the book, advising Darrell of his rights at every turn, applying no untoward pressure. At one point Mary took the stand, but nothing came of it beyond a momentary brightening of Darrell's day. She exercised her Fifth Amendment privilege and refused to testify. In the end the affair hinged on credibility, and in the credibility department Darrell was clearly no match for Jack and Chip. In his order overruling the motion to suppress, McGuire stated that the court "finds beyond reasonable doubt that [the] defendant was lawfully arrested; that he was properly advised of his rights; that his statements were given freely and voluntarily; and that they were not the result of force, threats or promises."

There was more bad news to come. Sometime prior to the hearing Wendt had arranged for Darrell to be examined by a psychiatrist, Dr. William Clary, and a psychologist, Dr. David Reuterfors. Both men were regarded in local legal circles as "defense-friendly" medical professionals, willing to go the distance in finding evidence of mental illness. In the crunch, it was rumored, they'd be capable of finding a medical excuse for a traffic light stuck on red. This was what Wendt was counting on—a diagnosis of mental illness for Darrell. That way he could mount a psychiatric or diminished-capacity defense and hopefully persuade the court that his client shouldn't be held criminally responsible for his actions. Maybe sneak him out the back door. But it wasn't about to happen. The medical reports, which Wendt received shortly after the hearing, weren't even close to what he'd been hoping for. While conceding that Darrell tended to be paranoid, Clary and Reuterfors concluded that it wasn't likely he was suffering from any mental disease or defect at the time of the killings. As best as they could determine, he had been capable of conforming his conduct to the requirements of the law. Wendt didn't see much point in shopping around for another opinion. If Clary and Reuterfors couldn't deliver the goods, it was probably best to pursue another avenue of defense entirely.

Whatever avenue of defense this might be, Wendt wasn't likely to get much help from Mary. In early January 1990, he tried taking Mary's deposition at his law offices in Springfield. It was like squeezing water from a stone.

"What is your name, please?" Wendt asked once they got started.

"I plead the Fifth."

"Mary, your name is Mary Epps, is it not?"

"I plead the Fifth."

"Okay. Don't be embarrassed. Where do you live?"

"I plead the Fifth."

Seven more questions, each one receiving the same response. All Wendt could do was smile and call it an afternoon. He had a pretty good idea which way this was headed.

In early March, Wendt swung another pre-trial hearing, this time so he could challenge the legality of Darrell's arrest. The two felony warrants Darrell had been picked up on in Arizona? Child support and carrying a concealed weapon? No question about it, Wendt argued, these were "pretextual" warrants, bad-faith numbers, issued for the ulterior motive of getting Darrell in custody so investigators could grill him about the Lawrence killings. Were Jack and Chip and Jim really interested in nailing Darrell for non-support? Or for a two-bit weapons violation? Forget about it—not a chance in the world. Darrell had been living on the road with Mary for months prior to the killings. Where was the posse then? How come there was no paper out on him all this time? The warrants came when they did because investigators suspected him in the Lawrence homicides and were looking for an excuse, *any* excuse, to lasso him for questioning. The arrest was invalid under the Fourth Amendment, Wendt argued, and all evidence procured as a result of it must therefore be ruled inadmissible.

A good sales pitch, but Judge McGuire wasn't buying. He ruled here just as he'd ruled previously: the arrest was valid and so was the evidence stemming from it. If Wendt were going to get his client off the hook, it would have to be through some other means.

Darrell wasn't much troubled by these setbacks. He had a difficult time even seeing them as such. Ultimate victory, after all, was already assured. The only thing that troubled him about all this pre-trial fuss and bother was Mary. Not her stonewalling of Wendt; he didn't mind that a bit. He just wished everyone would give her some breathing space, back off, loosen the vise. He wanted her out of the torture chamber.

Aside from his concerns for Mary, Darrell was actually faring pretty well in the Taney County jail. The food was a disappointment ("your basic slop"), but he didn't mind the company. Sharing the maximum-security unit with him these past several months were a couple of unruly cons named Tom and Henry, and Darrell got a kick out of some of their shenanigans. Tom and Henry would sometimes get plastered on jail-brewed buck—made from tomatoes, yeast, and sugar—and then squabble and fight like an old married couple before one of them passed out or maybe got knocked out by the other with a sucker punch. The next morning, regardless of how it had turned out, they'd always be the best of buddies again.

Every Wednesday Darrell joined other prisoners, though usually not Tom and Henry, for a midday prayer service that was presided over in the jail kitchen by a Baptist minister named Jim Minor. Minor was a gentle and humble soul who lived in semi-retirement with his wife in a trailer on the outskirts of nearby Rockaway Beach. He'd come to the ministry relatively late in life, receiving ordination at the age of forty-three, and he enjoyed the prayer service probably as much as any of the prisoners. He especially enjoyed getting to know Darrell, whom he found polite and respectful. "Darrell was a regular at our meetings, and he'd occasionally let me know how much he appreciated my prison ministry," Reverend Minor would subsequently recall. "I knew he'd recently converted and professed belief in Christ. Some people assumed it was because of me. I'd love to take credit for it, but I can't. Someone else—I don't know who—had gotten to him first."

Darrell was still praying, and reading now, too—the Bible sometimes, and anything else of a religious bent he could get his hands on. The pickings were slim at the jail, but three or four items left a lasting imprint on him. One of these was a book called *Power in Praise*, which Roscoe had brought along on his visit and then left behind. The book fit Darrell's needs perfectly. Far from being an old-fashioned scold, a repent-or-be-damned jeremiad, it was a best-selling paean to positive thinking. Its message was tantalizingly simple: You're sick or in prison? Broke and depressed? Lost and forlorn? Don't fret about it. Simply praise God. Praise and thank God for your grief and your failures, for every situation you happen to be in—regardless of how tragic or evil it may appear. That way you show confidence in God; you demonstrate trust that God has a perfect plan for your life. In return God will convert your difficult circumstances to joyous and prosperous ones. Be steadfast in your praise, never waver in your confidence—God will take care of the rest.

Darrell was so impressed with *Power in Praise* that after a second or third reading he sent it to the front desk with a note asking Roscoe to hand-deliver it to Mary.

The jail had a small bookshelf near the kitchen, and rummaging through its contents one afternoon Darrell dug out two palm-sized pamphlets written by a Tulsa-based preacher named Kenneth Hagin. Pastor Hagin was the spiritual godfather of the so-called Faith movement, a new sensation that was just then sweeping across the southern and southwestern regions of the country. His message was so bright and jaunty, so lustily optimistic, that it made *Power in Praise* seem almost grudging in comparison. The message was addressed to born-again Christians. The world is your oyster, it advised them. You have miraculous powers at your disposal; unlimited blessings are yours for the taking. Simply stand on your faith, master the art of positive confession—and tell God what you want. That's right: don't beg or cajole but rather *tell* God. *Name it and claim it, brothers and sisters.* Don't resign yourselves to poverty or disease or any other earthly affliction. Let God know your heart's desires, shout them from the rooftops. If properly confessed, your wish is God's command. This is your birthright as Christians; this is what has been wrought for you through Christ's atonement.

Hagin's message almost took Darrell's breath away. This is precisely what he'd been doing: telling God in no uncertain terms what he wanted, confessing his heart's desires. He'd been telling God that he wanted to be spared execution, freed from prison, and reunited with Mary. And he had no doubt that God would deliver. Imagine now finding these pamphlets—in the Taney County jail of all places. It couldn't be a coincidence. They had been miraculously placed here, as nourishment for his soul, corroboration of his convictions. He couldn't read them often enough.

On April 11, in preparation for his trial, Darrell was transferred to the Greene County jail in Springfield. The jail was located in a large rear wing of the old sandstone courthouse on Boonville, just a few blocks north of the city square. After playing musical cells for a few days, he finally settled into a fifteen-by-nine, six-man unit down a dingy corridor in the old section of the jail. Three two-man racks crowded the cement floor, and a sink and toilet were set off in an alcove to the left of the steel entrance door. From the waist up along the back wall a window with heavy bars looked out onto a walkway for guards. It was tight, claustrophobic living, but Darrell wasn't complaining. After so many months waiting, he was anxious to get the show on the road. Not only that, he liked his new cell mates and even tried his hand at religious witnessing with a couple of them—something which not so long ago would have been utterly unthinkable.

The trial started on April 24, a Tuesday. Judge McGuire's was the largest courtroom on the second floor of the old courthouse, a trim and dignified room with oak paneling, high windows, and a swinging gate separating the gallery from the judicial bench, counsel tables, and jury box. A portrait of Thomas Jefferson hung on the front wall. More than sixty spectators, a packed house, were on hand the first day, including a dozen representatives from the regional news media. Michelle Beth Katzenell wasn't among them. She'd hoped to cover the trial for the *News-Leader*, but a more veteran reporter, Barbara Clauser, had been given the assignment instead.

Bill Wendt had realized from the start that he'd be facing long odds, but several recent developments had lengthened them even further. Just a few weeks earlier, on March 23, Mary Epps had finally signed her long-anticipated deal with

Jim Justus: immunity from prosecution in return for her trial testimony. Jim had notified Wendt's office of the deal and offered to make Mary available for a deposition. Wendt had declined the offer. At this late hour deposing her seemed more trouble than it was worth. He'd read the statement Mary had given Jack and Chip in Arizona. He knew how damning it was to his client. What else was there to know?

And then, in an eleventh-hour maneuver, Judge McGuire had approved a motion by Jim to sever the three murder cases, which meant that Darrell would be tried at this point for the death of Willie Lawrence only. This arrangement worked to the advantage of the prosecution in two ways. Willie was clearly the most sympathetic of the three victims, not nearly as susceptible as Lloyd (or even Frankie) to being dirtied up by the defense. And if Jim, for any reason, failed to convict Darrell for Willie's murder he could always go after him later on for the other two.

Jim and Wendt gave their opening statements, and then Jim summoned his first witness, Retha Lawrence, who described finding the bodies of the three victims at Lloyd's farm. Jack Merritt testified next, followed by pathologist Jim Spindler, Chip Mason, and then Charles Durham, a ballistics expert from the Highway Patrol's forensics laboratory.

The star witness for the state took the stand after lunch. Mary looked elegant in a black dress, her hair tied back in a braid—and also very nervous, struggling for her composure, dabbing her eyes with Kleenex. The direct examination was handled by Bill McCullah, a young prosecutor from Stone County who was assisting Jim with the case. In response to McCullah's careful prompting, Mary tearfully recounted how she and Darrell first fled Missouri and then returned so Darrell could "settle things with Lloyd."

"Did the two of you discuss any further what settling things with Lloyd might entail?" McCullah asked.

"Yes."

"What?"

"He started talking of ways that he could stop Lloyd from ever hurting us."

"Did he get more specific than that?"

"Yes, he said the only way to stop Lloyd was if he was dead."

"Was it talked about in the abstract like that or more specifically?"

"He was—said he had to kill him."

"What conversation would you have with the defendant when he would say things like that?"

"Well, I wanted to take the money we had and get a house in California, but he said he had to go back and take care of business."

"Do you recall when that conversation took place?"

"Well, when we were in California, I said I wanted the house and the closer we got to Missouri, the more he was obsessed, and so by the time we were in Louisiana, he had figured out what he had to do, and by that time, you know, I didn't think that he was really serious. I thought, you know, how some people say they're going to kill somebody when they're mad. I thought we were just going back to that area kind of as to satisfy maybe an ego or something of being seen."

Mary left nothing out. Dropping Darrell off near Lloyd's farm and then picking him up. Their heartbreak days as fugitives in Nevada, Colorado, and Arizona. Their arrest in the desert outside Phoenix. She covered all the bases.

Sitting at the prosecutor's table, Jim Justus couldn't help but feel pleased. Mary was coming across precisely as he and McCullah had hoped: sincere and vulnerable—a young woman clearly susceptible to being manipulated by an outlaw such as Darrell.

Bill Wendt, on the other hand, courtroom-dapper in a light blue suit and wire-framed glasses, seemed almost ready to throw in the towel. Up to this point, he'd still been devising strategies for keeping Darrell's videotaped confession out of evidence. But now he wasn't so sure it really mattered. Mary's performance, in and of itself, had been damaging enough.

Out in the corridor, with the court adjourned for the day, Wendt spoke with an interviewer for KY3 TV, sounding very much like a guy who'd just missed the last train.

"With her testimony it makes no difference whether that videotaped statement by Darrell comes in before the jury," he said. "It just pretty well closes up the first stage of the case. That's my belief."

Criminal trials in Missouri are divided into two stages: the evidentiary stage in which a verdict is reached; and then, if the defendant is found guilty, the penalty stage in which a sentence is imposed. Even without Mary's testimony, winning the first stage would have been tough sledding for Wendt. His options were severely limited. The state's evidence was strong enough that a straight acquittal was a long shot at best, and he'd already abandoned the possibility of a psychiatric defense. He couldn't very well argue self-defense, especially now that the cases had been split and Darrell was being tried here just for the death of Willie. His only realistic option, especially after Mary's testimony, was to somehow create reasonable doubt that Darrell had acted with deliberation, that his killing of Willie had been cold-blooded and premeditated. Get him off the hook for first-degree murder and instead finagle a conviction for murder in the second degree.

He planned on pursuing this strategy during his cross-examination of Mary on Wednesday, fully aware that it would take some nimble footwork. He had gone after Jack and Chip aggressively in cross-examination, all but accusing the two investigators of having played mind games with Darrell, extracting his confession through emotional extortion. A similarly aggressive approach clearly wouldn't work with Mary. She'd already proven herself a sympathetic witness, so sweet, so vulnerable, so naïve. If he tried discrediting her, impugning her testimony, he'd risk alienating the jury. Not aggressive or hostile, then, but firm and avuncular: that's how he'd approach it the next day.

In the days leading up to the trial the defense had been concerned that Jim Justus might have Rocky Redford waiting in the wings, ready to hit the stand and testify against Darrell. As a precaution Wendt had arranged for Rocky's younger brother, Rick, to be brought in from a prison in

Kansas, where he was serving serious time on a kidnapping rap. Rick knew Darrell, he knew Rocky, and, if need be, he'd take the stand himself and tell the jury which of the two men he'd side with when the truth was on the line. Not the ideal rebuttal witness, perhaps, but the best Wendt could come up with on short notice. Rick was being held in a cage in the Greene County jail, which Darrell now passed on his way back to lockup after the first day of testimony.

"How's it going so far?" Rick asked.

"The trial's going down the toilet," Darrell said.

"That's pretty rough, man."

"Nah," Darrell said, smirking. "I'm not worried about it."

Rick stood there deadpan, watching as Darrell passed out of view, not quite knowing what to make of his old buddy's apparent unconcern.

With R.J. sticking it out at home, folding in on himself these past few months, Lexie was attending the trial with her daughter, Rita. On Wednesday morning a reporter caught up with the two women outside the courtroom, wanting to know how Lexie was holding up under the pressure. Wearing a crisp blue jacket over a white blouse, looking even thinner than her normal hundred and ten pounds, Lexie said that she was holding up just fine, her voice not giving away so much as a flutter of anxiety.

"I've put all of this right in God's hands, and God is supreme," she said. "So whatever God's will is, this is what we're waiting for."

At ten o'clock Mary, in a purple blouse and white skirt, took the stand for Wendt's cross-examination. The defense attorney wasted no time throwing his strategy into gear.

"You, in your testimony yesterday, Mary, mentioned that prior to these deaths, or prior to the time at least that you dropped Darrell off and later heard the radio report, you used the word 'obsessed.' Was Darrell obsessed with his relationship with Lloyd Lawrence at the time you dropped him off?"

"Yes."

"Wasn't he mad and upset and disturbed, as well as obsessed, with his problems with Lloyd Lawrence at the time you dropped him off?"

"Yes."

So far, Mary was cooperating nicely. Wendt decided to shift direction just for a moment.

"Many months ago didn't Darrell say to you, 'Mary, if this ever comes to the courtroom I want you to turn on me and to tell the truth and get yourself out of this'? Wasn't that your agreement with Darrell?"

"He told me to tell the truth," Mary said, her voice buckling.

"And he encouraged you, if there was an arrest, to go ahead and testify even though you had to testify against him, did he not do that?"

"Yeah, he told me to tell the truth."

Indeed, it was so. On at least two occasions during their fugitive days—once in Tucson, and again immediately after the arrest outside Phoenix—Darrell had communicated as much to Mary. If she ever found herself backed up against the wall, she should tell everything she knew, without worrying about the consequences. He expected she'd be reluctant to do so, but he gave her the green light, insisting this was what he wanted. Bringing this out here, Wendt was hoping to show the jury a side of Darrell, honorable, selfless, ingenuous, that might give them pause later on when they were chalking up the final score.

Wendt now returned to the main business of the morning, trying to show that Darrell was so freaked out by Lloyd, and so addled by crank, that he couldn't possibly have killed Willie with cool deliberation.

"Now, then, Darrell was also concerned about Lloyd converting you into his girlfriend, was he—did he express that concern to you?"

"Darrell did, yes."

"And I really don't want to embarrass you but did you ever ingest any of these Lloyd Lawrence drugs at all? The— I guess it's called crystal—do you remember, did you ever do that?"

"Yes."

"Okay. Does—in your experience with Darrell, he was—there was a time during his relationship, was there not, with Lloyd Lawrence that he was—that Darrell was taking these drugs frequently?"

"Yes."

"Didn't that cause a kind of a—I'll use the word mental upset or emotional upset? When you—I call it paranoia . . . do you know what the term *paranoia* is?"

"Yes."

McCullah objected to this line of questioning, saying it was a matter for expert testimony. Mary wasn't competent to address a technicality such as paranoia. Judge McGuire brushed him off, one of the few times during the trial that the prosecution didn't get its way.

"Now," Wendt went on, "did Darrell get paranoid during this period of time building up to when he felt that it was either him going to get killed or someone else? Did he get paranoid and very suspicious?"

"Yes."

Of course, as Wendt took pains to establish at this point, Darrell's fear of being killed by Lloyd wasn't entirely unreasonable. He may have been prone to paranoia, he may have been corkscrewed by crank, but the threat was acutely real. Lloyd was after them, and both Darrell and Mary were fully aware of it.

"Were you personally afraid for your own life prior to [the killings]?" he continued, driving the point home.

"Yes."

"In fact, that's why you and Darrell were running, is that not true, afraid of Lloyd and his crew?"

"Yeah, I was more afraid after the drugs were taken."

Wendt took another slight detour at this point, trying to fill in some gaps in the narrative, then once again returned to his main theme.

"All right. Would it be proper for me to say that within—or to suggest, I'm going to suggest—and tell me if it's the truth—within a two- or three-month period prior to these deaths that you and Darrell were crazy with fear about being killed yourselves? Isn't that true?"

"Yes, he was. I didn't really know what was going on, I—"

"When Darrell spoke to you about Lloyd Lawrence the last three months before this terrible death or deaths, did he become upset, mad, and angry about Lloyd, not at you, about Lloyd?"

"Yes."

"And he was that way when you dropped him off immediately prior to the deaths, wasn't he?"

"Yes. He didn't—he was—didn't say nothing, really."

"But he was a different man those two or three days before you dropped him off, was he not?" Wendt asked, leaning in now. "From the man you knew and wanted to marry previously, he was a different man, wasn't he?"

"Yes." Mary losing it momentarily, sobbing, Judge McGuire handing her a box of tissues, Darrell thinking, *Forget about it, Bill. Leave her alone. It's not worth it.*

"If you need a break, I'm sure the judge would give you one," Wendt said, consolingly.

"I'm okay." Mary, sniveling, apparently over the worst of it.

Maybe it was Mary's small emotional outburst, but Wendt seemed to start sputtering here, the momentum he'd built up strangely halted.

"Okay," he said. "And you and Lloyd at one time had planned to marry, I believe. Faux pas there, Judge—but had you and Darrell planned to marry?"

"Yes."

"Had you ever dated Lloyd?" Wendt asked, incongruously.

"Dated Lloyd?" Mary said, voice raised, incredulous.

"Yes."

"No."

Wendt's moment had passed. He continued to press Mary, even taking a second shot at her in re-cross before lunch, but nothing much came of it. At one point Mary confirmed that Darrell "was insanely obsessed with the fact that Lloyd had men trying to kill us," but mostly she took refuge behind one-word, yes-or-no answers, rarely elaborating. Wendt never stopped trying but his resolve seemed weakened. He was like a guy dutifully seeing some unpleasant business through to the finish, perhaps wondering why he'd taken it on in the first place. In the end the road he'd been trying to take the jury down petered out in a thicket of detail. Bad drugs, shady arrest warrants, backroom deals: everything was laid out, but the thing he'd most wanted to impress the jury with, namely Darrell's manic and fearful state of mind prior to the killings, had been lost in the scenery. He'd pointed it out, danced around it some, but he hadn't succeeded in fixing it as a primary point of reference.

All eyes in the courtroom had been trained on Mary throughout the morning, but Bill McCullah occasionally stole a glance over to the defense table, trying to get a read on Darrell, to see how he was reacting to being betrayed by his girlfriend. If Darrell was hurt, angry, or disappointed, if he even saw Mary's testimony as a betrayal, he wasn't letting on. He simply sat there, calm and dignified, almost stoical, watching Mary intently, flashing her smiles of encouragement, silently cheering her on.

With Mary's testimony wrapped up, the court was recessed for lunch. Escorted off the witness stand by Jim Justus's wife, Mary was forced to pause for a couple of seconds by the defense table, waiting out a bit of congestion as people in the front rows of the gallery filed out into the aisle and made their way to the door. All morning long and the day before, Mary had avoided making direct eye contact with Darrell, but now here she was, practically standing in his shadow, Darrell looking up at her from his chair, wordlessly pleading for some kind of connection, anything. Perhaps feeling his hopeful gaze brushing the side of her face, Mary turned and for a brief moment, three or four seconds, they locked in.

"You done good, baby. I love you," Darrell said, grinning broadly.

Mary nodded, a trace of a smile on her lips, then she was hustled out the door and into the corridor.

With its long counter, private booths, and bargain-priced menu, Hamby's Steak House was a favorite lunchtime hangout for the courthouse crowd. The place was usually a smorgasbord of gossip, but today it was the Mease trial and not much else. An old-time lawyer, white-hair and three-piece suit, sharing a booth up front with a younger colleague and a reporter, the old courthouse visible across the street, suggested that a guilty verdict was all but signed, sealed, and delivered.

"It's all over but the crying," he said. "The girlfriend did him in. Wendt can call in the cavalry now, it's not gonna do him any good."

"It wasn't the girlfriend," the reporter volunteered. "It was a lost cause to start with. If Wendt can save the guy from the needle, get him life without parole, he's done more than anybody could have expected."

"I don't know, let's not sell Wendt short," the younger lawyer said. "He might still have a card or two up his sleeve. I'm going back over for the summing up, see how it comes out."

"You're wasting your time," the first lawyer said, wiping the corner of his mouth with a napkin. "When it's done, it's done. And this one's good and done."

If anyone still had a card up his sleeve, it was Jim Justus, not Wendt. After lunch Jim called Jack Merritt to the stand again. He questioned Jack in detail about the circumstances surrounding the taking of Darrell's videotaped confession and then played the videotape for the jury. Wendt tried roughing Jack up in cross-examination, accusing him of wheedling the confession out of Darrell, but the investigator stood his ground, insisting that he'd played it strictly by the book.

With the case for the prosecution now completed, the ball was in Wendt's court. He wasn't able to do much with it. He had no moves left—at least none he thought worth making. He summoned no witnesses, and he decided against putting Darrell on the stand. Wendt had taken his best shots, almost worn himself out, cross-examining the prosecution's witnesses. Anything he had left, he'd save for the closing argument.

By this point Jim and McCullah smelled blood; they were eager to go straight for the kill. During a brief conference in the judge's chambers they told McGuire that they wanted an instruction for first-degree murder only. They didn't want the jury to have the option of convicting Darrell for murder in the second degree. It was all or nothing—a calculated risk, but the two young and hungry prosecutors were oozing confidence. They felt they couldn't lose. Over Wendt's protests, McGuire acceded to their request. The jury would have the option of either acquitting Darrell or convicting him of first-degree murder—nothing in between. The odds for acquittal were about a million-to-one. Under Missouri law there were only two possible penalties for a first-degree murder conviction: life without parole, or death by lethal injection.

Wendt's closing argument wasn't one of his finer moments. He sputtered and stuttered, never quite finding his stride, three times referring to Darrell as Lloyd. *Lloyd! Calling his own client Lloyd again!* Only toward the end did he muster a bit of the flourish for which he was famous, insisting there was reasonable doubt that Darrell had acted with deliberation, the key element in first-degree murder.

"Now, then, we're talking about deliberation," he said, facing the jury. "What did the State's own witness say about the defendant's state of mind? I'm talking here about cool reflection upon the matter for any length of time: What did she say, Mary Epps, about Darrell's state of mind at the time he was let out of the car prior to these deaths? She used the word 'obsessed.' And then I asked her, I said, well, was he extremely disturbed mentally?—and I think Bill here complained about the use of the term 'mentally,' but she said, yes, he was disturbed mentally. I said, Was he mad? Yes. Was he frightened? She said, Yes. I said, Was he upset? She said, Yes. So, the last evidence that we have on the state of mind, this element of deliberation, Darrell, is from Mary. Now if you believe that Mary's telling the truth, if you believe that she was in fear of her own life from Lloyd Lawrence and that Darrell was in fear of his own life, you're not going to be able to find deliberation beyond a reasonable doubt. And I ask you to find him not guilty and let the prosecutors go to the law books and start all over again, however the law will let them do that."

Jim Justus, summing up for the prosecution, wasted no time coming to the point.

"Willie Lawrence is asking you to protect him," he told the jury. "He was killed because he could identify Lloyd's and his grandmother Frankie's killer. That killer is Darrell Mease, who intentionally planned, who for a period of three days laid in wait in the woods with the arsenal that he had for the one sole purpose of killing someone. And has the State proven beyond a reasonable doubt that he deliberated on it? They most certainly have. And that's why when you go from this room to deliberate, we're asking you to come back with a finding of guilt of first-degree murder."

The jury of nine women and three men left for the jury room at five-forty. Less than an hour later, early-evening sunlight slanting through the courtroom's high windows, they returned with their verdict.

Guilty. Murder in the first degree.

Willie's dad, Buck, was in the courtroom when the verdict was read, a stocky, big-faced man wearing glasses and a sports shirt open at the collar. Several minutes later, surrounded by reporters out in the corridor, he said, "I just feel like it was a fair verdict. It couldn't come out any other way." Not sounding vindictive, taking no real pleasure in it, just breathing some relief.

Buck's wife, Anita, was an exemplar of class and compassion. After the verdict was announced she sought out Darrell's mom and sat with her for a couple of minutes on a wooden bench in the corridor, commiserating, whispering words of condolence, one deeply religious woman to another. A bit later, buttonholed by a reporter, tearful, her voice quaking, she expressed sympathy for Darrell's family.

"I feel for them because I know what I had to go through losing my son," she said, "and I'd hate to think anybody else has to go through what we have had to go through."

Lexie was momentarily shaken but when she stood to face the cameras, Rita beside her with mascara-streaked tears running down her cheeks, she spoke with brave conviction. "Darrell still has his faith in God, and we just go from here," she said.

The penalty phase of the trial took place the next day. Since there were only two possible punishments for Darrell's murder-one conviction, execution or life without parole, Wendt's job was straightforward: save his client from the execution chamber. The key was to present as many mitigating circumstances as possible, lighten the load of guilt, so to speak, and also to humanize Darrell, show the jury the boy behind the man, the man behind the outlaw. Show them the sweet hillbilly kid, the kid with the infectious smile who aced Bible drills every Sunday at his hometown church, the Vietnam veteran who couldn't catch a break after returning home from a war he'd wanted nothing to do with in the first place.

In preparation for just such an eventuality, Lexie had been rounding up character witnesses, putting in the call to old friends and family members, folks who knew Darrell before the sky caved in and who'd be happy testifying on his behalf. In a matter of days she'd landed more than forty people; she easily could have managed twice that number. Boyhood friends such as Mike Langston; old stomping buddies such as Ronnie Dickens, Keith Thurman, and Bruce Broomfield; cousins and aunts and uncles: they all said they'd be pleased to help out any way they could. Nobody turned her down.

And there they were Thursday morning when Darrell was escorted down the courthouse corridor, more than forty strong, lined up awkwardly along the walls. Some of them hadn't seen Darrell in years; few could recall him looking quite so respectable. Clean-shaven, his hair slicked back, and wearing an ill-fitting tan jacket over a white shirt and brown tie, he smiled and raised a hand in greeting, happy to see there were people from his past who hadn't yet given up on him.

The prosecution called just four witnesses during the penalty phase, saving their trump card for last. Jim Spindler, Jack Merritt, and Lee Stephens took the stand, Jim and Jack for the second time each in the trial, and then Chief Deputy Jerry Dodd of the Stone County Sheriff's Department, the same Deputy Dodd who had videotaped the crime scene no more than an hour or so after the killings. Justus and McCullah wanted to play Dodd's gruesome footage now for the benefit of the jury, and Judge McGuire gave them the go-ahead, over the strenuous objections of the defense. Wendt argued that the video was superfluous, and also wildly inflammatory. The jury had already looked at stills of the crime scene; they'd already heard graphic testimony from the pathologist, Jim Spindler. Was it really necessary, Wendt asked, that they now be subjected to this five-minute horror film, with its depiction of "head wounds wherein most of the cranial cavity is removed and exposed with the brain tissue outside of the head?"

The jury viewed the video, as grisly as advertised, and then Wendt went to work, calling one character witness after another, each one hopeful of finding the right words, the magical phrase, that might persuade the jury to spare Darrell's life. Although impressive in sheer numbers, the exercise fell decidedly flat. The overall effect was rather like a procession of out-of-town mourners showing up at a funeral parlor in a strange city to pay respects to a deceased they barely knew. Part of the problem, of course, was that many of the witnesses had lost touch with Darrell over the years and they were frankly mystified by the frightful turn his life had taken. For the vast majority, moreover, Judge McGuire's courtroom was strange and forbidding territory. They were coming in cold, without truly knowing what was expected of them. Most hadn't exchanged so much as a single word with Bill Wendt prior to being thrust on the stand.

So there they were, Darrell's brigade of well-wishers, done up in their Sunday best, giving it their utmost, but unable to muster the words that might have turned the tide in his favor. Only two or three succeeded in breaking through the stifling formality of the courtroom with a breath of insight; a glimpse into the life of the man the jury knew only as a murderer. One of these was Danny McCrorey, a dairy farmer who had had only brief and sporadic contact with Darrell since high school.

"Now, how far did you stay in school with Darrell?" Wendt asked.

"Twelve years," McCrorey answered. "We graduated together."

"And did you socialize with him, go to any other places or have other meetings?"

"We—cave explorers, you know, we done a lot, we was together a lot. We went to church together. That's been—like I say, the twelve years I was around Darrell quite a bit. He was a—what stood out to me about Darrell was, I was taught to do right when I was growing up but I didn't do the things right. But now Darrell—he was taught by the same rules, his mother went to church where mine did, but Darrell drew a line when it come to drinking, anything. I never knew of Darrell saying one cuss word the whole twelve years of school. And that's why Darrell stood out in my life and that's why I'd like to say everything I could to help Darrell because he was a number one guy."

"You're here to try to save his life, aren't you?"

"That's right."

Alma Tolbert, one of Darrell's many aunts and the youngest of Frank and Lizzie Mease's seventeen children, did a feisty turn on the stand, raising eyebrows with her talk of blood bounties and family treachery.

"Do you remember about the time that Darrell went into the military service?" Wendt asked her.

"Yes."

"Prior to that time what kind of reputation did he have for

being a law-abiding citizen and Christian and a good school-boy?"

"Well, I would say one of the best."

"And what's his reputation now insofar as the people in the community say with regard to truthfulness? Good or bad?"

"Well, they don't— Very few if any holds anything against him."

"And you're thinking now in terms of the Lawrence deaths, aren't you?"

"Yes."

"Prior to the Lawrence deaths, did you ever hear of any threats against Darrell?"

"I certainly did."

"What did you hear?"

"I heard he had a ten-thousand-dollar price on his head, just to tell him which direction he went in, and he told our relation."

"He did what?"

"It was told to my relation, he asked my relation to give him the directions, if he knew where he went, he was on the run."

"By whom, who told you that, your family?"

"My nephew, he was a friend of Lawrence. I think, to be honest, they had dealings."

Darrell's mom spoke on his behalf, as did his sons Shane and Wesley, and finally, in one of the trial's odder developments, Darrell took the stand. He testified for several minutes, nothing earthshaking, answering questions about his family background and military service, taking the Fifth on anything having to do with the Lawrence killings, and then Wendt, McGuire, and the two prosecutors adjourned to the judge's chambers to thrash out a technical point of procedure.

Sitting up there alone, Darrell cast a sidelong glance at McGuire's bench: he almost did a double take. Impossible, he thought. A snub-nosed .38 in a holster, strung up in the kneehole under the bench, clearly visible from where he was sitting. Right there, right there, easily within his grasp. With a snap of the fingers, he could have the .38 in his hand, ready for business.

Tempting, unbelievably tempting, but Darrell wasn't up to it. Most of the fight had been knocked out of him since the arrest in Arizona. Not only that, some quick figuring convinced him it was too good to be true. It had to be a setup. Why would the judge have left the .38 within easy pouncing distance of a mad-dog killer and a noted pistolero? There could be only one answer: McGuire had wanted him to see the gun. He'd been banking on him making a lunge for it in a last desperate bid for freedom, assuming Darrell would jump at the chance to blast his way out of the courtroom and onto the street. The only problem was, the gun would be unloaded. Sure, plain as day, it had to be unloaded. Get him to take the bait, face down the courtroom with an empty pistol. This would be an excuse for the plainclothes troopers standing along the back wall to kill him right there. That way nobody would have to worry about the jury voting against the death penalty. Or maybe an honest appellate judge ordering a new trial. Gun him down, take care of business here and now, save everybody a lot of trouble. *Convicted murderer killed trying to escape.* Was anybody going to protest?

Puzzling it through, the pieces started to come together. They were all part of it: McGuire, the prosecutors, even his own lawyer. Why had Wendt put him on the stand in the first place? To ask a few piddling questions of no value whatsoever to the case? And why had Wendt and the rest of them cleared out of the courtroom, leaving him up there all by himself? Easy: they knew the deal was on and they didn't want to be caught in the line of fire. Everybody was trying to play him for a sucker. Not this time, though. This time he'd seen right through it.

With Darrell opting out of a courtroom showdown, there was nothing other than for the trial to advance to its final stages. While acknowledging in his summation that the Lawrence killings were "the worst [he'd] ever seen, no question about it," Wendt pleaded with the jury to spare his client's life, arguing that Darrell was a fundamentally decent person whose moral sensibilities had been crippled by a tragic chain of circumstances, beginning with Vietnam and ending with his entanglement with Lloyd. "Mitigating circumstances, no question about it," he said. "Think about those mitigating circumstances. In thinking about [them] you can even think about any fact, any fact, in the first stage of this case, in the second stage of this case, which would soften the ultimate verdict. You can even say, Well, Darrell, you deserve to die, but I just don't want to take you away from your boys even though they can only visit maybe once a month.

"Don't play God," he concluded. "There's not a God on this jury. You have the right, but don't play God."

Now the prosecution's turn.

"The worst he's ever seen," Jim Justus said, making Wendt swallow his own words. "The man said, in thirty years it's the worst he's ever seen. We're standing here today saying, we agree. It's one of those times, one of those few times where the law allows the imposition of the death penalty." Neither Vietnam nor paranoia nor anything else save "the oldest motive in the world" was behind the killings, Jim insisted. Darrell was motivated by greed, pure and simple. He was determined to take over Lloyd's drug empire, and nothing was going to stand in his way. "And I say for the final time that's why as a prosecuting attorney of Taney County, Missouri, I can stand up and say he deserves to die. Because the law and the facts say so and because you said you could follow it if this is the case. It is."

Close to two hours later the jury reached a verdict, which McGuire read aloud to the packed courtroom.

"We the jury, having found the defendant, Darrell Mease, guilty of murder in the first degree of William Lawrence, now assess and declare the punishment at death."

Darrell showed no emotion. He sat stock-still, avoiding eye contact with the jurors as they left the jury box and filed past him.

Lexie caught up with Jim Justus by the courtroom door. "Do you realize you've just done what you've accused Darrell of doing?" she said to him. A couple of minutes later, sitting alone on a bench in the corridor, a picture of grim dignity in a pale blue dress, she told reporters that she'd said a prayer for the jurors when they started deliberating and another one when it was all over. "I think that this was handled wrong because had it not been split up it would've been a whole different story, and I feel that Darrell has really been railroaded," she added.

Asked by the press for his parting words, Jim Justus said, "When you have a brutal homicide such as this, with that much drugs involved, and that much premeditation, with mutilation of the body, I could in good faith stand up and look that jury right in the eye and say, 'This man deserves to be put to death.'"

When Darrell was led out of the courtroom in handcuffs and a chain around his waist, the media scrum in the corridor wasn't expecting him to stop and talk. Up to this point, no one in the press, outside of Michelle Beth Katzenell more than a year earlier, had been able to coax a single word out of him. But with the death verdict in, Darrell decided that the time was right to deliver a brief message.

"Mary is my friend," he said, microphones and notepads snapping to attention, "and I'm proud of her for telling the truth." His armed escort jabbed him in the ribs, trying to get him to move along, but Darrell managed to squeeze in one more sentence. "Jesus Christ is my best friend," he said, "and I trust God now more than ever before."

And that was that. Back in his cell Darrell picked up a snapshot of Mary, smudged and crinkled, and whispered, "Someday, I will be with you." Then, sitting there on his rack, eyes closed, his mind seized on a passage of Scripture, Mark 11:23–24: "I solemnly assure you, whoever says to this mountain, 'Be lifted up and thrown into the sea,' and has no inner doubts, but believes that what he says will happen, shall have it done for him. I give you my word, if you are ready to believe that you will receive whatever you ask for in prayer, it shall be done for you."

Reciting the passage silently, caressing the words, he

suddenly felt a sweet and luxuriant sensation washing over his body, almost as if a bucket of warm oil had been poured on his head and then soaked down to his knees. He'd never experienced anything like it, but from his Pentecostal boyhood he was almost certain he knew what it was. A Holy Ghost confirmation: in this hour of need, the Holy Spirit was anointing him with strength and resolve and passionate purpose. *They've just pronounced the death penalty on me,* Darrell thought. *It doesn't matter. They can put a thousand death penalties on me and it doesn't make a difference. I'm walking free and I'll be reunited with Mary.*

Bill Wendt wanted twenty-seven grand to handle the appeal. The well was almost dry: no way at this stage could Lexie come up with that kind of money. A few days after the death penalty was handed down she came to see Darrell with the bad news. "We're not abandoning you but that's a lot of money," she told him. "We're going to have to figure out the best way of proceeding."

Darrell was momentarily jolted. He'd grown to like and trust Wendt. Over the past year, almost despite himself, he'd put quite a bit of faith in the smooth-talking attorney. But thinking it over later that day, he decided that a clean break was probably for the best. He didn't need Wendt starting out; he certainly didn't need him now. No sense confusing the issue: God was his lawyer, and God was going to carry this thing through to its miraculous conclusion. "I don't care if the janitor handles the appeal," he told Lexie over the phone the next morning. "God can't be stopped."

A couple of weeks later Darrell and Wendt met briefly in a conference room in the basement of the Greene County jail. By this point Wendt had already filed a motion for a new trial, standard procedure after a homicide conviction, and he wanted to know definitely one way or the other where he stood with Darrell.

"I'll be fine without you, Bill," Darrell said. "God is my lawyer."

"That's good," Wendt shot back. "You're going to be needing all the help you can get."

PART
FOUR

PART
FOUR

TWELVE

Darrell was transported to Potosi Correctional Center on June 1, 1990, after a formal sentencing hearing in Judge McGuire's courtroom earlier the same day. The vehicle he was riding in turned off I-44 at St. James and cut southeast through thickly forested country for fifty-five miles before hitting the sad-sack town of Potosi. A left at a county road past the far edge of town, then half a mile more—and there it was. A low-slung stone structure with tiny window slots, recreational yards at one end, and a gigantic water tower standing off to the side, the whole complex enclosed by perimeter fences and coils of razor wire. Darrell's first hard look at the place that was supposed to be his final mailing address.

If there were ever such a thing as a good time for entering a maximum-security prison, Darrell was hitting it just about right. Potosi had opened for business only the previous year and state corrections people weren't too far off the mark in proclaiming it the cleanest, brightest, and best-equipped facility of its kind in the entire country. Compared to the ancient and decrepit Missouri State Penitentiary in Jefferson City, it was practically lush living. MSP, or "the Walls," as hard-timers usually referred to it, was cramped, squalid, and violent, the kind of place where simply making it through dinnertime without getting raped or stabbed generally counted as a good day.

No sense, however, pressing the point too hard: although definitely a step up in class from Missouri State Penitentiary, Potosi was hardly a bed of cheer in its own right. Despite its well-stocked law library, two music rooms, and impressive gym facilities, despite its brightly lit visitation center and central air-conditioning—despite all of its frills and conveniences, the place was marked by a fundamental gloom. Everyone knew that Potosi was the end of the line. Each and every one of its three hundred inmates had been sent there either to be executed or to rot away with no chance of parole. Brand spanking new, sure, but also the most forlorn of institutions—no exit, no mercy, no return ticket.

Not by accident, moreover, was it located in one of the most forlorn parts of the state. At one time a national leader in lead mining and shoe manufacturing, the Potosi region was now depressed and run down. The mines were long abandoned, the factories shuttered or razed. Little wonder then that the local citizenry had actually lobbied for the new maximum-security prison to be built in their very own backyard. Better this than nothing—at least some jobs would come of it, and maybe some collateral benefits down the road. As for the Missouri Department of Corrections, the idea of putting the facility in this remote and rural corner of the state, sixty-five lonely miles southwest of St. Louis, held a certain appeal. The new prison was where state-sanctioned killings would henceforth be carried out, and the lonelier and more remote the location, the better. Opponents of capital punishment would think nothing of staging protests if the execution site was conveniently situated somewhere just off an interstate; only the most dedicated would bother venturing all the way down here.

Darrell spent his first two weeks quarantined and under observation in One House, standard procedure for any newly arrived capital-punishment prisoners. An additional fortnight of observation on the top floor of Two House, and he was finally let out with the fellows. Not that he was exactly chafing for company. He wasn't planning on sticking around very long anyway; no sense chumming it up too much. The best approach was to play it cool, keep a low profile—and, above all, avoid altercations.

Easier said than done. At a place such as Potosi altercations have a habit of sneaking up on you. On the top walk of Two House there was only one other prisoner for a while—a white guy about ten years younger and twenty pounds lighter than Darrell. The guy had a TV in his cage and since he spent most of his time downstairs playing cards anyway, he told Darrell, "Be my guest, man, feel free to go in and watch it anytime you want." Darrell was grateful for the offer. He was looking for ways to pass the time and wasn't much interested in weathering the strife and cheating of the interminable poker games. Later the same week the guy walked into his cage while Darrell was watching television and said, "What would you do if I raped you, old man?"

Not the best way of endearing yourself to a onetime hillbilly hooligan from Stone County. Darrell instantly flew mad—and not just because of the physical threat. The guy actually had the temerity to call him an old man. He jumped to his feet saying, "I have no sexual desire for your body at all," and stormed out of the cell. The guy must have seen the anger in Darrell's eyes. He stood back and let him pass without saying a word.

Darrell didn't stay angry for long. Over the next couple of weeks, as he learned more about the guy with the TV, he actually found himself growing sympathetic. He learned that the guy had been sent to prison as a kid and had been turned out as a punk at Missouri State Pen. His cellblock daddy would pimp him out for cigarettes and whatnot and charge people to watch while the kid, who was inordinately flexible, performed sexual acts on himself. Daddy-o eventually killed a couple of fellow cons and received a death sentence. He told the kid to follow suit so he could join him on death row. The kid obliged, murdering the fellow who happened to be his cell mate at the time, which is how he came to be at Potosi when Darrell arrived—no longer a kid but still lost and confused, still desperate for respect and belonging. Darrell never went back to the guy's cage to watch television after their run-in but the two of them got along pretty well from then on—right up until the time the guy was executed.

Darrell was transferred to Four House after a few months, which was the unit with the largest population of death-row prisoners. All around him he saw guys who, one way or another, had made their peace with prison life and settled in for the long haul, trying to make the best of a situation they assumed they couldn't change. Even their griping had a ritualistic quality, like it was something they figured they were supposed to do but couldn't quite muster the proper enthusiasm for. Darrell was different. From the moment he arrived he was determined that he wouldn't become acclimated to life on the inside. *Keep your eye on the door*, he'd say to himself. *Don't let them break you. Stand firm.*

Standing firm came relatively easy to Darrell. He detested everything about prison life—truly and fully detested it. The sexual squabbling and the constant one-upmanship, the stall-feeding at meal times, the nighttime screaming and muttering—every inch of it a stone-walled hell. Where other guys were finding niches for themselves by joining the prison band, hitting the weight room, or boning up on case law in the library, Darrell was gritting his teeth and counting the days. There was no relenting on his part—just because he happened to be in prison didn't mean he was obliged to cash in his manhood. Any way he could stand apart, so much the better. Shortly after arriving in Four House he even tried setting his own schedule. By this point he had his own television, courtesy of the folks back home, and he took to staying up most nights watching reruns of the old *Bob Newhart Show*, doing some reading, and then grabbing snatches of sleep during the day. Not the most conventional of prison routines, but then again, Darrell was hardly known for playing to expectation.

Neither, for that matter, was Robert Maurer. A smallish, chain-smoking man in his late thirties, Maurer wouldn't have met anyone's expectation of a public defender. Crusader for justice? Champion of the underdog? Youthful idealist? Forget about it. Robert Maurer was none of these things. He'd taken a job in the capital appellate unit of the public defender's office in Columbia, Missouri, for two basic reasons. First, it was a high-stakes job that promised plenty of action. Second, it was available when he needed it. All things being equal, he would have been just as happy taking a gig in a prosecutor's office somewhere. Come to think of it, this probably wouldn't have been such a bad idea. Working out of the public defender's office, he sometimes felt like a marked man. Maybe it was his witty and acerbic manner that had turned some of his oh-so-earnest colleagues against him. Or maybe it was his politics, which he didn't mind advertising as being "somewhere to the right of Barry Goldwater." Or maybe it was his permissive views on capital punishment. Whatever the reason, it definitely wasn't a comfortable situation. Never mind that he was one of the sharpest lawyers on staff: in the view of some of his co-workers he didn't quite fit the bill—not righteous enough, not pious enough, certainly not left-lib enough. No sense kidding himself: he knew that his days in the office were numbered. If he listened hard enough, he could almost hear the knives being sharpened.

Right now, however, office politics weren't Maurer's chief concern. He'd recently been assigned the toughest challenge of his career: representing a hillbilly named Darrell Mease in post-conviction relief. For death-penalty cases in Missouri, post-conviction relief was one of the earliest and most critical stages of the appeals process. Maurer was determined to make the most of it, though he was too much the realist to be excited by his chances of success.

Darrell's case hadn't actually been his to start with. After Bill Wendt's motion for a new trial was denied and Wendt had withdrawn as attorney of record, the case had gone to the public defender's office, where it had been assigned to a young woman named Leslie Delk. But then Delk had left the office under hurried circumstances and the entire business had landed on Maurer's desk.

In the two or three months since then Maurer had covered a lot of territory. He'd dropped down to Potosi a couple of times and met not just with Darrell but also with a prison buddy of Darrell's, Doyle Williams. Williams was a near-legendary figure in Missouri public defender circles. A native of North Carolina, he'd received a death sentence some years back for allegedly handcuffing, pistol-whipping, and generally terrorizing a guy named Kerry Brummett to the point where Brummett, in a frantic effort to escape, threw himself into the Missouri River and drowned. In his years on death row Doyle had immersed himself in legal studies and become one of the best jailhouse lawyers in the entire country. He'd assisted more than a dozen inmates, guys otherwise lost and helpless, with the early stages of their appeals. On March 20, 1991, just a few months prior to Maurer visiting, Doyle had taken what was supposed to be his last meal and bidden farewell to his family and friends when the U.S. Supreme Court gave him a last-minute stay of execution. While waiting for another execution date to be set, he'd been helping Darrell gear up for post-conviction relief.

The meetings at Potosi had gone well. Maurer was pragmatic and unsentimental, definitely not a lawyer prone to bonding with his clients. Nevertheless, he'd come away impressed with Darrell.

"I found Darrell somehow appealing and sympathetic," he recalled. "This wasn't necessarily my initial impression but it was the impression I walked away with. It's tough to say why. He spoke about his religious conversion, which seemed to me completely genuine, but this wouldn't have swayed me one way or another. I've always prided myself on being agnostic about this sort of thing. I'm not the easiest guy to win over. Force me to pin it down, I'd say he struck me as being very modest and very honest, not a conniving bone in his body. You see some guys in prison, they strike you right off as manipulative and malicious. But not Darrell—he didn't fit the profile. I thought to myself, 'Something terrible has happened here, but this guy doesn't have the makeup of a murderer.' I was intrigued, and really motivated. I wanted to do everything I possibly could to help him. I was working solo at the time, the woman who was supposed to be my investigator had just gotten fired, so I went down by myself to the area Darrell was from and started digging around."

Maurer spent about a week in southwest Missouri, sleeping most nights at a twenty-dollar motel in the tattered old resort town of Rockaway Beach. His second day in the area, a broiling hot afternoon, he dropped by to see Lexie, who was working as a cook at a Christian summer camp on the rim of Lake Taneycomo. They sat and talked in the camp's screened-in cafeteria, perched high atop a cliff overlooking the lake. It was an encounter Maurer wouldn't soon forget: the aching contrast between the idyllic setting and the grim subject matter of their conversation; Lexie so strong and hopeful, so grateful to Maurer for his efforts on Darrell's behalf; and Maurer himself, wishing he had something more to offer than merely good intentions, something concrete, a promise he could keep.

The next day he drove over to Reeds Spring. As an outsider, a guy who'd grown up in the St. Louis area, it was like entering a storybook world. The breakdown bend on Route 13 smack in the center of town, the walled-in spring and the small weather-beaten stores, the crumbling motel next to the take-out dairy joint, the wooden houses jutting crazily out of the rocky hills: the place looked like it had been frozen in time for fifty years. He visited with Lexie and R.J. at their house in the hollow, and then with a dozen of Darrell's old school chums at a house on the edge of town. Sitting with these folks, listening to them, Maurer felt almost humbled. *Salt of the earth*—for the first time, he felt he truly understood what the phrase meant. Darrell's long-ago school friends: authentic Ozarkers, people with legacies, people of few words and nothing to prove—if they didn't fit the bill, it wasn't likely anyone did.

After digging around some more over the next few days, Maurer started to get a clearer picture. Darrell had been a good and lovable kid, everybody's favorite hometown son.

But then Vietnam, marital calamity, and drugs had worked
their nastiness, pushing him closer and closer to the edge.
Hooking up with Lloyd had finished the job. One thing Maurer was now virtually certain of: Darrell hadn't carried out
the Lawrence killings in a state of cool reflection or deliberation. He may have been legally responsible for the killings,
but not to the point where he deserved the death penalty.
This, he decided, was the main angle he'd pursue in post-
conviction relief. Darrell was mentally unhinged when he
shot the three Lawrences, and if Bill Wendt hadn't given up
so easily on the idea of a psychiatric defense the trial might
have had a different outcome. He gave Mary a call, hoping
she would be willing to elaborate on Darrell's mounting
paranoia prior to her dropping him off on Bear Creek Road.
No dice: Mary was cordial enough but left little doubt that
she wasn't interested in picking at the scabs. Maurer, no sen-
timentalist, couldn't pretend that he was surprised. No matter—he still had his ace in the hole: William O'Connor, a
crackerjack psychologist out of Kansas City. He'd arrange
for O'Connor to evaluate Darrell at Potosi. Forget about the
two local yokels Wendt had signed on: the true expert was
coming to town.

On his way back to Columbia, Maurer stopped by the old
courthouse in Springfield for a sit-down with Judge Tom
McGuire. McGuire was slated to preside over Darrell's post-
conviction relief hearing in October, less than two months
away. Why not get to know the judge beforehand, Maurer
reasoned, maybe rack up some schmoozing points? They sat
together, smoking cigarettes in McGuire's second-floor
courtroom. Maurer found himself liking the judge, a brassy
and candid old boy, the kind of guy you'd enjoy having a
drink with after work. Darrell had told Maurer that McGuire
had tried tempting him with an unloaded pistol during the
trial, the judge banking on him making a grab for it and then
being gunned down by troopers ringing the courtroom. Now
Maurer ran the same story by McGuire—as good a show-
case as any other, he was thinking, for Darrell's runaway
paranoia.

Crazy or what? he said.

The judge laughed. Maybe not so crazy, he said. He'd always kept a pistol under the bench, so Darrell wasn't just imagining it. But you can be damned sure of one thing, he added, the pistol would have been fully loaded. This was where Darrell was dead wrong. The pistol was always fully loaded.

As often as not, the dominant issue in post-conviction relief proceedings is ineffective assistance of trial counsel. To some extent, this is what Robert Maurer was planning on arguing in Darrell's case: that Bill Wendt had fumbled the ball and cost his client the game. He was planning on arguing it, even though he wasn't entirely convinced of it himself. In truth, as he would recall more than a decade later, Maurer believed that Wendt had actually done a decent job.

"The guy was facing incredible odds. Forget the confession, the corroborating evidence, and all the rest of it, and just consider the videotape of the crime scene. I have never—*ever*—seen anything that matched the devastating impact of this. You cannot explain evidence of this sort away. The prosecutor plays a few minutes of this to a jury, you'd need a miracle to save Darrell. No way a jury could look at this and not give death. But having said this, Wendt still fell short in a couple of areas. For one thing, he failed to present Darrell as a real flesh-and-blood human being. Read the trial transcript, and where's Darrell? Darrell is the missing element of the trial. Wendt didn't succeed in bringing Darrell to life—a fatal flaw in a murder case. What's more—and here's where I really wanted to push—he could have done a much better job working the psychological angle. If only he'd arranged for someone such as my man O'Connor to evaluate Darrell, it could have been a different story."

If only, indeed. A trim, soft-spoken, and articulate man in his early fifties, William O'Connor was a criminal defense attorney's dream. Not only was he a top-notch diagnostician and an accomplished researcher, with enough publications on his résumé to match the output of many a tenured professor, but he was also as thoughtfully impassioned an opponent of the death penalty as one was likely to come across in the state of Missouri. He'd started evaluating defendants in death-penalty cases in 1983, motivated in equal measure by moral indignation and a strong sense of professional obligation.

"It was something I felt I had to do," he said at his offices in Kansas City, where he still maintains a private practice with his wife, Sharon, a first-rate psychologist in her own right. "A lot of the psychiatric and psychological evaluation that was being done at the time was grossly inadequate—really terrible, incompetent work. There were guys on death row who hadn't even been assessed for mental retardation. So I was troubled by this, but by other stuff, also. In Missouri it was always black guys and poor white guys who were getting charged with the death penalty, quite often—and not just coincidentally—when county prosecutors happened to be up for reelection. Where's the justice in that? I was also convinced, and I still am, that capital punishment is destructive to the families and friends of crime victims. It doesn't provide genuine resolution—it traumatizes and brutalizes. So I started doing evaluations and also serving as an expert witness, quite often at the request of people such as Rob Maurer in the public defenders office. This is how I came to be involved with Darrell."

O'Connor met with Darrell four times at Potosi prior to the post-conviction relief hearing, in one of the small windowless rooms in the visiting area that were reserved for such occasions. He gave him a battery of tests, everything from the Minnesota Multiphasic Personality Inventory (MMPI) to the Hare Psychopathy Checklist. Darrell submitted cheerfully enough to all this mental poking and prodding, but not without telling O'Connor the same things he'd already told Robert Maurer, and before Maurer, Bill Wendt. He'd come back to Missouri to kill Lloyd out of sheer necessity. Lloyd was gunning for him, and for Mary, too. Lloyd, being Lloyd, undoubtedly had a contract out on them, with no shortage of lowlifes itching for the chance to deliver on it. They had nowhere to run, nowhere to hide. Going to the law for help was out of the question; everyone knew that Lloyd was tight with the authorities in Stone County and probably half a dozen other local counties. Everyone knew that law enforcement in the Ozarks was bought and paid for. Darrell had only one option: take care of business the old-fashioned way, the way people had traditionally taken care of it in the hills of southwest Missouri. Somebody's threatening to kill you, you kill him first. This was his one viable move, and once he'd fixed on it there was no turning back. It was as simple as that, he told O'Connor. He'd done what he'd done because he had no other recourse. There was nothing crazy about it.

O'Connor wasn't buying it—at least not entirely. He didn't doubt that Lloyd was a nasty guy and that Darrell and Mary had good reason to feel threatened by him. Nor did he doubt that the legal system on Darrell's home turf was due a vigorous spring-cleaning. Nevertheless, there was something about Darrell's account that didn't quite ring true. It sounded almost biblical, Manichean—a dualistic epic of absolute good locked in fateful conflict with absolute evil. Was the real world, O'Connor wondered, ever so starkly black and white? Was it not possible, moreover, that Darrell had exaggerated in his own mind certain elements of his saga? Lloyd's criminal omnipotence, for example: in Darrell's telling, the backwoods, cockfighting bully was every bit as dangerous and well connected as Al Capone. And what of Darrell's conspiracy theories, such as his unflagging conviction, which he'd also run by O'Connor, that his trial was rigged and that even his own attorney had been party to a plot to destroy him? Going just by his interviews with Darrell, O'Connor strongly suspected that something was amiss.

The test results didn't cause him to think otherwise. The MMPI clinical profile, the Brief Psychiatric Rating Scale, the projective testing—they all pointed in the same direction: Darrell was suffering from a chronic and deeply entrenched mental disorder, more specifically, a delusional disorder of the persecutory type. "This is a longstanding disorder which would have been present at the time of the alleged offense and at the time of [the] confession," O'Connor wrote in his formal mental health report. "In the opinion of the examiner, the degree of incapacity was not sufficient to render Mr. Mease incapable of knowing or appreciating the nature, quality, and wrongfulness of his act; however, the degree of incapacity is, in the opinion of this examiner, sufficient to substantially diminish his capacity to conform his conduct to the requirements of the law. While Mr. Mease was not out of touch with reality or poorly organized, his Delusional Disorder did not allow logical consideration of alternatives. Further, it is the opinion of the examiner that this condition would have obtained at the time of his statement; while he was undoubtedly fully aware of his rights, his beliefs allowed him no alternative but to 'sacrifice himself' because of complex events which he constructed into a fixed and rigid belief system compelling his behavior."

And so here it was—not the most glamorous of diagnoses perhaps, but a diagnosis nonetheless. O'Connor knew that Maurer had been counting on something along these lines; he was pleased that he'd been able to deliver the goods. Now came the supremely more difficult task of trying to sell it at the hearing.

The post-conviction relief hearing (or, more technically, the hearing on Darrell's 29.15 motion to vacate the verdict and the sentence) was held on October 9, 1991, a typically hot and cloudless early-fall afternoon in Springfield. The presiding judge wasn't Tom McGuire, after all, but rather a colleague of McGuire's in the Circuit Court of Greene County, J. Miles Sweeney. For reasons still not entirely clear, McGuire had recused himself at the eleventh hour. There was one other significant roster change. Representing the state of Missouri was Donald Clough, a lawyer from Rockaway Beach who'd just recently taken over from Jim Justus as prosecuting attorney for Taney County. According to some folks, Justus had come up short in his reelection bid because he hadn't moved fast enough to shut down a male strip club that had opened in Branson. According to others, it was due to voter unhappiness over the expenses he'd run up going after the death penalty for Darrell.

Darrell had been transported to Springfield the day before and given a temporary cell in the Greene County jail. He'd have enjoyed the five-hour drive a lot more, his first real scenery in sixteen months, if not for the black box, a little contraption that locks on between the handcuffs and holds them rigid. The box was ostensibly a security device; Darrell saw it more as a mechanism of torture. Halfway along I-44 the two officers charged with transporting him stopped at a roadside toilet and asked if he needed to relieve himself.

"Sure do," he said, "but I can't see pulling it off strung up to this box. Would you fellas mind taking it off for a minute or two?"

They shook their heads no.

"In that case, I'll try holding off until we reach Springfield."

As anticipated, the highlight of the hearing was O'Connor's testimony, which took up almost half the afternoon. Wearing a blue suit and striped tie, cool and polished, a veteran at the expert-witness game, O'Connor described Darrell as a bright and articulate individual ("well above average" in intelligence) who had been laboring for years with "delusional or paranoid beliefs." Some of these beliefs might very well have been based in fact, O'Connor conceded, but Darrell had stroked them and stretched them and then stitched them together into a fabulous plot of conspiracy and persecution. It was a plot that Darrell believed in absolutely, indeed, one that he was powerless to question. It held him in an iron grip.

"What happens with a delusion is, you are compelled to believe it," O'Connor said. "If someone presents to you absolute positive evidence that it's not true, you have to find other evidence that it is. You have no choice about whether you believe it or not. And you are then compelled to act on that information."

"So, compulsive and obsessive behavior and thinking is part of this process?" Maurer asked.

"Yes. It does not impair your ability to know reality. You know what you're doing. You don't misidentify people. You are not hallucinating. What it does is compel your behavior. It—it impairs your capacity to—to appreciate alternatives and make decisions with respect to your behavior, and it impairs your capacity substantially to conform your behavior to any external standard that's not consistent with your delusion."

O'Connor, pulling out all the stops now, also testified that Darrell was suffering from chronic post-traumatic stress disorder (PTSD) as a result of his experiences as a combat engineer in Vietnam. This had been a "major contributor in the development of his delusional disorder," he said.

"As do almost all individuals with significant PTSD, Mr. Mease has what's called 'survivor guilt.' He's rather unhappy that he's been alive. He can't exactly justify it, and so he tends to want to do somewhat grandiose or great things. He's prone to want to get into great struggle between good and evil to somehow undo the survivor guilt that traumatized combat veterans have."

"How about the post-Vietnam experiences, the marriage and the failed marriages?" Maurer asked. "Would that have been a contributing factor?"

"All of these things contribute, because when someone comes out of a situation like that, disturbed, guilty, with a rather confused view of life, then the more failures you accumulate, jobs, marriages, et cetera, the more that's going to affect your mental status and the more you have to compensate. What a delusion does is give you some way of compensating for a life and world, I suppose, that you just can't accept. You adopt a set of beliefs with a certain amount of grandiosity, because you have to think you're important if everyone's plotting against you, that somehow explain away the unusual degree of failure and guilt that you experience."

"How about—how would the history of drug abuse fit into this?"

"Well, that can't do anything but make it much worse, particularly with amphetamines, since they tend to disorganize thinking and produce a lot of paranoia and extreme emotional reactions anyway."

Late afternoon now, the natural light beginning to fade in Judge Sweeney's second-floor courtroom, Maurer led his expert witness into the murkiest territory of all. If Darrell had come back to Missouri to kill Lloyd, his great scourge and nemesis, why hadn't he stopped there? Why hadn't he simply killed Lloyd when the opportunity arose and then left it at that? Why the extra killings?

"It's a hard question to answer," O'Connor said. "Anything that happened in the situation would have been an act of the moment. It's rather like being in a combat situation where you're fighting the enemy but you don't particularly think the individual soldiers on the other side are bad guys; they're just the people that you have to shoot at so that they don't shoot you. So there's kind of a two-level belief: you're fighting forces of absolute evil but you don't really consider very much individual soldiers—it's not your plan to kill individuals, only to fight evil in general."

If the brusqueness of his cross-examination was any indication, five minutes in and out, Taney County prosecuting attorney Donald Clough was hardly bedazzled by O'Connor's expert riffing.

"Doctor," he said, fairly dripping with derision, "I want you to assume that there is an associate circuit judge here in Greene County, and that [this] associate circuit judge is a combat marine veteran, having gone through Marine Corps boot camp, learning how to kill people; and that this judge either thought, or actually it happened, that the circuit clerk had made derogatory remarks about his wife, and this judge tried to pick the circuit clerk up and throw him over the rotunda. Would that person be suffering from a disillusional [sic] thought disorder?"

"No. I mean, you're asking hypothetically, but I doubt it."

"Thank you, sir."

Maurer trotted out six additional witnesses, friends and

relatives of Darrell's, all of whom gave it their valiant best. Then Clough, wrapping up the afternoon's proceedings, called Bill Wendt to the stand.

Of course he'd done a good job on Darrell's behalf, Wendt insisted. Could anyone reasonably suggest otherwise? He'd busted his tail, played every imaginable angle, used every courtroom ploy at his disposal. From the very start, however, it had been a losing battle. The evidence against Darrell had been overwhelming.

Maurer took a crack at Wendt in cross-examination but he might just as well have saved himself the trouble. Wendt, the old smoothie, didn't even come close to breaking a sweat. An insanity defense for Darrell? Of course he'd considered going this route. Tough pulling it off, though, when his own experts threw cold water on the idea. And it wasn't as if he'd tapped the wrong experts. Dr. Clary, for one, was widely recognized in Springfield's criminal law community as "a defense-oriented psychiatrist who would always find mental illness." So what was he supposed to do? Shop around endlessly for a friendly diagnosis?

Darrell was transported back to Potosi immediately after the hearing. A month later he got the bad news. He got it through the mail, which is how death-row inmates usually get bad news regarding their appeals. Judge Sweeney had ruled against his petition for post-conviction relief. His conviction and death penalty were upheld. Darrell permitted himself just five minutes of disappointment before digging in once again and revving up his resolve: it didn't matter how the appeals went, he said to himself. He knew, beyond a twinkling of doubt, that he had nothing to worry about.

The next year, almost exactly a year later, Darrell had more disappointment to overcome. In late November 1992 he received word that his direct appeal to the Missouri Supreme Court had also come to naught. This was a rough blow. Losing in post-conviction relief in Judge Sweeney's courtroom was one thing, but the highest court in the state ruling against him? How could this happen? It didn't take a legal genius to realize he'd been arrested illegally. How could an illustrious panel of judges possibly miss something so obvious?

The way the system of appeals for capital cases was structured at the time in Missouri, direct appeal to the state supreme court came directly on the heels of post-conviction relief proceedings. For death-row inmates, this was getting pretty close to the quick. Lose here, and the chances of obtaining a reversal or possibly a reduced sentence later on in federal review were slim to none.

Darrell's direct appeal had been handled by Craig Johnston, a slim, laconic man in his late thirties who'd been working out of the public defender's office—first in Joplin, then Columbia—since graduating law school in 1984. Like many of his colleagues in the office, Johnston was overworked and overstressed, too many three-hundred-hour months with a deadline perched on his shoulder. He'd approached Darrell's appeal with a wary, fingers-crossed optimism. While certainly not banking on winning, he'd gone to Jefferson City in September for oral hearings at the state supreme court building thinking he at least stood a fighting chance. It wasn't to be. In its decision of November 24, the court shot down Johnston's arguments one after another, like wooden ducks at a two-bit carnival booth.

No, the court ruled, Darrell had not been coerced or manipulated into confessing after he'd invoked his right to an attorney. It was Darrell himself who had initiated the conversation with law enforcement officials that resulted in his videotaped statement at Troop D headquarters in Springfield. No, Judge McGuire had not erred at trial in refusing an instruction on second-degree murder. The evidence supported only a finding of deliberate or first-degree murder. No, for the last time, no, Bill Wendt had not been derelict in abandoning the possibility of a mental defect or insanity defense.

At one point the court was forced to resort to some fancy footwork. Johnston had argued, as had Bill Wendt two years earlier, that Darrell had been arrested in Arizona on pretextual or bad-faith warrants, issued for the ulterior motive of questioning him regarding the Lawrence homicides. If the warrants were invalid, it meant that the arrest and all evidence stemming from it, as "fruit of the poison tree," were also invalid. The court argued in response that the arrest warrants, for non-support and carrying a concealed weapon, were *objectively* valid and that the *subjective* motivation of law enforcement officials in issuing them was completely beside the point. The kicker here was that in two previous cases, *State* v. *Blair* (1985) and *State* v. *Moody* (1969), the very same court had ruled that the subjective motivation of officers was indeed relevant in determining the validity of an arrest. But that was then and this was now, and the court, overruling itself on *Blair* and *Moody*, stated: "It is certainly incongruous to say that police may make a valid arrest of any person under the authority of a lawful arrest warrant, but if police are also motivated by a desire to question the person regarding an unrelated offense, the arrest is invalid."

Finally, after dispensing with all of Johnston's arguments, the court affirmed the death penalty for Darrell. "Where there are multiple homicides, the killing of a person who is disabled, or an intricate, well thought out plan of how the killing is to be committed, all of which existed here, the death penalty is not at all unusual."

Ninety miles down the road at Potosi, you could almost hear the buzzards gathering in the trees.

THIRTEEN

Back home, things would never be the same. Darrell heard about the changes now and then, from letters his mom sent and from the occasional visitor, but sitting in a prison cell, it was hard for him to appreciate just how extensive they really were. The world he'd grown up in was being transformed into something he'd scarcely recognize. Tourists were flocking to the Ozarks, especially down by Branson, and to make way for them, hills were being bulldozed, twisty two-laners straightened and widened, and brush land paved over and fenced off. There was no telling, once all the new development was finished and the ceremonial ribbons cut, how much of the old countryside would be left.

It's not that tourism was brand new to the region—its sweet clean streams and rolling hills had always been a draw to outsiders—but this was something different: a veritable stampede. People were descending in droves on the Branson area and relatively few had any interest in fishing or hiking or swimming. They were coming to test the beds in one of the fancy new hotels on the main drive, to dine out in one of the new steakhouses or theme restaurants, and to catch a couple of shows in one of the gleaming new music palaces. Almost overnight Branson had become an entertainment mecca—country-music cute, biscuits and gravy beneath the neon, Nashville without the ghetto, Vegas without the hustle, a place where you could take the kids and never have to worry about covering anyone's ears or eyes.

It began in the mid-eighties when a handful of country-music celebrities, sick and tired of touring, decided to cast about for a nice spot where they could settle in and set up permanent shop. Branson seemed to fit the bill as well as anywhere else. It was centrally located, not too far from Nashville, and just about as unsullied a place as you were going to find in middle America: all those hills and lakes and glistening streams, none of Nashville's smoke and noise. Not only that, the surrounding area was thick with genuine down-home hillbilly charm. Folks could drive in for some music and have plenty of local atmosphere to soak up besides. Roy Clark and Boxcar Willie were first off the blocks, opening theaters on what would eventually be known as the Strip, and they were soon followed by stars such as Mickey Gilley and Mel Tillis and a supporting cast of lesser lights, has-beens, corny comedy acts, and Elvis impersonators. By the early 1990s sleepy old Branson had become one of the hottest tourist destinations in the land. Show up during the busy season and it was bumper-to-bumper traffic, half-hour waits at mini-golf, and more strumming and chorusing and orchestrated goofiness than you'd ever dream of.

Things, so Darrell heard, would never be the same: visitors pouring in by the busload and leaving their money behind, fast-food outlets and giant chain stores springing up for miles around, illuminated billboards strung out along the roadsides as far as the eye could see. Once proudly and defiantly remote, a thing of mystery far off the beaten path, the traditional hillbilly culture of southwest Missouri was in danger of being smothered into submission. More and more, it was becoming something not so much to be lived as rather something to be rented out to visitors from Florida and Ohio, a weekend at a time. Quaintness on demand—a piece of secondhand nostalgia available at group discount rates.

The deal, to be sure, wasn't completely done—at least not yet. There were still backwoods areas where tourists dared not tread, still twisty blacktops guaranteed to make

your tires ache, still cockfighters and outlaws and preachers
in plaid shirts presiding over Sunday service at clapboard
churches. There were still secrets left untold, mysteries
buried deep in the hills, and honest-to-goodness hillbillies
who knew fakery when they saw it. But for how long? With
the Branson boom spilling out in all directions, and the
Springfield suburbs creeping steadily southward, how long
would it be before the hillbilly culture of southwest Missouri
ended up as an adorable, fun-for-the-whole-family theme
park?

In early December of 1994, having spent more than four
years at Potosi, Darrell was confronting environmental pressures of a rather different kind. Up to this point, each of Potosi's roughly three hundred prisoners had enjoyed the
comparative luxury of a cell entirely his own. This, however,
was soon to change. Faced with prison overcrowding across
the state, the Missouri Department of Corrections was intent
on significantly increasing the inmate population at its flag-
ship institution. In practical terms, this meant converting
many of the single-man cells into two-man units. It also
meant easing up on the stringent entrance requirements by
bringing in prisoners who had been sentenced to something
less than death or life without parole.

For many of those inmates already in place, this was un-
welcome news. In a maximum-security prison, where your
every move is closely monitored, where even the walls have
eyes and ears, and trouble incubates in every corner, a cell of
one's own is no small thing. The chance to stretch out unmo-
lested and dream of greener pastures, to arrange your belongings just so on the single wall shelf, to use the stainless
steel toilet with some degree of privacy—it makes all the
difference in the world. It's a matter of holding the madness
at bay, carving out a zone of dignity. If you're forced to ride
double, there's no telling whom you're going to wind up
with. Some druggie, maybe, fussing and fidgeting all day
long, or some pretty boy with a jealous daddy down the
walk. Or some wacko bleating and braying till three in the

morning. If your cell mate gets caught with a shank or a little bit of "girl" (cocaine), you'll get written up, too. If he's up all night with diarrhea, you'll be up all night with him, fending off the growl and stench of his guts.

Even if you luck out and land a cell mate you get along with, someone you might actually count as a friend, it's still a losing proposition. Two grown men stuck together day after day, endless hours at a time, in a fourteen-by-six-foot cement-block cage: not much chance of a happy outcome. After the first couple of weeks you're both all talked out, and then the edginess creeps in. Little things, the way the guy slurps his carton of milk from the canteen, or sniffs back his snot when you're trying to read—they build and build until they're unholy annoyances. Pretty soon the cell is enveloped in a smog of tension. You're like two tomcats cornered in an alley: you've no longer got any choice in the matter. You can't help but provoke one another.

The lifers in general population were doubled up first, starting in late December. It was a lengthy process. In one housing unit after another, individual cells were vacated and stripped clean so that bunk beds could be brought in and bolted to the floors. Over time the new inmates started arriving. They were a ragtag bunch. Some were violent offenders, serving thirty years or longer. Others were doing lighter time but had earned reputations as troublemakers in their previous places of incarceration. While all this was going on, the capital-punishment prisoners were watching and waiting. They knew they were next in line for doubling up, probably in a year or so. Not all of them, however, were planning on surrendering their single-man cells without a fight.

For the time being, Darrell carried on much as before. By this point he'd long given up on his earlier routine of staying awake until the wee hours watching reruns of old sitcoms. Instead he was usually asleep by eleven, up at six sharp and off to the mess hall for breakfast. Then two hours of yard or recreation, which, weather providing, he usually spent outdoors, where there was a football field encircled by a quarter-mile asphalt track, volleyball and horseshoe pits, handball courts, and picnic tables. Then back inside for lockdown and a head count before lunch, and after lunch three more hours of rec, which some days he'd split between the law library and the chapel library. A final hour of rec after supper and, finally, back into the cage until morning.

Darrell was on friendly terms with just about everybody at Potosi, in a casual kind of way, much like you might be on friendly terms with your fellow passengers on a cross-country bus trip. But that, for the most part, was as far as it went. He didn't go out of his way to cultivate deeper friendships and he steered clear of all the usual prison cliques. He even kept his distance from the born-again crowd and their Sunday chapel services. As far as Darrell was concerned, death row was a place he just happened to be passing through. He didn't want to have too much dirt to shake off when it came time for moving on.

His best friend, the guy he felt most comfortable talking with, was a death-row prisoner named Bert Leroy Hunter. Hunter was a former state computer programmer who'd pleaded guilty to killing an elderly woman and her middle-aged son during a robbery at their home in Jefferson City. Clinically depressed and suicidal at the time of his plea hearing, he waived his right to an attorney and a jury trial and told the court that he wanted to be executed. "Being strapped on that gurney at Potosi would be a blessing to the State and myself," he said. The court apparently found no reason to disagree.

Hardly anyone on death row admitted actually committing the crimes for which they'd been sentenced. Many of them spent half their waking hours protesting their innocence. Bert Leroy Hunter was one of the very few Darrell took seriously in this regard. Hunter insisted that he hadn't killed the old lady and her son and that he'd pleaded guilty only because he had a death wish at the time. Darrell believed him. He thought Hunter was too sweet natured to kill anyone, too delightfully loopy. "Just a couple clicks away," he'd say, "from being a real good man." Not that Hunter couldn't occasionally get on your nerves. He'd cruise the prison yard bragging about his genius-level IQ, which he claimed would be even higher were it not for years of cocaine abuse. Intensely competitive, he'd cheat in a heartbeat at Scrabble or poker or any other recreational game, like he was playing for millions in some back room at Atlantic City. He liked telling people that he was a split personality, and when Darrell once suggested that it must be quite a burden being a split personality, he snapped, "No, it isn't—well, yes, it is." Mostly Darrell just appreciated Hunter's company, one of the few things that made the time pass easier.

There were quite a few names and faces at Potosi that Darrell recognized from back home. Marty Strange, for example—from the Taney County jail days. Strange, convicted of murdering his wife and kids, was now doing life and working in the prison library on the side. Another long-ago acquaintance, Glennon Paul Sweet, was stashed away in the housing unit next to Darrell's, awaiting execution for the 1987 slaying of Missouri · highway patrolman Russell Harper. While he was still on the loose, Sweet had been a full-time menace, running crank down to Texas and New Orleans, scheming it up with Lloyd Lawrence and Bill Gold. He reportedly had a hand-painted sign outside his house north of Springfield that read NO NIGGERS ALLOWED. Darrell had seen him at Joe Dean's a few times, bumping or rolling bulldogs—letting the dogs go at it for five or ten minutes, no betting, just checking them out, seeing if they had the right stuff for a contract fight.

And then there was sweet Mary's cousin, Red Stephens, who'd killed a Reeds Spring deputy some years back. Darrell had known Red long before he met Mary. He once showed up drunk at Red's house in Galena only to be sucker-punched by Red or one of his buddies and knocked off the front porch. A month or so after Darrell arrived at Potosi, Red sent word to him, "Anything you need, just let me know." Later on, while they were walking the track together, Red said, "You know, it wasn't me who knocked you off the front porch that time."

"It doesn't matter," Darrell said. "It was my fault anyway."

So Darrell held nothing against Red—and he certainly held nothing against Mary. This was where a lot of folks back home had it wrong. They assumed he'd be feeling betrayed, abandoned. They assumed he'd be angry. His sweetheart selling him out? Cutting a deal with the state to save her own skin? Of course he'd be angry.

Not a chance. Darrell wasn't close to angry. He was grateful—and more deeply infatuated than ever. Mary had given him the best two-year run of his life. He'd idealized and romanticized every single moment of their time together. It was his constant fantasy; something to light a candle to. She was his sweetheart for all time, his one and only. His being imprisoned and on death row didn't change a thing. He was grateful for what she'd given him, and grateful also that she wasn't locked up somewhere. He was the one who had led her into the wilderness, not the other way around. He'd taken her through hell, and she'd stuck by him every inch of the way. How could he possibly resent Mary? How could he be angry with her for playing the only card she'd been dealt?

Outgoing phone calls are restricted at Potosi. Prisoners can only dial numbers they've been authorized to dial. One day Doyle Williams phoned his sister and had her patch a call through to Mary. Doyle handed the receiver to Darrell. Mary picked up on the other end. Darrell said, "Hi, baby." Mary hung up.

Darrell was momentarily jolted. But just for a minute or two. He was a true believer. He believed in unconditional love. The time wasn't right.

The time would come.

Darrell was packing on the pounds. Part of the problem was the starchy prison diet. The other part was his innate extremism—"whole hog or nothing" he liked to call it. Some months he'd settle into a nice workout routine and fast-walk the track every day for an hour or two. But then he'd go months at a time just sitting around and eating. And that's when he'd balloon up. He'd come in at around one ninety-five, now he was pushing two thirty. He wasn't proud of the excess weight but he wasn't overly concerned, either. Put him in a more natural environment, it was sure to melt away.

Food—even more than sex—was a constant preoccupation at Potosi. Inmates would complain endlessly about the miserable prison fare and fantasize aloud about the thick-cut pork chops, crispy fried chicken, and juicy T-bones they could be digging into at their hometown restaurants. Sometimes guys got so worked up thinking about food that they hit the mess hall for supper tense and angry. Nerves could run raw and ragged at supper. It was a prime time for altercations.

Usually nobody messed with Darrell. He was regarded as a standup guy who'd never think of snitching anyone off. He wasn't involved in any of the prison drug or sex trade. He was on decent terms with both black prisoners and white prisoners. There was no reason, really, for anybody to mess with Darrell. Only once, at suppertime, did he ever come close to getting in a fight. He was standing second in the chow line, waiting his turn. The guy at the head of the line wouldn't budge. He was letting his buddies cut in front while Darrell and everyone else behind him smoldered.

Finally, after five or six dudes had crashed the line, Darrell said to the guy, "I'll be going next. It looks like you're not interested in eating."

The guy stepped back and flexed his shoulders, setting himself for some serious action.

"You know what you gotta do," he said.

"Yow, I do," Darrell said, ready to go.

They stood there ten or fifteen seconds, facing each other down, before they both eased up and let the moment pass. Afterward, Darrell reprimanded himself. He'd just come within inches of precisely the kind of fracas he'd been trying to avoid. He'd try his best to make sure it wouldn't happen again.

Drugs were another preoccupation—and considerably easier to come by than pork chops, fried chicken, or T-bones. Occasionally guards would smuggle drugs inside and pass them off to a prisoner they were trying to impress or a prisoner they were trying to buy sexual favors from. More often it was visitors who did the smuggling, tucking the goodies into body cavities and sweating their way past the security checkpoints, praying they wouldn't get singled out for a full body search. They'd then hand the stuff over to the guy they were visiting who at first opportunity would keister it—shove it up his rear end. In a slightly classier variation, a wife or girlfriend would tuck a condom containing drugs into her mouth and then transfer it during the brief "greeting" kiss in the visiting room. Her man would swallow the condom and later on fish it out of the toilet in his cell.

Darrell knew all about the drugs. He knew who was bringing them in and who was taking them and who was making a profit off them. A few years ago it would have been exciting knowing all of this. Now it bored him. The whole scene left him cold. He couldn't care less about the drugs.

The doubling up of capital-punishment prisoners got under way in late 1995, just before Christmas. It seemed unlikely to go off without a hitch. Seventeen prisoners, Darrell included, signaled their intention to protest the new policy. They were supposed to be hard-knock guys; here was their chance to prove it. There was no way they were simply going to roll over and take whatever the institution decided to dish out. They'd hang tough, stand up to the prison bosses, and insist on their right to their own cells.

The test of resolve came several months later, in May, when the superintendent of Potosi issued an ultimatum: either double up without fuss or suffer banishment to the administrative segregation unit, more commonly known as *isolation* or *the hole*. This was serious business. Banishment to the hole meant being locked in a tiny cell virtually twenty-four hours a day, with canteen, visiting, and basic walking-around privileges severely curtailed. It was a stiff price to pay for joining a fight that probably wasn't winnable anyway. Far too stiff, apparently, for most of the would-be protesters. One after another, they caved in. Being consigned to the hole—the very idea of it—was more grief than the malcontents could handle. There was just one holdout. Of the seventeen guys who'd initially locked arms, Darrell alone stood his ground. Refusing to double up, he was thrown into isolation. He'd remain in isolation for three long years.

Anyone who knew Darrell, truly knew him, wouldn't have been surprised. Of course he'd refuse to back down. Once he zeroed in on something, there was no knocking him off course. Going to the hole didn't faze him a bit. He'd been in training half his life for precisely such a punishment, hanging out by himself in the brush back home, surviving by his wits, playing by his own rules. He'd deal with the hole: How rough, after all, could it be?

Quite a bit rougher, as it turned out, than Darrell had anticipated, especially at night. At ten o'clock, when the lights in administrative segregation were switched off, the howling began. The unit became a bedlam of shouting and weeping and tortured sexual release. Guys would be hollering at their long-lost lovers; they'd be taunting imaginary demons and wailing for mercy and crying out for their mommas. They'd be screaming blood-curdling fantasies of revenge and violence. Darrell would wad up pieces of toilet paper and stick them in his ears; he'd stuff his prison-issue blanket under the door. Try as he might, however, he couldn't block out the noise. Some nights he'd try reading himself to sleep by the shaft of light that came in through his window slit from the security lamps outside. He'd usually manage to drop off at two or three, and then wake up at five when the lights were switched back on.

All meals were served through slots in the cell doors. The food ranged from dismal to inedible, but it seemed to have a tranquilizing effect on the shouters and weepers. The three- or four-hour stretch after breakfast was the most blessedly quiet period of the day. Darrell would frequently take advantage of the lull in lunacy by grabbing some sleep until ten-thirty or thereabouts, which was when the lunch trays were brought to the unit. Then it was largely a matter of killing time until supper at four-thirty, after which he'd top out the day by answering his mail, reading his Bible, and losing himself in thought.

Communicating with other prisoners was a tricky proposition. Some guys would simply holler from their cells for one and all to hear. Darrell preferred subtler methods, such as writing kites, or notes, which he'd hand off to wing workers, who were prisoners assigned tasks such as passing out food trays and picking up laundry. The wing workers would deliver the kites to Darrell's buddies in other housing units. On good days he might receive something in return, a kite from Bert Leroy Hunter, maybe, or a treat from the canteen socked away in his parcel of fresh laundry.

Anyone so inclined could also conduct cell-to-cell conversations through the unit's air vents. The hole was designed so that groups of four cells, two on the bottom walk and their twins directly above, shared the same vent. Hearing your vent mates, providing it wasn't howling time, was seldom a problem; the problem was picking up something actually worth hearing. During all of Darrell's time in the hole, the only guy whose conversation he found even halfway interesting was a serial killer named Joseph Paul Franklin. Franklin was on death row for the 1977 killing of a man outside a synagogue in Clayton, Missouri. He'd been linked to more than twenty murders or attempted murders all told, including the 1978 shooting of *Hustler* magnate Larry Flynt. Darrell enjoyed talking with Franklin now and again through their shared vent, though that was as close as he really cared to get. "The guy could be civil but he could also snap easy—hard and fast," Darrell recalled of their time together in the hole. "Out on the street, you'd definitely want a gun on him at all times."

Despite being physically separated from one another, prisoners in isolation were still able to exchange smokes and lighters and other contraband. Their main way of doing so was through the use of so-called Cadillacs. Here's how it worked: Your buddy in the cell down the walk wants a couple of cigarettes. You put the smokes in an envelope weighted down with a packet of ketchup or whatnot and tie the envelope to the end of a cord, fashioned out of strands you've pulled from your sheet or mattress. You then throw the weighted end of the cord, or Cadillac, out onto the walk. The guy in the next cell reels it in and transfers the smokes to his own Cadillac and guns it out again. On and on down the walk, until the cigarettes reach their destination.

Darrell had long since given up smoking, and he didn't much care for some of the other goodies that were being chauffeured up and down the walk. But this didn't stop him from making a Caddy of his own and becoming a pretty decent hand at the wheel. It was one of the very few diversions available to him. He had no radio or TV, and precious little in the way of reading material. He was limited to just one phone call per month, and to basics such as soap and paper and pens from the canteen. He was permitted out of his cell occasionally, cuffed and under escort—barely long enough to shake off some rust and then right back in again.

He was allowed visitors, but on a strictly no-contact basis—over the phone and behind glass in one of the little caged-in cubicles off the main visiting area. His most frequent visitors were his mom, and Larry and Sophia, who usually came up together from Stone County. His dad had enjoyed making the trek with them the first few years, before dying of a ruptured stomach in 1993. A few other people from back home dropped by from time to time: his sister Rita; his daughter, Melissa; an occasional buddy. But never the person Darrell would have been most thrilled to see.

With all the time in the world on his hands, those dead and empty hours begging to be filled, Darrell took to reading his Bible with greater purpose than ever before. And the more he read, the more astonished and outraged he became. How was it possible that so many Bible-believing Christians in the United States supported the death penalty? How could they fail to see that capital punishment was a scandal to the basic tenets of their faith? Were they reading the same Bible he was reading?

Check it out—it was plain to see. During his earthly ministry, Jesus preached a message of unconditional love and mercy. He rejected the old rule of "an eye for an eye, a tooth for a tooth" and called on his followers instead to forgive and pray for anyone who may have caused them harm. Mere mortals, Jesus taught, had no business casting stones, tightening nooses, pulling the switch; final condemnation was the prerogative of God alone. And it was never too late, this side of eternity, for the most hardened of sinners to repent and be born anew as sweet children of grace. God could work miracles in the hearts of monsters. No one was beyond hope of redemption and transformation. Even the Apostle Paul was converted on the road to Damascus, the very same guy, according to the Bible, who was "breathing threats and murder" against the earliest Christians. Would execution-happy churchgoers in contemporary America have denied Paul his encounter with the light? Given the chance, would they have preferred stringing him up on a tree?

And life without parole was hardly much better. If a monster was spiritually transformed, truly and fully so, and hence no longer a monster, what was the point of keeping him in chains until his dying breath? Pious churchgoers never tired of bragging about the new life of joy and hope that was available to anyone who turned their heart over to God. But what of life-without-parole prisoners who had turned over their hearts? Where was the joy in growing old and feeble behind bars? The hope in endless days of moldering confinement? Locking a guy up and telling him he didn't stand a sliver of a chance of ever walking free: this was as contrary to the spirit of the Gospels as whatever crime the guy may have committed in the first place. And smug Christians who thought otherwise were in for a rude awakening. The God of the Bible was a God of redemption and liberation, a God of surprise. It was only a matter of time before God started busting born-again prisoners out of death row and out of life-without-parole sentences, busting them into freedom.

Darrell had no doubt about his own situation. He'd always known that he'd be delivered from death row, and eventually delivered from prison altogether. He'd always known that he'd be given a second chance. But now he also knew what he was meant to do with it. For the first time in his life he felt the conviction of a genuine calling. He'd been especially chosen by God to spread the word—on the fundamental evil of capital punishment, primarily, but also of life without parole. And why not? Who better to spread the word than a hillbilly—a onetime death-sentenced hillbilly—from Stone County?

So there it was. All those long years since Vietnam, all those false turns and tough breaks and horrible decisions— all those woebegone years and Darrell seemed finally to have come full circle. When he was growing up, his brother and his mom and even some of his classmates had assumed he'd become a preacher. Now, an eternity and three gruesome murders later, a preacher was what he felt called to be. He had a message to spread, and as soon as he got off death row he'd be taking it to the streets. He'd be a crazy man for God, shouting out from the rooftops—shouting no more death penalty, no more mandatory life without parole, shouting forgiveness, forgiveness, forgiveness.

FOURTEEN

No more death penalty. Not exactly the sort of message the state of Missouri was hankering to hear. Not these days anyway—not since George "Tiny" Mercer. Ever since Tiny, Missouri had been on something of a death-penalty kick.

Tiny was put to death in early 1989. He'd been convicted of murdering a young woman some biker buddies had abducted and handed over to him as a birthday present. His execution was the first in Missouri in more than twenty years.

It wasn't that Missouri had somehow gone soft on capital punishment in the two decades or so prior to Tiny Mercer. The biggest reason for the long stretch between executions was the U.S. Supreme Court. In its landmark *Furman* v. *Georgia* decision of 1972, the court put the kibosh on capital punishment nationwide, ruling that it had hitherto been applied unfairly and arbitrarily, with poor and black defendants generally drawing the short end of the stick. For several years after *Furman*, execution chambers across the country were put in mothballs, as individual states scrambled to bring their death-penalty laws up to constitutional snuff. In 1976 the Supreme Court gave the go-ahead for executions to resume, ruling that the revised laws of several states, by stipulating the conditions under which a death sentence could be imposed, had succeeded in eliminating much of the older bias and inequity.

Missouri's revised Capital Murder Law became effective in 1977, and then it was another dozen years before Tiny Mercer's number came up. For Tiny it was a double whammy: not only was he the first person slated for execution under the new law, but he also had the dubious distinction of being first in line for the state's brand-new, state-of-the-art lethal injection machine. Executions in Missouri had previously been carried out by lethal gas, and before that by public hanging. But now, in these gentler post-*Furman* days, lethal injection was suddenly the method of choice, not just in Missouri but nationwide. Coast to coast, individual states were boarding up their gas chambers and putting their electric chairs—their Old Sparkys and Yellow Mamas and Sizzling Jacks—into deep storage. The future of capital punishment had come calling and damned if it wasn't wearing a white coat and toting a black medical bag. The future of capital punishment looked for all the world like a scrubbed-down lab technician.

But, of course, a lab technician. This was the great appeal of lethal injection. It took the death—the X-rated-ness—out of execution. No more bulging eyeballs or sizzling flesh, no more heads bursting into flames or bodies writhing in cyanide-induced agony. With lethal injection, the entire business was smooth as silk, medicalized, sanitized, over and done with in scarcely a whisper. Strap the victim onto a gurney and put him under with a nice solicitous shot of sodium pentathol, then some pancuronium bromide to shut down his respiratory system, and, finally, a carefully measured dosage of potassium chloride to stop his heart. Nothing cruel and unusual about this punishment. Not much different from having an old dog euthanized at the neighborhood veterinary clinic.

Missouri's lethal injection machine was designed by a dweeby New Englander named Fred Leuchter. During the 1980s Leuchter had fashioned a nifty living for himself handcrafting customized execution devices out of his basement workshop in Boston. Any state after *Furman* looking to get back into the execution business and needing an upgrade in equipment could always count on Leuchter. A new electric chair, perhaps, a lethal injection machine, even a full-assembly gas chamber: he'd build it and he'd install it; he'd even conduct on-site training sessions to ensure that prison officials got the hang of operating it. Anyone doing business with Leuchter would almost certainly walk away a satisfied customer. Nobody in the United States was a greater expert on the hows and wherebys of killing a man. If old Fred hadn't gotten sidetracked by anti-Semitism during the early 1990s and frittered away his credibility denying the Holocaust, there's no telling how far he could have gone.

Leuchter would build almost anything you asked for, but his real pride and joy, the thing that brought him greatest professional satisfaction, was his lethal injection machine. It was something to behold, Leuchter's machine. With the press of a button, it swung into action—its hi-tech delivery module dispensing the lethal drugs, its control panel with color-coded phase lights monitoring the procedure from start to finish. And best of all, the machine worked its magic with a minimum of fuss and bother. In keeping with Leuchter's business motto—"capital punishment, not capital torture"—its efficiency gave execution all the drama of watching some guy nodding off after Sunday dinner.

Tiny Mercer was lethally injected on January 6, 1989, in a small rock-walled gas chamber on the grounds of Missouri State Penitentiary in Jefferson City. Nicely warmed up now, Leuchter's machine was all set to really prove its worth. A couple of months after Tiny's execution, it was moved to the brand-new death chamber at Potosi, an eighteen-by-twelve-foot, cinder-block room located in the prison's hospital wing. Four guys were strapped down, hooked up, and carted out in 1990, and twelve more over the next five years. Doyle Williams headed up a class of six lethal injectees in 1996, and the following year there were six more, including a big good-looking guy named A.J. Bannister, who'd become a minor celebrity during his final years on the row. Sentenced to death for a fatal trailer-park shooting that he insisted was accidental, Bannister had been featured in two documentary films and had received public support from Sean Penn,

Gregory Peck, Ed Asner, and a number of other Hollywood personalities. "The state of Missouri is committing as premeditated a murder as possible," Bannister said in his final statement, "far more heinous than my crime."

The traffic was somewhat slower in 1998, with only three guys ticketed for the gurney. One of these was the convicted cop-killer from southwest Missouri, Glennon Paul Sweet. In a last-ditch gambit for survival, Sweet wrote the Vatican pleading for the pope's intervention. The pope responded with a letter to Missouri governor Mel Carnahan requesting clemency. The letter apparently didn't do the trick. Sweet was lethally injected on April 22.

Darrell received his warrant of execution on November 12, 1998. The warrant was issued by the Missouri Supreme Court and hand delivered to his cell in administrative segregation. It stipulated that he was to remain incarcerated at Potosi until January 27, 1999, at which date he was to "suffer death."

The warrant was hardly a bolt from the blue. Since failing in his direct appeal to the Missouri Supreme Court, Darrell had suffered one legal disappointment after another. First, in September 1996, the U.S. District Court for the Western District of Missouri had denied his petition of appeal. Then, several months later, the U.S. Eighth Circuit Court in St. Louis had done likewise. Finally, in October 1998, just one month prior to the issuance of the execution warrant, the U.S. Supreme Court had declined to hear his case. Getting brushed off by the highest court in the land was pretty much the end of the line. It meant that Darrell had exhausted his avenues of relief and that the state of Missouri was now free to set a firm date for his lethal injection.

The string of defeats had actually been rougher on Darrell's new attorney, Laura Higgins Tyler, than on Darrell himself. A strong, bright, attractive woman in her midforties, Laura had been appointed in 1995 by the U.S. District Court for the Western District of Missouri to represent Darrell in federal appeals. The appointment was not without a certain irony. Laura's dad, Andrew Jackson Higgins, had just recently, in 1991, retired from the Missouri Supreme Court after a long career as one of the most formidable jurists in the state. He'd written the opinion in the Tiny Mercer death-penalty case, and were it not for his stepping down he might very well have been tapped to write the opinion for Darrell's case, too.

Laura had jumped at the chance to represent Darrell. Working on behalf of the underdog—it's what she knew best as a lawyer. She'd spent seven years as a public defender after graduating law school in 1981, and even in more recent years, since hooking up with a top-notch law firm in downtown Kansas City, she'd dedicated the bulk of her practice to standing up for poor lost souls in juvenile court.

It was a long way from the firm where Laura worked, with its plush lobby and smartly polished hardwood floors, its perfectly appointed offices and perfectly creased lawyers, all the trimmings of prosperity—it was a long way from downtown Kansas City to Potosi Correctional Center. Laura was nothing if not game, however, and she was determined to do this thing right. Whereas some other attorney might have preferred conducting business through the mail or over the phone, Laura always made a point of dropping by to see Darrell in person. Sometimes the purpose of the visits was to discuss legal strategy; too often, however, it had come down to delivering bad news.

The worst was when she learned that the Supreme Court had declined to hear Darrell's appeal. She'd realized from the start that it was a long shot. Of the thousands of cases that came knocking at its door every year, the Supreme Court would normally take on no more than a hundred. The trick in making it into this select group was to dress up one's case as provocatively as possible, give it the appearance of having some broader constitutional significance. This is what Laura had tried doing with Darrell's case, and as insurance against missing an angle, she'd enlisted the help of a brilliant death-row attorney out of Kansas City named Kent Gipson.

No one knew the angles on death-penalty appeals better

than Kent Gipson—though seeing him for the first time you'd be hard-pressed to guess it. Baby-faced and pudgy, and hanging out most days in sneakers, jeans, and a T-shirt at his office bungalow on the south side of Kansas City, he could easily give the impression of a graduate student in no big hurry to finish his thesis. Listen to him talk a few minutes, however, and the truth came crashing through. Not many graduate students had seen the things Kent had seen. For almost a decade, he'd been a key player with the Missouri Capital Punishment Resource Center, an agency founded in 1989 for the purpose of providing expert legal representation for poor people on death row. Kent knew all the guys on Missouri's death row and had been involved in most of their appeals. Some of them he liked, some he didn't. Some he thought had been unfairly convicted, others he wouldn't relish bumping into on the street. All of them, without exception, he was committed to keeping alive. Fighting the death penalty was Kent's passion. He was accustomed to putting in sixty hours at the office Monday through Friday, and then cramming in extra hours on weekends. For Kent it was the work above all else, driving out to Potosi in a car he knew was running on borrowed time, not making nearly enough money to think of buying a replacement, not caring about the car, not caring about the money, the work was enough, the work was its own reward.

So of course Kent had said yes when Laura asked for his help. Kent always said yes, and, besides, he had some added incentive for working on Darrell's case. He'd grown up in Stone County, the oldest of three kids. His dad was the town barber in Crane, just twenty miles up the road from Reeds Spring. Kent remembered some of the outlaws that Darrell had fallen in with, guys such as Lloyd Lawrence, Bill Gold, and Kendall Schwyhart, guys with big reputations as badasses and the don't-mess-with-me swagger to match.

"These guys were larger-than-life characters where I was raised," he said recently, sitting in his office behind a desk stacked with legal files. "They did pretty much as they pleased. The local cops were afraid of them. Unless they committed a major felony right out in front of the police station, the cops would leave these guys alone. Plus there were the rumors, about the local sheriff being on the take, deputies being on the take, which meant, if the rumors were true, that Lloyd and the boys had a lot of room to operate. As far as I could tell, the rumors were well founded. So Darrell's story hit close to home. I had no trouble believing that Lloyd had done terrible things to him, and was planning on doing even worse, and that Darrell had good reason for not going to the police."

Teaming up, Laura and Kent put their very best material into the petition to the Supreme Court: the highly irregular jury instructions at trial, whereby jurors were denied the option of convicting Darrell of murder in the second degree; the troublingly long time it took before Darrell saw an attorney after being apprehended in Arizona; the questionable legality of the arrest warrants. And when it all came to naught, and the Court turned down the petition without comment, Laura was disconsolate. This was rough news, the roughest yet, and she found herself making the lonely drive to Potosi not knowing how she'd break it to Darrell.

She needn't have worried. Darrell spent their hour together trying to pick up *her* spirits. No reason to feel disappointed, he said. She'd given it her best shot. She'd done all she could. She was first-rate all the way. Plus, it really didn't make a speck of difference, the Supreme Court turning them down. It didn't change a thing. He wasn't going to get executed—no chance in the world. Might as well sit back and enjoy the ride, he told Laura. Things were heating up. Things were bound to get interesting.

It was a few weeks after Laura's bad-news visit that a prison official delivered the death warrant to Darrell's cell in the hole. The guy might as well have been delivering a dozen roses, for all Darrell cared.

Bring it on, brother, he said to himself. *Hallelujah, bring it on. This just forces matters to a head.*

Once a death-row prisoner received a firm execution date,

the usual procedure at Potosi was to take him out of population and put him in protective custody. In the protective custody unit, isolated and monitored round the clock, he'd be certain to stay alive until the appointed hour. No chance of suicide, no risk of getting shanked out in the yard. Prisoners on the row delighted in the macabre irony of the arrangement, the institution going to so much trouble to prevent some condemned guy from dying prematurely and thereby cheating the executioner.

Darrell had a firm execution date of January 27, two and a half months hence, and since he'd spent most of the past three years in the hole anyway, protective custody was a romp in the park. It was like moving into a higher rent neighborhood—quieter, more decorous; it even had a better view from the window. As another bonus he also got his personal property back, the radio and other stuff that had been confiscated when he was exiled to the hole. The first thing he did on settling into his new cell was to turn on the radio and pick up a song by a Christian recording artist named Clay Crosse. "It must have been Your hands," the chorus went,

> *Turning my world in perfect time*
> *I know it was Your hands*
> *Holding my heart in our design.*

This was the first song Darrell had heard in three long years, and it was all he could do to contain his emotions. He knew the guards would be coming soon to bring him to the prison psychiatrist, standard procedure for a guy who's just been given a kill date, and he didn't want them or anyone else seeing him choked up and red eyed. He didn't want anyone mistaking the joy he was feeling right now for something else—least of all fear or uncertainty. He wasn't afraid, and he'd never doubted, not for a second, that he was going to escape the death chamber.

The psychiatrist asked Darrell if he wanted some medication to relieve the strain and anxiety. Keep the meds, Darrell said. He'd never felt better. He wanted to experience this ride with a clear head.

"I've got one bit of advice for you," the psychiatrist said as Darrell was leaving. "Don't give up hope."

Darrell grinned and said thanks.

He couldn't help but note the irony. This day of all days, the very day his kill date had come down—it was shaping up as his best day ever in prison.

Later on Darrell was called out of his cell to have his picture taken. For publicity purposes and so forth, Potosi liked having on file an up-to-date shot of any prisoner who was slated for imminent execution. Something gray and sober, preferably, something befitting the gravity of the occasion. But Darrell wasn't feeling gray and sober. He was out in the corridor joking and goofing around with the guy assigned to take the picture, a Potosi investigator named Gary Reed. Soon Reed got caught up in the fun himself and was swapping one-liners with Darrell. The next day he returned with his camera and said, "We'd better take another photo. You're laughing in the one we did yesterday. We don't want people thinking we're crazy."

So Darrell put on his best poker face and Reed finally got the picture he was looking for.

January 27, 1999, turned out to be not quite so firm an execution date after all.

On November 16, four days after issuing Darrell's original death warrant, the Missouri Supreme Court issued a new and amended warrant changing the date of execution from January 27 to February 10. There was no word of explanation or clarification—simply a new warrant stipulating a new death date. Issued about as ceremoniously as a notice for traffic court.

Okay, sure, Darrell said, with a slight frown of puzzlement, when the amended warrant was brought to his cell in protective custody. No big deal, he thought. So they're monkeying around with the timing. So what? It's not happening anyway.

Afterward, sitting on his bed, he decided it was time to get down to work. Forget the death writs: he knew he wouldn't be executed. With God as his lawyer, a miracle was bound to happen. So why not begin spreading the news right now? It was a golden opportunity for testifying. Tell people on the outside what was in store for him before the walls started shaking. Tell them in advance so that when it happened, as it surely would, they'd recognize it for what it was.

The Faith preachers, he decided, should be first to know, big-time television evangelists such as Kenneth Hagin, Kenneth and Gloria Copeland, and others of their ilk. He'd write a letter alerting them that there was a miracle waiting in the wings. Any stage setting that might need doing, he'd leave up to them.

Darrell sent the letter on November 27, eight defiant pages riveted with biblical citations. He hit his punch lines right off the top.

"It just got better, Praise God! Lucifer's own set a date to try to murder this child of God but they and their father are beat . . . [The execution date] forces this deal to a head and people shall see God show Himself strong on my behalf with one of His 'suddenlys' . . . Satan and his death penalty sons don't have enough power, money, or people to murder me here or anywhere else! I am telling you before it happens so you will believe."

The letter was sent to ten evangelists. If any of them actually got around to opening it, they could hardly be faulted for abandoning it halfway through. The letter showed Darrell at his resolute best, but also at his grinding, self-righteous worst. As testimony it fell dead flat—there was no mention that Darrell himself may have done something wrong, not a whimpering word on the triple homicide. Regret? Remorse? Not here—not in this letter. It was all about Darrell's grievances, Darrell's pilgrim's progress in a land of liars and hypocrites. All about Darrell the persecuted one, Darrell the target of evil forces in law enforcement and the courts.

But, still, there it was again: Darrell's clenched-fist guarantee that somehow—miraculously—he'd be spared execution. With the death date less than two months off, he hadn't wavered an inch. Whether out of monumental stubbornness, sheer delusion, or something else altogether, he was just as confident as ever. And now, with the letters sent, no one could say he hadn't gone on record during countdown time.

Darrell had no idea why his date of execution had been pushed back, and neither at first did most anyone else. After a while, however, you would've had to be almost willfully obtuse not to figure it out. In setting the date initially for January 27, 1999, the Missouri Supreme Court had committed a colossal blunder of timing. January 27 was precisely the date Pope John Paul II was scheduled to visit St. Louis. One of the most celebrated spiritual leaders of the age was coming to town, and the state supreme court had inexplicably set Darrell's execution for the very same day.

Now what were the odds on this? Not just that the court could screw up so badly, but that the pope was coming to St. Louis in the first place? Not New York or Los Angeles, not Chicago or Washington, no, not any of the usual suspects, but St. Louis, poor old St. Louis, shrinking and bedraggled, the twenty-seventh city, a city whose best days were gone and mostly forgotten. Never before had a pope visited St. Louis. Never before, it would seem, had a pope even come close to visiting St. Louis. But now Pope John Paul II was coming, and St. Louis was the only city in the United States in his travel plans. It was a one-stop itinerary—St. Louis and nowhere else. John Paul II, famously opposed to the death penalty, was visiting St. Louis on January 27, and the Missouri Supreme Court had chosen that precise date for Darrell's execution.

It wasn't as if the court hadn't been given advance notice. St. Louis archbishop Justin Rigali had announced the papal visit in late April, and anticipation had been running high ever since. Everybody in Missouri knew the pope was coming, and everybody with any imagination knew the main reason for his coming was none other than Archbishop Rigali.

The Los Angeles–born Rigali had spent nearly a quarter of a century in the Vatican before being named archbishop of the St. Louis diocese in 1994. He'd worked closely with John Paul II during much of that stretch, accompanying the pope on his extensive travels and sometimes serving as his English-language translator. From 1985 until his departure for St. Louis, moreover, Rigali had served as president of the Pontifical Ecclesiastical Academy, overseeing the instruction of future Vatican diplomats in the delicate arts of international protocol. By most accounts, Rigali was an ideal man for the job, a master of Vatican-style protocol in his own right. The precise formulation, the deft pause, knowing exactly what should be said and, better, what should be left *unsaid*—Rigali had it down to a science.

Some observers found it odd that a man so perfectly suited to Rome, the consummate Vatican insider, should be transferred to the relatively unglamorous precincts of St. Louis. Rigali seemed to take it in stride, however, and in early 1998 he saw a chance for St. Louis to shine as never before. The pope was scheduled to visit Mexico City in January 1999 for a meeting with Catholic bishops from the Western Hemisphere. Since he was going to be over in this part of the world anyway, why not invite him to swing by St. Louis for an impromptu visit? He could fly directly from Mexico City on January 26, the day the bishops' meeting was scheduled to wrap up, and then spend most of the following day in St. Louis before heading back to Rome. Rigali extended the invitation, and then, on April 23, 1998, the news hit the front page. The pope had said yes—a gesture of respect and appreciation, undoubtedly, for an old and valued friend.

One can only imagine the sense of chagrin in both the court and the governor's office when, four days after the first warrant was issued, the gaffe finally struck home. A once-in-a-lifetime papal visit to St. Louis, and they'd marked Darrell's calendar for the very same day. If they'd deliberately been trying to insult the pope, they could hardly have done a better job. There seemed only one way out of the mess. Push back the execution. Finesse the date. Issue a new warrant setting the lethal injection for February 10. Let the pope have his visit on January 27 . . . see him safely off to Rome . . . allow a decent interval of time to pass . . . then execute Darrell. If everything went right, nobody would be the wiser.

But this, of course, was probably asking too much. In the Sunday, December 6, edition of the *St. Louis Post-Dispatch*, the editorial page featured an eight-panel cartoon of a supreme court judge standing beside a corrections official and waving farewell to a departing jet.

"Goodbye, John Paul!" the judge is crying out. "Thanks for visiting Missouri . . . We'll never forget your message of love . . . peace, brotherhood . . . and forgiveness!" A two-beat pause while the jet disappears from view, and then the judge, big smile dissolving into a scowl, rips out an execution order and says, "He's gone now—let's fry Mr. Mease."

The papal visit was still almost two full months off, and already the press was tuned in to the deal.

On the second Saturday in January, Darrell's brother drove over to Potosi with a pep talk in his pocket. Actually, more like a get-real talk. Larry figured it was long overdue. All this stuff about God-is-my-lawyer and divine intervention, about Darrell miraculously escaping the death chamber: for almost a decade now, he'd gone along for the ride. If it gave Darrell hope, and their mom hope—hey, where was the harm? But enough was enough. Time to check out of fantasyland and come to grips with reality. The death warrants had convinced Larry. There'd be no sudden burst of thunder, no hand from heaven plucking Darrell to safety. The execution was due to come off on February 10, and wishful thinking wasn't going to stop it. If not for his own sake, then surely for their mom's sake, Darrell had to accept the inevitable and start making his peace.

Right now Lexie was the person Larry was most concerned about, and he wasn't alone. A lot of folks back home were concerned about Lexie. Darrell's execution was as sure as tomorrow, but she'd refused to prepare for it. She'd refused even to consider its possibility. There wasn't a chance in the world of it happening, she'd say. They can take Darrell in and strap him to the gurney—it doesn't matter. It won't happen because God won't let it happen. She'd bought completely into Darrell's fantasy. She was as convinced as he was that the death clock would be stopped by one of God's "suddenlys." But where did this leave her when the execution went off as scheduled? Larry and his wife, Sophia, had tried coaxing her into reality the past few weeks, even to the point of talking about the need to make funeral arrangements, but she hadn't heard a word they'd said.

So that second Saturday in January, Larry did his best to get through to Darrell. He tried talking with him about final farewells, about family burial plots, about all the sad and somber details of impending death. It was like running into a stone wall. Don't be planning any funeral services, Darrell said. Don't even be thinking in that direction. It would only betray a lack of faith.

Back home, a couple of days later, Larry quietly got down to work. With Sophia's help, he began making the necessary arrangements. Time was running short. Somebody had to take charge.

The state of Missouri managed to sneak in one more execution just two weeks prior to the scheduled papal visit. On Wednesday, January 13, at one minute past midnight, a thirty-seven-year-old hard case named Kelvin Malone was lethally injected at Potosi. Malone had been convicted of killing three people, including a St. Louis cabdriver, during a cross-country crime spree almost two decades earlier. A dozen people showed up outside the prison for a candlelight protest. It was tough keeping the candles alive in the cold wind, however, and by the time Malone was officially pronounced dead, shortly after two, most of the protesters were already long gone.

The Reverend Larry Rice certainly hadn't meant any harm. At the time it had seemed the decent thing to do, sending a goodbye card. His plan all along had been to go down to Potosi and hang out with Darrell the eve of the execution. Time and again since starting his death-row ministry, this is exactly what he'd done with guys on the brink. Show up at the prison around eight, sit with them an hour or two, talking, praying, singing, and holding hands, anything they wanted. Anything that might bring some solace during those last few hours before strap-down time. He'd intended doing the same thing with Darrell, but when the court set the final execution date he knew he wouldn't be able to make it. Larry was scheduled to be in India on February 10, visiting orphanages and spreading the Gospel, and there was no way he could get out of it. The trip had been in the works for months. So he'd sent the card, a heartfelt gesture of affection and regret. He certainly hadn't meant to upset Darrell. He'd simply been trying to do the right thing.

Larry Rice was widely known for trying to do the right thing—especially since moving to the St. Louis area from his native Texas years earlier and, as a newly ordained Pentecostal preacher, starting up a hugely ambitious street ministry. In two decades on the beat, working the grittier and more forlorn sections of town, he'd been the guy you'd most likely turn to if you were broke, despairing, or otherwise down on your luck. If you had nowhere to stay, nothing to eat, or nothing to wear, you could always turn to Larry. Show up at his New Life Evangelistic Center, housed in an old YWCA building on Locust Street in downtown St. Louis, and chances were you'd be taken care of. Or if your needs leaned more toward the straightforwardly spiritual, you couldn't go wrong tuning in some religious programming on one of Larry's television or radio stations. One way or another, Larry would have the answer.

Not everyone, however, was always open to listening. For someone so manifestly well intentioned, Larry had built up quite a list of detractors over the years. It was partly a matter of style. Always in a rush, talking a mile a minute, and preternaturally self-confident, Larry was simply too overwhelming a presence for some people. Among his fellow social activists, the biggest complaint was that he wasn't a team player. Try working with Larry on some issue, they'd say, and you'd be lucky getting a word in edgewise. Larry knew what he wanted done, and how he wanted it done, and he wasn't one for considering alternatives. If you worked with Larry, you did it his way—or not at all.

If fighting poverty was Larry's greatest social passion, fighting the death penalty ran a close second. He'd embraced the abolitionist or anti-death-penalty cause in the mid-1990s, and he hadn't eased up a bit since. Nobody in Missouri was more fervently opposed to capital punishment than Larry Rice. Not that his high-energy style always played well among other leading abolitionists. For the most part, veteran death-penalty opponents in Missouri were a ragtag band of old-time peaceniks, left-leaning academics, and social-justice Catholics who prided themselves on knowing the political ropes, knowing what could be accomplished today and what might need putting off until tomorrow. But then along comes fast-talking, hard-praying Larry, who had no time for compromise and little patience for negotiation. And then there were his political ambitions, which he certainly made no secret of. Larry was planning on making a run for governor, and he seemed always to be plotting his course, calculating the odds. He was a tough guy to figure out—an anti-death-penalty Pentecostal preacher in cowboy boots with glory on his mind. More than a few old-line death-penalty activists weren't sure he was worth the trouble.

One thing nobody could deny: the guys waiting out the

clock down at Potosi had nothing but good to say about Larry. They loved his commitment and his sincerity and, above all, they loved his personal touch, the way he took the trouble to get to know them and their families, the way he published their stories in his *Cry Justice Now* newspaper and filmed their death-row testimonials for broadcast on his statewide television network. Larry was real, they'd say.

Larry took pride in his good relations with death-row prisoners, which made his falling out with Darrell all the more troubling. The two men had exchanged frequent letters since the mid-1990s, and the depth and quality of Darrell's faith had impressed Larry. So he'd sent the card when Darrell's execution date came down, thinking it was a final chance to say goodbye and lend some pastoral support. Larry knew that Darrell had always insisted that God was his lawyer and that he'd never be executed. Now that the execution was a foregone conclusion, he didn't want Darrell falling into despair. "Don't for a second doubt God's love for you," he'd written on the card. "Believe with all your heart, even as you prepare to be executed, that God has not abandoned you."

Larry had been pleased with the card, thinking that it hit just the right tone. He hadn't anticipated getting a chiding, chastising letter from Darrell in return. For almost a decade now, Darrell wrote in the letter, he'd been holding fast to his God-given belief that he'd be spared execution and eventually freed from prison altogether. And now this card? What had Larry been thinking? What had he been hoping to accomplish? Was he trying to tempt him into doubt? Throw him off course? The card was shameful. It betrayed an astonishing lack of faith. How could Larry, a Pentecostal preacher, have sent such a thing?

"Do you realize that sending me a 'goodbye' card is shooting a fiery dart of doubt at me?" Darrell wrote. "It's about like throwing a rock at a man who is swimming for the shore. Satan uses Christians, at times, as well as his own. I've caught him using me on occasion. I say what I say to you with sadness and in a spirit of love and I pray that you receive it that way, that your eyes are opened to the truth."

A lesser person might have been offended by an upbraiding like this, but Larry seemed to take it in stride. He dashed off a note of apology to Darrell the first chance he got, hopeful of patching things up.

Monday evening, January 25, Laura Higgins Tyler attended a meeting of her Christian women's fellowship group. She'd always looked forward to these get-togethers, never more so than now. The truth was, she needed some patching up herself. A couple of weeks earlier she'd submitted a petition for executive pardon to the governor's office. This was the last thing she could do on Darrell's behalf, and she wasn't exactly brimming with optimism. Though she'd worked long and hard on the petition, she suspected it wouldn't make a whit of difference.

Not a whit of difference: this, Laura confided to her fellowship group, was what it appeared all her efforts had amounted to. She felt guilty for letting Darrell down, and guilty also for not fully subscribing to his belief that there'd be some sort of miraculous intervention. She felt a shortcoming as a Christian. Next to Darrell's, her own faith seemed timid and frail. Try as she might, she couldn't match his confidence—his sublime, unswerving confidence—that the execution wouldn't take place.

Laura unburdened herself for a good hour, the other six women in the group, all members of the same Disciples of Christ congregation, giving her a sympathetic hearing. Then, just before the meeting broke up, the women shared several minutes of silent prayer, which Laura closed by saying aloud, "Thy will be done."

Driving home, Laura could already feel the difference. The guilt, the sense of failure, the pressure—all gone, evaporated. She felt stronger and more at peace with herself than she had for months. The closing prayer had done the trick.

She'd put everything in God's hands. There would be no more second-guessing, no more scolding herself for weakness of faith. She was through agonizing over whether or not Darrell would be executed. God's will be done.

PART
FIVE

FIFTEEN

Charles Jaco was dying for a cigarette. Knocking elbows with the other journalists on the papal flight to St. Louis, an hour out of Mexico City, he was having a tough time fighting back the urge. Maybe it was the boredom. For a guy who'd made his reputation covering war and mayhem on three continents, this was pretty tame stuff. Two weeks on the beat, all the way from Rome to Mexico City, and now finally zeroing in on St. Louis—no bullets to duck, no death squads on his tail, nothing, nothing at all. It almost made him nostalgic for the good old days of tromping around the jungles of Nicaragua.

Still, Jaco knew something was in the works. He'd been picking up the signals for months, ever since November when the Missouri Supreme Court set January 27 as the date for executing Darrell Mease, then four days later switched it to February 10. "These clowns screwed up and now they're counting on nobody knowing the score," he'd thought at the time. But Jaco knew the reason for the change in date, and just to make sure others caught on, he'd talked it up on his KMOX radio show out of St. Louis. "What happens when the Vatican gets hold of this?" he'd said. "When the pope finds out they've been playing games with the execution date? This thing isn't done yet." Then two weeks earlier in Rome, a Vatican functionary had told him: "Certainly we're aware of the Mease case. We're aware of the entire situation regarding execution in Missouri. We've been keeping tabs on it ever since Glennon Paul Sweet wrote the pope asking for help."

So Jaco knew something was up. This thing wasn't close to being done. Chances were the pope was going to reprimand top state officials for their trigger-happy approach to capital punishment. Or, better yet, he might even make a pitch for sparing Darrell Mease, a guy Jaco wasn't alone in regarding as tailor-made for execution. One way or another, it was shaping up as an interesting visit.

Seventy-five minutes into the flight, a guy from one of the news services pulled back the curtain separating the journalists from the bigwigs up front. Sure—it figured. Some of the people up in "Bishops Class" were puffing away. That's all Jaco and the other journalists needed to know. They took down the cardboard no-smoking signs and lit up. He still would have preferred Mozambique or Panama or Kuwait, but Jaco was starting to enjoy himself. That story at the end of the trail was smelling sweeter all the time.

Through plumes of cigarette smoke, Patricia Rice spotted Joaquín Navarro-Valls, director of the Vatican press office, come through the curtain out of "Bishops Class" and start hobnobbing his way down the aisle. She waited for him to get closer, deciding this was an opportunity she couldn't afford to pass up. As chief religion correspondent for the *St. Louis Post-Dispatch*, Rice had been on top of the story for months. She figured she had as good a line on what was happening as anyone else.

Check it out: The pope is scheduled to visit St. Louis at the invitation of Archbishop Rigali. The state supreme court messes up on its initial execution date for Darrell Mease and then, anxious to avert a public relations disaster, tries sneaking through a new date. Patricia Rice knows Archbishop Rigali from covering the local religion beat. She knows that he's strongly opposed to capital punishment, and that he's well connected in Rome. What's more, she's been tailing the pope closely for the past few years, reporting on his travels, living and breathing his every public utterance. She knows where the pope stands on the death penalty, one of the great evils of our time, he's been saying. He spoke out powerfully on the subject the previous Christmas in Rome, again just this past Saturday in Mexico City, and he's taken to intervening personally in specific cases involving capital punishment in the United States, most famously the Karla Faye Tucker case in Texas. All of which means that the pope is tuned in to the Darrell Mease case, the snafu with the date, everything. Archbishop Rigali would have contacted him about it. A case involving capital punishment, directly impinging on the visit to St. Louis—of course Rigali would have contacted him.

Navarro-Valls was right beside her now, looking down, registering recognition. They'd spoken several times in the past.

"Hello, Dr. Navarro-Valls."

"Hello. You're enjoying the flight, I hope?"

"Very nice, thanks. I have a question. Do you mind?"

"Not at all."

"Why is the pope coming to St. Louis?"

"I'm sure you're aware of the historic importance of the St. Louis archdiocese to Catholicism in America."

"Yes, of course, but could the visit also have something to do with Missouri having the highest per capita rate of execution in the United States?"

"*You* can say that." Confidingly, putting his hand on Rice's forearm.

"And something also to do with Darrell Mease?"

"We're aware of the situation involving Mr. Mease. The pope is quite disturbed about it. The postponement of his execution is a mockery. Postponement is not good enough."

Other reporters were leaning in at this point, as Navarro-Valls poured on the indignation.

"What do you do? First you are going to kill him, but then you give him a Valium and say, 'Wait.' And then after the pope is gone, you kill after. No! Whenever he is executed, the state must know that what it is doing is morally wrong."

An hour later, at an airport arrival ceremony attended by Bill and Hillary Clinton and Governor Carnahan, the pope delivered a short speech, focusing his remarks primarily on abortion and euthanasia. Not a word on the death penalty or Darrell Mease. It was the same thing later that evening during a Catholic youth rally at the Kiel Center downtown. Inspiring words from the pope on prayer and family life and other matters; silence on capital punishment.

Seven the next morning, January 27: it was shaping up as a bright clear sunny day in eastern Missouri.

Darrell would have been dead already, lethally injected hours ago, if the initial execution date had stood. Instead he was lying back after breakfast, the iron-willed man of Potosi, waiting on a miracle. He realized the pope was visiting St. Louis today, and he was vaguely aware by now that this was why his date had been put off. Beyond this, however, the papal visit meant nothing to him. Nothing, that is, in a positive vein. In his wild ride of a life, one of the few constants had been anti-Catholicism. He'd been raised to think of Catholicism as a wayward cult, a sham religion, and the pope as its master manipulator. Most kids of his generation in the Ozarks had been raised to think likewise. Anti-Catholicism was a cultural orthodoxy from which he'd never deviated.

Once or twice in recent months, guys on the row had suggested he write the pope asking for help. The very idea had seemed astonishing—and repugnant—to Darrell. He'd no more dream of asking the pope for help than he would some fly-by-night swami. There was authentic Christianity, of which Darrell was a part, and then there was fakery and falsehood, with Roman Catholicism at the head of the class. Darrell would be receiving his help from God, and God alone. There was no sense in getting anyone else involved, the pope least of all.

Sixty-five miles up the road from Potosi, the pope and his entourage were preparing to leave Archbishop Rigali's residence on Lindell Boulevard for a papal mass at the Trans

World Dome in downtown St. Louis. Hats and coats were still being sorted out when Joaquín Navarro-Valls approached Monsignor Richard Stika, a high-ranking aide to Archbishop Rigali, with a special assignment: contact Governor Carnahan and arrange for him to come by Rigali's residence sometime around noon. Why? The Vatican secretary of state, Cardinal Angelo Sodano, was interested in meeting personally with the governor on a matter of utmost importance. A couple of moments later, lest there be any doubt, Cardinal Sodano himself spoke with Monsignor Stika and urged him to take care of it as soon as possible.

At half past nine, Joe Bednar dropped by his office at the capitol building in Jefferson City, planning on picking up some files and then whisking out to the airport. He had business late that afternoon in Washington, D.C. But before he could get to the files, Bednar was corralled by Governor Carnahan's press secretary, the smart and affable Chris Sifford.

"Glad you're here, Joe," Sifford said. "The governor's been looking for you. Something's come up."

"What is it, Chris?"

"We got a call from Archbishop Rigali's office. They want the governor over there for a sit-down with some of the pope's people."

Capital punishment, Bednar immediately thought, maybe even some fallout from the Mease affair. As the governor's chief legal counsel, he knew this could be tricky business.

He grabbed his files and went directly to the governor's office.

"The request came first thing this morning," Carnahan said, appearing just a tad ruffled. "We're not talking a social call here, Joe. It looks serious. They really want me over there."

"Have you decided what you're going to do?"

"What do you think, Joe? Should I go?"

"Yes. I think you should."

"Will you come with me?"

"Absolutely."

"Join me on the state plane then?"

"No, thanks. I'll drive over and we can hook up before the meeting."

"Okay. I'll have Chris tell them we'll be there around one."

An hour later, driving eastbound on I-70, Bednar was feeling an excitement that likely would have taken some people by surprise. Around Jefferson City he was widely considered shrewd and unflappable. If you were on his side, he could be the sweetest guy in town, but line up against him on some legal issue or another and he'd calmly skin you alive. When it came to the law, nobody in Jefferson City was sharper than Joe Bednar. But this meeting at one o'clock had the makings of something bigger than the law, bigger than politics. Though he wasn't much for advertising it, Bednar was a practicing Catholic. His younger brother, Tom, was a Holy Cross priest at Notre Dame, and Bednar had once thought of becoming a priest himself, spending summers during his teens at a Benedictine monastery in north-central Missouri. So this meeting at Archbishop Rigali's really was something to be excited about. Who knew? Maybe even the pope would be there.

A few miles east of Wright City, Bednar got stopped for speeding. He played it straight, not mentioning his connections to the governor. The trooper let him off with a warning, telling him to take it easy.

At twelve-fifteen he met up with Governor Carnahan and another of Carnahan's legal advisers, a young woman named Angie Heffner, at a restaurant in Clayton.

Bednar left his car at the restaurant and joined Carnahan and Heffner in a black Chevy Suburban driven by a St. Louis cop, Tom Malacek, who sometimes did security for the governor. On the way over to Archbishop Rigali's, it was all nervous speculation. Would the pope be making an appearance? Would the conversation be limited to capital punishment? Or might abortion also enter into it? Not exactly ice-breaking topics, either one. Since becoming governor in 1992, Carnahan had presided over twenty-six lethal injections, making Missouri one of the most execution-intensive states in the country. There'd been no indication this trend was about to change. Only once, in the case of two-time killer Bobby Shaw, had the governor commuted a death sentence—on the grounds that jurors hadn't been properly apprised of Shaw's mental retardation. If the governor had been having moral qualms lately about the death penalty, he'd done a good job of keeping them to himself. And it was tough imagining the subject of abortion going over any better. Carnahan was a strong supporter of reproductive rights, and he'd recently run afoul of Archbishop Rigali and other leading Catholics in Missouri by vetoing a measure that would have outlawed the mid- to late-term procedure known as "partial-birth abortion." One way or another, the governor and his crew suspected they were in for some tense moments.

Here they were—the big stone house at the southwest corner of Lindell and Taylor, a block from the Cathedral Basilica, both sides of the street lined with motorcycle cops, Secret Service lurking in the shadows. They rang the front doorbell and Joaquín Navarro-Valls ushered them into the vestibule, a framed photograph of Pope John Paul II on the far wall, another of the pope with Archbishop Rigali on the wall by the front door. Off to the left, a parlor opening onto a large dining room, a swirl of red and white, bishops and cardinals seated at three round tables finishing their pasta lunch. The smell of Polish sausage from breakfast six hours earlier was still lingering in the air. Navarro-Valls led them through a sliding door into the Glennon library, an oak-paneled room to the right of the vestibule, and invited them to sit on a plush sofa with flowered upholstery beneath the front window.

He thanked them for coming and apologized for the short notice. The pope was resting, he said—it had been a big morning, with the mass at the Trans World Dome, and another event coming up later that afternoon. He said that he'd be back with Cardinal Sodano and Archbishop Rigali in just a moment.

It had indeed been a big morning for the pope, who was

now taking a nap in an upstairs bedroom, his personal nurse, a valet, and two Swiss Guards near at hand. At the papal mass, he'd given a vibrant homily highlighted by some of his strongest comments yet on capital punishment.

"[The] dignity of human life must never be taken away, even in the case of someone who has done great evil," he'd said. "Modern society has the means of protecting itself, without definitively denying criminals the chance to reform. I renew the appeal I made most recently at Christmas for a consensus to end the death penalty, which is both cruel and unnecessary."

Joe Bednar hadn't attended the papal mass. Neither had Angie Heffner or the governor. They'd have to wait until later for word on the pope's homily. For now there was nothing to do but take in their surroundings. Bednar couldn't help but be impressed by the elegance of the room. Crystal chandelier, pale beige carpet, white drapes. Oak bookshelves—along the far wall and next to the side window—crammed with creaking hardbacks: Shakespeare, Chaucer, Tennyson, Bonaventure, Chesterton, Belloc, Aquinas. Alabaster marble fireplace to the right, matching alabaster clock atop the mantel sounding out the seconds like time entranced.

Navarro-Valls came back, Cardinal Sodano and Archbishop Rigali with him. After a round of handshakes, Sodano thanked the governor for taking time out from his busy schedule. The churchmen sat opposite the sofa in three white-cushioned chairs, Rigali in the middle, Sodano to his left directly across from the governor. They engaged in some banter to get things started. Sodano praised the wonderful hospitality of St. Louis and the state of Missouri. The governor pointed out that while he himself was Southern Baptist, both Angie and Joe were Catholics, and Joe's brother, Tom, was a priest. Both men remarked on the fine January weather, crisp, sparkling, made to order for a papal visit.

Bednar, sitting beside Angie Heffner, and across from Navarro-Valls, was struck by the respect the two men were showing one another. Their exchange was so polite and so honorable—what was referred to locally as Missouri Proper.

Then, three or four minutes into the conversation, Cardinal Sodano got down to business.

"The case of Mr. Darrell Mease has been brought to our attention," he said.

Patricia Rice had been right all along—though Sodano didn't mention it here, Archbishop Rigali had personally contacted the Vatican about the Mease case shortly after the execution date was changed.

"We understand that Mr. Mease was scheduled to be executed today," Sodano went on. "We also understand that the date was changed because of the pope's visit. The pope is very concerned. He doesn't want to be in a position where he flies out of St. Louis, then a week or so later Mr. Mease is executed."

Carnahan, attentive, hands folded in his lap, looked the cardinal straight in the eye. He'd been dreading this meeting all morning. He displayed no sign of discomfort now, though—just executive composure through and through.

"Governor," Sodano continued, "we've invited you here today in a spirit of friendship and good will, not confrontation. We're not asking you to change your personal views on capital punishment. We're not asking you to change the laws of your state."

Bednar was impressed. This tall, bespectacled cardinal—the Church's top-ranking diplomat—was hitting all the right notes.

"We're asking one thing, and one thing only. On behalf of the pope, on the occasion of his historic visit to St. Louis, we're asking that you exercise your mercy and authority in regard to Mr. Darrell Mease."

Carnahan remained impassive, giving nothing away.

"Our appeal, on behalf of the pope, is that you permit Mr. Mease to live. We're sure you're aware, Governor, that throughout history pardons have sometimes been given on exceptional occasions. On this exceptional occasion, we ask that you pardon Mr. Mease."

A brief pause. Silence except for the ticking of the clock on the mantel.

"Again, it is not a question of capital punishment in general. Our appeal is very specific. We are not asking you to do anything beyond your prerogative as governor. Please exercise your mercy and your authority to permit this one man to live."

It was Carnahan's move now and Bednar wasn't at all certain how the governor would respond.

"Well, the Darrell Mease case is before us now," he said. "Joe and Angie review these cases very carefully—"

"Yes, of course," said Cardinal Sodano.

"—and we'll give Darrell Mease every consideration. I'm sure you know where I stand on capital punishment—"

"Yes."

"—but I will take your request seriously. Give me some time to reflect on it, and I'll get back to you with my answer as soon as possible."

"Fine," Cardinal Sodano said, standing and shaking Carnahan's hand. He then excused himself, returning a moment later with commemorative medallions and rosaries for the three visitors.

Bednar was concerned about the media getting wind of the request. He didn't want the governor facing any added pressure.

"What are your plans on publicity?" he asked Navarro-Valls.

"We won't publicize this until we return to the Vatican," Navarro-Valls said.

Just before leaving, Carnahan turned to Sodano and said, "I have a request of my own, Cardinal. I'd appreciate it if the pope could somehow communicate this plea to me directly."

"I'm quite certain this can be arranged," Sodano said, knowing how much the Mease case meant to the pope. "This afternoon, possibly, after the prayer service at the Cathedral Basilica."

Outside, going down the front walk, Carnahan said, "That was interesting."

"Yeah," Bednar said.

Then, on their way back to the restaurant in Clayton: "What do you think, Joe?"

"I have to tell you, Governor, I'm conflicted here. I'm your legal counsel and I'm also Roman Catholic. So however I advise you, I'm afraid you'll be left wide open to criticism."

"Uh-huh."

"Remember the JFK campaign in 1960? The fear that the pope would be running the country? I was just a kid and I can remember. So even though you're Southern Baptist, not Catholic, I'm concerned that you'd be setting yourself up for some real grief."

The governor shifted sideways in the front seat of the Chevy Suburban. Resting his left arm on the seat back, and looking directly at Bednar behind him, he said, "Joe, we fought that fight back in 1960, and I think we won."

Half a mile farther along, Carnahan called his press secretary, Chris Sifford, on his cell phone and ran through the meeting with him.

"So this is what they're asking, Chris," he said. "Think about it and we'll talk later on."

At the restaurant parking lot now: "I'll think about this the rest of the day, Joe," Carnahan said, "but I don't want to know everything about the case—"

"Okay."

"—because, Joe, are the facts ever good in a death-penalty case?"

"No, Governor, they're always bad."

Still intent on seeing to his business in D.C., Bednar shot out to Lambert–St. Louis International Airport. With a bit of time to kill before his flight, he ate a hamburger and scanned a newspaper. There it was, on the front page: Patricia Rice's piece on her in-flight conversation the day before with Joaquín Navarro-Valls. Interesting, Bednar thought—the Vatican's top media dog, as savvy as they come, scoring some advance press points on the Darrell Mease deal. It looked like there was even more to this than met the eye.

Bednar hit the nearest pay phone and put through a call to Chris Sifford.

"Look, Chris," he said, "I'm out here at the airport in St. Louis but I'm thinking maybe I should forget about my trip and drive back to Jeff City instead."

"Good idea," Sifford said. "Why don't you come on back? There's a good chance we'll be needing you."

It was midafternoon, bright and chilly, when the slow prop plane carrying Chris Liese and five other local politicians hit the runway in St. Louis. Liese was bristling with anticipation. The short flight from Jefferson City had lasted all of a heartbeat. Now it was simply a matter of hanging in for a few hours and he'd finally have a chance to meet the pope when he came out to the airport later that day for the official departure ceremony.

There was some confusion outside the Midcoast terminal building, as people jockeyed for rides over to Lambert's main terminal where Vice President Al Gore and his wife were scheduled to arrive on *Air Force 2* at any moment. Liese jumped into a black Chevy Suburban that pulled up to the curb, and as the vehicle looped east and then north along a service road toward the main terminal he suddenly realized that he was sitting directly between the governor and the governor's wife, Jean, who had just come in on a separate plane.

Liese said hello. He and the governor knew one another professionally. As fellow Democrats, they'd worked together over the years on various pieces of legislation.

The governor turned to him and said, "Chris, you're Catholic, what can I tell the pope about executing Darrell Mease?"

Liese was stymied. He knew nothing about the Mease deal. Recognizing as much, Carnahan filled him in on some of the details. He told him about the meeting with Cardinal Sodano earlier that day at Archbishop Rigali's residence. He said that he was on his way right now to an ecumenical prayer service at the Cathedral Basilica, and that Sodano had contacted his office an hour or so ago confirming that the pope would be approaching him after the service and requesting that he spare Darrell Mease.

Then, as best as Liese months later was able to recall, Carnahan said: "The pope is going to ask me this even though it's undisputed that Darrell Mease committed these crimes. And, Chris, these were heinous crimes. Mease is guilty under the law, and he deserves to die."

Liese took a deep breath, wanting to measure his words carefully. Never before had the governor asked his advice. And never before had he seen the governor so tense. So what to say? From the little the governor had told him, Liese felt torn. As a good Catholic, he wanted to advise the governor to heed the pope's request. As a politician, however, he knew that doing so could prove costly. He knew that Missourians could play rough at election time with any candidate deemed soft on the death penalty. In his own career, representing a suburban St. Louis district in the state legislature, Liese had studiously avoided any appearance of softness on the matter. He also knew that Carnahan was wrapping up his second term as governor and was planning on making a bid for a seat in the U.S. Senate. Letting a guy like Darrell Mease off the hook could be just the thing to scotch his chances. But still . . . this was the pope. How could the governor possibly say no to John Paul II, a superstar among religious leaders if ever there was one?

Finally Liese made up his mind. He knew what he'd tell the governor, though he seriously doubted it was what the governor wanted to hear.

"This is no ordinary pope," he said. "If I were you, Governor, I would do what he asks you."

The governor said nothing in response. He merely sat there, turned toward the side window now, grimly nodding his head.

The Chevy Suburban came to a stop outside the main terminal and the Secret Service took the governor and his wife inside to meet Al and Tipper Gore. Liese was escorted to a secured VIP tent, already filled to near capacity, where he'd spend the next three hours over cookies, coffee, and lemon-ade waiting to say goodbye to the pope.

It got under way at four-thirty in the afternoon—the perfect capstone to the papal visit: an interfaith prayer service at the Cathedral Basilica of St. Louis, a grandly ornate building with a glittering green dome on Lindell Boulevard in the city's central west end. Wearing a cope and stole, the pope went to the main altar and chanted the doxology praising the Trinity. He then sat facing the congregation on a simple wooden throne, Archbishop Rigali and Cardinal Sodano flanking him, his entourage seated in choir stalls off to the side. Governor Carnahan, wearing a dark suit and glasses, was in the front pew to the left of the center aisle, his wife and Al and Tipper Gore alongside him.

The pope read his homily with a shaking hand and a qua-vering voice, closing with a ringing entreaty to all Ameri-cans: "If you want peace, *work for justice*. If you want justice, *defend life*. If you want life, *embrace the truth*—the truth revealed by God."

There was no explicit reference in the homily to capital punishment.

It was a stirring event—the comparative intimacy of the cathedral, with its byzantine mosaic-clad interior, the sump-tuous music that both preceded and followed the homily, the passage from Isaiah expertly rendered by a prominent local rabbi. Everything was in perfect pitch, graceful and harmo-nious, with not a single note off-key. Then, a little before six, after the last canticle had been chanted and the last prayer recited, the pope struggled to his feet, gingerly negotiated the steps in front of the altar, and slowly made his way over to the front left pew where he chatted briefly with the Gores before moving on to Governor Carnahan.

The two men exchanged greetings, and then the pope, his face a scant six inches from Carnahan's, said: "Governor, will you please have mercy on Mr. Mease?"

And that was it. *Will you please have mercy on Mr. Mease?* The most direct request imaginable. The most specific request imaginable. It wasn't about the death penalty in general. It wasn't about sparing anyone else on death row. Just Darrell—nobody but Darrell.

The governor nodded, almost imperceptibly, and the pope moved on, working his way laboriously to the rear of the cathedral with his entourage in tow.

At just a few minutes before seven, Chris Liese's patience was finally rewarded when the pope came into the VIP tent at Lambert for the departure ceremony. It didn't matter to Liese that he wasn't able to get much closer than gawking distance. Simply being in the pope's presence for a few precious moments was thrill enough.

Afterward, needing a lift back to the Midcoast terminal building, Liese was whisked into the same black Chevy Suburban that he'd hitched a ride in earlier. Once again, he took the middle seat of the second row. The governor hurried in after him and shut the door. Several minutes of tense silence passed while Carnahan waited for his wife to wrap up a conversation she was having with someone on the pavement outside. Neither Liese nor the passengers behind him—state attorney general Jay Nixon and state treasurer Bob Holden —breathed a word. Finally, his agitation apparently getting the better of him, Carnahan uncharacteristically barked: "Jean, get in the car."

Jean Carnahan took the empty seat next to Liese and sat with her arms folded. The ten-minute drive to the Midcoast terminal was about as cheerful as a funeral cortege. Liese was dying to ask the governor about his meeting with the pope, but he didn't dare break the silence. Nevertheless, he had a strong hunch that the deal had already been struck. The governor had decided to grant the pope's request and was now contemplating the political implications.

Flying back to Jefferson City, Liese kept turning it over in his mind. If his hunch was right, there was a good chance that Darrell Mease was just the beginning of a major shift in Missouri's death-penalty policy. Let Mease live, and the walls could soon start tumbling.

• • •

At seven o'clock, Terry Ganey had all his assignments tidied away and was preparing to shut down for the evening when a tip came through. Somebody had contacted *Post-Dispatch* gossip columnist Jerry Berger saying that members of the pope's entourage had met with the governor a few hours earlier urging him to put a halt to capital punishment in Missouri. Berger had passed the tip on to the city desk where an alert editor immediately thought of phoning it in to Ganey. Ganey was an old hand at covering government in Jefferson City for the newspaper, so if anybody could get to the bottom of this, he was the guy.

The first thing Ganey did was put a call through to the governor's press secretary. Kiddingly, he told Sifford that it was a tradition for the governor's office to give the *Post-Dispatch* a couple of exclusives toward the end of a second term.

Interesting tradition, Sifford said. He asked Ganey if he had anything particular in mind.

Now that you mention it, Ganey said, and he ran through the tip that had come in to Jerry Berger.

Perhaps hesitant about going any further without a green light from the governor, Sifford told Ganey that he'd get back to him within the hour.

Thirty minutes later, Sifford called back with the full scoop. It was true, he said. The governor had in fact met with Cardinal Sodano at Archbishop Rigali's residence earlier that afternoon. The meeting had been perfectly cordial and had lasted approximately twenty minutes. But it hadn't been about a state moratorium on capital punishment. In fact, nothing of the sort had come up in the conversation. It had been about Darrell Mease's pending execution—and nothing more. On the pope's behalf, Cardinal Sodano had asked the governor to grant Mease a commutation. What's more, the pope had personally requested the same thing of the governor at the interfaith prayer service that had ended less than two hours ago.

And what, Ganey asked, was the governor's response?

He was considering it, Sifford said.

He was considering it. Perhaps it was something in the way Sifford had said this, or that he had said it at all, but Ganey had the distinct impression that the headline writers at his newspaper would soon have their hands full. It wasn't every day that a death-row prisoner in Missouri received a reprieve through the direct intervention of the pope.

Late Wednesday, at about ten-thirty, Governor Carnahan met with his team around a big oval-shaped table in his private office at the capitol building in Jefferson City. The governor sat at the head of the table, with his chief of staff, Brad Ketcher, and Angie Heffner along one side, and Chris Sifford and Joe Bednar along the other.

The purpose of the meeting was to come to a decision on the pope's request. The governor did most of the talking.

"I'm really moved to grant this," he said. "I think it's the right thing to do."

He went on to say that he admired the precision of the request.

"This is something we can say yes to. They've asked me to do something that's entirely within my purview. I'm legally authorized as governor to grant executive clemency. They're not asking us to change the laws on abortion or the death penalty. Their request is very, very specific."

There was some frank discussion around the table on both the pros and the cons of granting the commutation. Nobody, however, tried pushing the governor very hard in one direction or the other. He seemed to know exactly what he wanted to do.

Finally, at eleven-fifteen, the meeting drew to an end. Joe Bednar said: "You give the word, Governor, I'll draft the commutation order. But I'd like to talk with Jim Justus, the prosecutor in the case, before making it public."

Carnahan agreed and then went home for the night to the governor's mansion, where he presumably gave it some more thought and talked it over with his wife.

First thing Thursday morning, January 28, the governor

spoke with Bednar and asked him to go ahead with the commutation order.

An hour later, at nine sharp, Bednar got through to Jim Justus. The two men knew one another personally. Back in 1987, while Bednar was working on the sex crimes unit out of the Jackson County Prosecutor's Office in Kansas City, Jim had asked for his help with a child molestation incident in Taney County. This was just a month or so after Jim had failed in his bid to secure a death penalty in the David Tate case.

After a bit of catching up, Bednar dropped his bombshell: Darrell Mease wasn't going to be executed. The pope had personally interceded on Darrell's behalf and the governor had agreed to commute his death sentence.

Jim was flabbergasted. "This was my only successful death-penalty case," he said.

Before ringing off, however, he assured Bednar that he had no hard feelings over the deal.

"Listen," he said, "if I was there, and the pope asked me, I'd say okay, too."

This first piece of business accomplished, Bednar now put the finishing touches on the commutation order. The final draft read as follows:

> I, Mel Carnahan, Governor of the state of Missouri, have had presented personally and directly to me by Pope John Paul II, a request for mercy in the case of Darrell Mease who was convicted of First Degree Murder on April 25, 1990, and sentenced to death on June 1, 1990. After careful consideration of the extraordinary circumstance of the Pontiff's direct and personal appeal for mercy and because of the deep and abiding respect I have for him and all that he represents, I hereby grant to Darrell Mease a commutation of the above sentence in the following respect: This commutation eliminates from the sentence the penalty of death and further causes Darrell Mease to remain incarcerated for the remainder of his life without the possibility of parole.

. . .

At ten o'clock on Thursday morning, Laura Tyler was interviewing a prospective client at an alternative school in Kansas City when she was summoned to the front office. There was a phone call waiting for her, she was told. A phone call? Laura was perplexed. Why would anyone be trying to reach her here? She certainly didn't consider herself an important person. She didn't carry a pager, and the only reason she had a car phone was to stay in touch with her husband and kids. She wasn't accustomed to having people track her down while she was out in the field.

It was a secretary from her law firm, saying Joe Bednar from the governor's office was on the line. Laura knew Bednar, and from their limited contact over the years she liked him a great deal. They'd first become acquainted when Laura was working as an assistant public defender in Jackson County and Bednar was interning for the county prosecutor's office.

"Have you been following the pope's visit?" Bednar asked.

"Well, a little bit," Laura said. "Why, Joe? What's going on?"

Bednar sketched out the crucial events of the past twenty-four hours, but it was almost too much for Laura to digest. The pope's people meeting in secret with the governor over the fate of her client? The pope interceding with the governor on Darrell's behalf? She'd had no idea any of this was happening. Her initial astonishment soon gave way to immense gratitude. She recalled the simple prayer with which she'd ended her fellowship meeting three days earlier. *Thy will be done.* She'd put everything in God's hands and this was the result. Her prayer had been answered, and Darrell's unflinching faith had been vindicated.

But perhaps not entirely so. At least not yet. In the thrill of the moment, Laura remembered that Darrell had been counting on more than getting off death row. He'd also been counting on getting out of prison altogether. He'd made this clear to her at their very first meeting. God was his lawyer, he'd said, and God didn't settle for halfway victories. In God's good time, he'd be dancing off the row, and dancing right out the front door. This was why Laura, in the petition she'd filed with the governor's office a couple of weeks earlier, had been careful to ask for a full pardon rather than just executive clemency. A full pardon meant release from prison, total freedom, no strings attached.

As grateful as she was, then, Laura still managed to keep the larger picture in focus.

"You know everything my client has asked for," she said.

"Laura," Bednar said, "you didn't get everything you asked for."

Bednar suggested she call him from her office so he could fill her in on all the details.

After phoning her husband from her car with the news, Laura drove back to her office and put the call through to Bednar.

He told her that her client wouldn't be going free. The governor's mercy had extended only so far. Darrell would be spending the remainder of his days behind bars.

Laura's next move was to call Darrell at Potosi. She felt some anxiety waiting for him to come to the phone, aware that the commutation wasn't everything he'd staked his faith on.

"Hi Laura," he said. "How you doing?"

"Just fine, Darrell. I've got some news. I think it's good news but it's not everything you wanted."

Darrell listened quietly as Laura laid out the commutation deal. He wasn't especially surprised. He wasn't jubilant. He didn't jump and shout. If anything, he was initially troubled over the way the deal had gone down. He'd always known that he wouldn't be executed. He'd always known that there'd be some sort of divine intervention. This had never been an issue for him. He'd never entertained a moment's doubt. But the pope's involvement was something he hadn't banked on. And this is partly what troubled him. It wasn't just that the pope was the head of a faith for which Darrell held little affection. It was also that he was so famous, easily the most recognizable religious leader in the world. Darrell had always wanted his release from death row to be a demonstration of the power and glory of God. Now he was worried that people would be missing the point. They'd be giving the pope credit whereas, in truth, the credit was all God's. Through no fault of his own, perhaps, the pope would be taking glory away from its rightful source.

This was a major concern of Darrell's, and so too was the matter of his sentence being reduced to life without parole. He'd always assumed that the miracle that sprung him from death row would also spring him from prison altogether. He'd assumed it would be a one-shot deal. Life without parole wasn't the total victory he'd been anticipating. He found it hard for the moment accepting it as a victory at all. He couldn't see himself spending the rest of his life behind bars, especially not when he'd been holding out for so much more.

He asked Laura what the commutation meant for the future. Would it foreclose all legal possibility of his ever being released?

Laura said she'd get Kent Gipson on the phone for a three-way conversation. Kent was the ranking expert on matters of this sort.

By the time Kent joined in, several minutes later, Darrell had already adjusted his thinking. He'd decided that the commutation was a good thing after all. God must have worked it this way for a reason. And who was he to question God? He'd been wrong to assume it would be a one-shot deal. He'd still be leaving prison, but on God's timetable— not his own, not anyone else's.

Kent was struck by how calm Darrell seemed, how remarkably under control. Anyone else who'd just been brought back from the dead would be bursting at the seams with elation. But then again, Kent knew Darrell. He knew that the possibility of actually being executed had never entered his mind.

He assured Darrell that the commutation was a marvelous stroke of good fortune. It had kept him alive, and so long as he was alive, there was always the chance of his finding some way out of prison.

Darrell returned to his cell in protective custody, grateful but hardly triumphant. The commutation, he was convinced, was only a partial and provisional victory. The full victory would come later.

SIXTEEN

Late Thursday morning, January 28, the governor's office put out a press release in Carnahan's name making it official.

"Yesterday afternoon," it began, "Pope John Paul II asked me to commute the death sentence of Darrell Mease. The Pope asked me to, in his words, 'have mercy on Mr. Mease' . . . I continue to support capital punishment but . . . I decided last night to grant [the pope's] request. I commuted the sentence of Darrell Mease to life in prison without the possibility of parole."

Later the same day the governor met with the media in Washington, where he'd flown on state business.

"It was one of those moments that one would never expect to happen in one's life and would never expect to happen again," he said of his encounter with the pope at the Cathedral Basilica. "I felt that this response from me was appropriate."

A reporter asked how he'd respond if the pope appealed to him sometime down the line on behalf of another death-row inmate.

"I will take care of that at the time," he said. "[Inmates] can expect to receive the punishment that was meted out by the court, unless there are extenuating circumstances or their trial was not fair or something of that nature."

In Rome, at roughly the same time, Joaquín Navarro-

Valls was telling reporters of the pope's delight with the commutation.

"On learning the news of the governor's generous decision," he said, "the holy father expressed great satisfaction for the gesture of high humanity on the part of Mel Carnahan, governor of the state of Missouri."

So there it was: Darrell Mease, one of the last true Ozark hillbillies, had become the first person in the history of the United States to have his death sentence commuted through the direct intervention of a religious leader from outside the country. And not just any religious leader, but the inestimable Pope John Paul II, certainly one of the most important spiritual figures of the age. Darrell, a most unlikely candidate for celebrity status, had suddenly become the talk of the nation.

Darrell's second wife, Donna, was visiting her sister's house when news of the commutation came on television. She remembers feeling thunderstruck, incapable of believing at first that what she was hearing was actually true.

"It was so incredible, Darrell always insisting that he'd never be executed, the pope's involvement, everything. Then, when it really sank in, I started crying. I'd lived with Darrell. I'd been married to him and had two kids with him. I was terribly conflicted. I was mainly happy for Lexie, who I love and think the world of. It was Lexie, I thought, who deserved the most credit for the commutation, this good woman who got down on her knees every night praying for Darrell's life to be spared. I was also happy for my kids—that they wouldn't have to go through the trauma and stigmatization of their father getting executed. This whole ordeal had been horrific for them, so terrible, terrible, terrible. I doubt Darrell even recognized what he'd put us through."

Darrell's sister was at home in West Des Moines, Iowa, when she heard the news. "Darrell's lawyer phoned my mama right after she talked to Darrell, and then my mama phoned me. She was happy, of course, but not really surprised. She and Darrell were the only people who knew all along that the execution wouldn't take place. Then my friends and co-workers asked me about it because they knew Darrell was my brother. They asked if I was shocked. I said no, but I'm very happy and very proud of my brother."

Early evening, January 28, Jack Graves had friends over at his house in Palmdale. He was regaling them with wild stories of some of his friends and relatives from back home in Missouri when something caught his eye on the TV set in the corner of the living room. It was recycled news footage of his cousin Darrell walking down the courthouse corridor in Springfield after his death sentence had been handed down. "Damn," Jack said. "That's old Darrell. Now what's this all about?" He hurried over and turned up the volume. The pope and Darrell—this was the wildest story of all. Even Jack had nothing to compete with it.

The Reverend Larry Rice had attended the interfaith prayer service at the Cathedral Basilica. He'd seen the pope descend from the altar and speak with the governor, and he'd wondered what it was about. Early the next afternoon he found out. Driving to an appointment in St. Louis, he heard the story on the car radio. Larry immediately thought of the angry letter that Darrell had sent a couple of months earlier chiding him for lack of faith. He thought of Darrell's absolute insistence over the years that he'd never be executed, that he'd be rescued by one of God's "suddenlys." And this, Larry thought, was exactly what had happened. Darrell had been right.

"I was blown away," Larry recalled. "Darrell had never asked the pope to say a word on his behalf. He'd simply continued to pray. Absolutely remarkable. And I thought there was a lesson here for all of us. The Scriptures are radical, and God's mercy is boundless. But most Christians don't truly appreciate this. We're too timid in our faith. We needed someone like Darrell Mease to drive it home."

The news media tended to draw a rather different lesson. Whereas Darrell and his supporters regarded the commutation as divinely inspired, most journalists regarded it instead as a monumental fluke of historical timing. Darrell just happened to be next in line for execution when the pope just happened to be visiting Missouri. It was as simple as that.

There was nothing providential about it. The commutation was arbitrary and capricious—and utterly undeserved. Given the ghastly circumstances of his crimes, Darrell was full value for his death sentence. There may indeed have been people on Missouri's death row worthy of special consideration, but Darrell, alas, wasn't one of them.

This didn't mean, however, that the news media were universally opposed to the commutation. Far from it: quite a few journalists commended the governor for making such a bold and uncalculated move. Support for capital punishment ran high in Missouri, to the tune of 70 percent among Catholics and non-Catholics alike. The governor must have known that he stood to lose far more than he would gain by letting Darrell off the hook. He must have known that the commutation could come back to haunt him at the polls. And yet he signed off on it, a rare instance of a politician throwing expediency to the wind.

The problem, then, wasn't so much that the governor had extended mercy to Darrell. The problem rather was that his mercy seemed perversely misplaced. If someone as monstrously guilty as Darrell could be given a free pass simply because the stars happened to be aligned in his favor, what about all the other prisoners on Missouri's death row? Should they be lethally injected when their dates came up? And if so, why? Because they weren't as fabulously lucky as Darrell? Because their executions weren't scheduled for the very same day the pope happened to be passing through town?

And herein lay the lesson: in the view of journalists generally, the commutation underscored the arbitrariness of the entire system of capital punishment in the United States. If the final decision to pull the switch could turn on something so fickle as a botched execution date, an accident of timing, the best move would be to eliminate capital punishment altogether. By all means, let Darrell live—but then let the others live, too.

The lead editorial in the January 29 edition of the *Post-Dispatch* summed up the thinking of most journalists on the matter. "While merciful, [the commutation] is also arbitrary and capricious," it read. "Is it fair, is it just, that Mease's life be spared just because the pope asked? Just because Mease drew a serendipitous execution date? Mercy must be informed by justice. If Mease deserves to live, so do the others on death row for whom the pope did not personally intercede. Surely some opportunistic lawyer should file suit for these inmates, making that precise point."

The Pope, the governor, and Darrell: for a solid week following the commutation, the three men were inseparable in the news. Where one was mentioned, the others were certain to be mentioned also. Their fateful collision in Missouri was written about in *The New York Times*, *People* magazine, and hundreds of publications in between and was featured on newscasts from Los Angeles to Bombay.

The Potosi publicity photo taken of Darrell in preparation for his execution received an extended workout, appearing in newspapers worldwide, sometimes alongside photos of the pope and the governor. There he was, wearing glasses and a neatly trimmed beard, balding a bit at the front, looking every inch his fifty-plus years but still recognizably the same Darrell of the high-school yearbook an eternity ago, the boy managing to peek through the accretions of advancing age and long imprisonment.

It was the kind of story that lent itself to the stunned reaction, the verbal double take, and there was no shortage of people willing to fill in with quotations.

"I'm disappointed with [the] decision, but I respect it," Jim Justus told a reporter from a prominent wire service. "I'm a religious person and I just have to believe that there is a reason this all happened . . . God works in mysterious ways."

Darrell's mom spoke with several enterprising reporters who succeeded in tracking her down in Mease's Hollow. "Oh, there are just no words to describe how thankful and happy we are," she said. "I've been listening and looking for it and today it came. We knew God was on Darrell's side and God is the best lawyer you can get. He's never lost a case."

"It was God at work," Laura Tyler told the *Post-Dispatch*.

"The whole turn of events that culminated in the pope's request for mercy didn't just happen because of luck or because [Darrell] happened to be at the right place at the right time. I think those events were very intentional, and they were acts of a more superior being."

David Lawrence, the younger of Lloyd and Frankie's two sons, had a rather different take. In the same *Post-Dispatch* article, he said that he was surprised by the commutation and distressed that neither the pope nor the governor had "considered the feelings of the family." "I don't think they looked into the background of the situation," he went on. "A man who killed three people, and did it brutally, is now allowed to go ahead and live."

On a more stridently partisan note, Daryl Duwe, a spokesman for the state Republican Party, told the press that Darrell was "the poster boy for the death penalty in Missouri." "If we can't execute Darrell Mease," he asked, "who can we execute?"

Everyone within shouting distance, it seemed, had something to say. Everyone, that is, except Darrell. True to form, he refused all requests for interviews. Only one reporter succeeded in making any headway whatsoever with him, and this only because of a memorable encounter in an Ozarks jailhouse a decade earlier.

Michelle Beth Katzenell was Michelle Beth Mueller now, married and raising a young family in a St. Louis suburb, a lifetime removed from the death-and-destruction beat of southwest Missouri. She was still plying her trade, contributing occasional pieces, on education mostly, to the *Post-Dispatch*. Hearing of the commutation, she thought back to that unexpected interview at the Taney County jail ten years ago when Darrell assured her that God was his lawyer and that under no circumstances would he ever be executed. It had been her most singular experience as a reporter. And now this: the most implausible of outcomes, the pope coming to St. Louis and Darrell's prediction coming true.

She wrote him at Potosi, suggesting a follow-up interview. Darrell's reply was dated February 1, four crowded pages in black pen, studded with biblical citations.

Of course he remembered her, Darrell said. How could he not after God had sneaked her into the jailhouse so she could put the word out about the miracle that lay ahead? And, yes, of course, he'd be happy to grant her another interview. But not right now—give it a bit more time. God was hatching another miracle on his behalf, one which would free him from prison altogether. Wait until then, he said, and he'd grant her a great interview. He'd tell her all about the death penalty: how it was fundamentally at odds with the Christian Scriptures. He'd tell her everything he'd learned during his time in prison. "When I come out of here," he wrote, "I'll come out a talkin'."

He wrote a few words about the commutation, reminding Michelle that he'd known from the first that he wouldn't be executed. The last thing he'd anticipated, however, was the pope's involvement. ("[It] caught me flatfooted, too," he said.) He added that he was "deeply touched" by John Paul II's intervention and that he planned on thanking both the pope and the governor by letter.

But again, Darrell said, this was only the beginning. God wouldn't be satisfied with anything less than total victory. The best was yet to come.

"Fasten your seatbelt," he wrote, "it's fixin' to get wild. What a ride, God, what a ride. You shall see me walk out of here totally free, in Jesus's Name."

Michelle did a piece for the *Post-Dispatch* on the letter, which must have induced a fair bit of head shaking. Everybody knew that the guy the pope had saved was a convicted murderer. But was he also crazy?

The abolitionist or anti-death-penalty crowd in Missouri was of mixed mind regarding the commutation. While delighted with the pope's intervention, abolitionists would have preferred if someone other than Darrell had been its direct beneficiary. In the worthiness rankings, Darrell was near the bottom. There were questions regarding the fairness of his arrest, sure, but none whatsoever regarding his guilt or the severity of his crimes. If the pope had singled out almost anyone else, anti-death-penalty activists would have been quite a bit happier. "Darrell Mease is the luckiest bastard in Missouri," a leading activist said not long afterward. "And he is *not* a sympathetic person."

Of course, most anti-death-penalty activists barely knew Darrell. He hadn't given them much opportunity. With God on his case, he'd seen little point taking up their occasional offers of help. While other prisoners were being adopted as favorites of the abolitionist cause—"death-row darlings"—Darrell had tucked in his chin and kept mostly to himself. He hadn't been anyone's darling.

Misgivings about Darrell aside, abolitionists were determined to make the most of the commutation. Here was something that defied all odds. It was a gift from heaven, the breakthrough for which they'd long waited. In a sense, Darrell's unworthiness only made it that much sweeter. If someone so far down the list could be plucked off death row, why not everyone else? If Darrell's life could be spared for ostensibly ethical and religious reasons, why not the lives of other death-row inmates, too? The sky was the limit. The commutation, they were convinced, augured a new moment in the debate over capital punishment.

The moment proved tantalizingly brief. On February 24, 1999, less than a month after the commutation, James Edward Rodden was lethally injected at Potosi while eighteen people conducted a vigil outside the prison walls. Rodden had been sentenced to death for the fatal stabbing, in 1983, of twenty-one-year-old Terry Lynn Trunnel in the west-central Missouri town of Marshall. His date of execution had been finalized on January 29, when the ink on Darrell's commutation order was still wet and the pope had not yet fully unpacked from his visit to St. Louis.

Two days before his execution, Rodden was interviewed from prison on a talk-radio show out of St. Louis. He insisted that he hadn't killed Trunnel and that he'd been convicted of the crime mainly through the stupendous unfairness of the criminal justice system. Nevertheless, he said, he was resigned to being executed. He knew he had no shot of receiving a commutation. After Darrell, no one had a shot. The governor would be packing guys off for lethal injection like it was going out of style, trying to mollify voters displeased with him for caving in to the pope. It wasn't Darrell's fault, Rodden said. Darrell was a good guy; everybody on the row was happy for him. It wasn't even necessarily the governor's fault. It was the politics of the situation.

Rodden appears to have been on to something. On March 10, a mere two weeks later, Roy "Hog" Roberts became the second person executed in Missouri following the papal visit. This one was especially hard on death-penalty opponents. Roberts had been one of the few guys on the row whose profession of innocence seemed entirely plausible. He'd been condemned for allegedly helping two inmates murder a guard during a riot at a medium-security prison in Moberly, Missouri. By any reasonable standard, the evidence against him at trial was paltry and contradictory. If there was anyone, on strictly legal grounds, deserving of a commutation, it was surely Roy Roberts.

And so it went—over the next six months the death chamber at Potosi was kept constantly busy. By the end of August, six more lethal injections had taken place, making a total of nine for the year. Death-penalty opponents had hoped that Darrell's commutation would slow down the killing machine, perhaps even grind it to a halt. Instead it was the exact opposite. Never before in Missouri had there been so prolific a stretch of executions. The machine was polished and primed, and operating as smoothly and efficiently as Fred Leuchter had promised it would. It was as if the governor, having spared Darrell, couldn't dispatch the others fast enough.

The pope wrote the governor on Roy Roberts's behalf. He might just as well have saved himself the postage. Safely back in Rome now, he was much easier to ignore.

And, of course, James Rodden was right. The governor wasn't necessarily to blame. Even if he'd wanted to spare Roy Roberts, spare any of the others, political realities dictated otherwise. With his second term winding down, he was planning on making a run for the U.S. Senate seat held by the hard-baked Republican John Ashcroft. No one was predicting an easy cruise to victory. A former governor himself, sturdily right wing, sturdily Pentecostal, Ashcroft liked presenting himself as a tough law-and-order guy, a capital-punishment guy, the kind of guy who would have told the pope thanks for the suggestion but we've got our own way of doing business in Missouri. He strongly disapproved of Darrell's commutation ("I wouldn't have granted him mercy," he'd been saying), he seemed confident that most voters disapproved of it also, and he wasn't above playing the deal to his own political advantage. It didn't matter that Carnahan, with Roy Roberts in the books, had presided over a whopping twenty-eight executions. Twenty-eight, and counting. The only thing that mattered was the one that got away. It made him look soft and impressionable. It made him look like a flunky, the governor who couldn't say no to the pope.

Kent Gipson represented James Rodden in his final appeals. Kent, too, saw it right away. Once Darrell's commutation was announced, he knew that no one else stood a chance. Given his political aspirations, how many commutations could the governor afford? He had extremely limited capital in this area, and he'd spent it all on Darrell. The Missouri electorate was *possibly* willing to forgive a single commutation. Catholic voters *might* make special allowance for a deal engineered by the pope. But that was surely it. One was the limit, and with Darrell the limit had been reached. The account was empty. Whatever small fund of mercy may have existed, it was completely exhausted.

On May 1, 1999, looking to get an early jump on the Senate race, Ashcroft held a public hearing in St. Louis on a proposed measure to strengthen the rights of victims of violent crime. He brought in Buck and Anita Lawrence as star witnesses.

Imagine their shock, they said, when they turned on the television several months back and found out that the very same man who had brutally murdered their crippled son,

Willie, along with Frankie and Lloyd—imagine their shock finding out on TV that Darrell Mease had been given a commutation. Never mind the sheer injustice of it, this cold-blooded killer waltzing off death row for no better reason than the pope's asking. Even worse was their having to hear about it on the nightly news, the governor's office not bothering to give them so much as a courtesy call. Finding out cold like that, with nothing to cushion the blow—who exactly was being punished here? Mease was receiving the break of a lifetime, and it was they who were being made to pay.

"When the news came on, this was the very first thing that came on and there was Mease's smiling face," Anita Lawrence said at the hearing. "It was kind of like learning they were dead again . . . I think if the governor would have just took the time to look at the pictures and hear our side, I think it would have come out different."

Joe Bednar attended the hearing on the governor's behalf. He apologized to the Lawrences, saying they had good reason to feel aggrieved. Of course they should have been properly notified, he said. The governor's office had assumed, mistakenly, that there were no surviving relatives.

With Bednar this was more than simply damage control. He truly regretted the oversight. Nevertheless, the damage was done. The governor's detractors were already accusing him of being soft on crime, soft on the death penalty. Now, thanks to Buck and Anita's testimony, he was also made to seem uncaring. He'd spared Darrell while leaving the Lawrences out in the cold.

Ashcroft had clearly gained the early advantage.

The less said about Darrell Mease, the better. This seemed to be the thinking of Carnahan and his team during the opening months of the Senate race. The early polls showed Ashcroft holding a decisive lead, with Darrell's deal the key factor. Almost 34 percent of respondents to a *Post-Dispatch* survey said they were more likely to vote against Carnahan because of the commutation; less than 8 percent said they were more likely to vote for him. Clearly the commutation had become a major liability—keep quiet about it, the thinking seemed to run, and maybe it would go away.

But of course it wouldn't go away, not with an election looming. The only thing left was to meet it head-on. On an overcast morning in late March 2000, Carnahan finally did just that. Halfway through a question-and-answer session at a Catholic high school in Kirkwood, Missouri, a student asked him about the commutation. Carnahan knew it was coming; the questions had been vetted in advance.

He ran through the events of January 27, 1999, beginning with his visiting Archbishop Rigali on such frightfully short notice, fully expecting a painful conversation on capital punishment or something similarly unpleasant. "I didn't much want to go because I did not agree with [the pope] and with the Church's position on the death penalty," he said. "I support the death penalty. I didn't want to get in a big discussion or theological debate about the subject. But I didn't think I ought to say no."

Then he described his surprise when the conversation, while still painful, turned out not to be about capital punishment in general but rather just about Darrell. "They didn't want me to open the whole of death row and didn't expect me to change [the death-penalty laws]," he said. And, finally, he recounted his decision to commute Darrell's death sentence after the pope's personal appeal at the Cathedral Basilica. "It was done on the basis of a one-time act of mercy for this prisoner at the request of the holy father. It had to be an act of mercy because this fellow lay in wait with a shotgun and blew away three people in a failed drug deal. There were no circumstances on the basis of justice to help him. But as an act of mercy, we could."

Carnahan didn't back down from his decision. He insisted that he'd made the right call, though it had not been easy. Death-penalty decisions, even under less pressured circumstances, were seldom easy. As governor, however, they came with the territory. "It's an awful thing for any one individual to have the power to cause an execution to go ahead or to stay it," he said.

Six months later, on October 13, Carnahan and Ashcroft appeared on Charles Jaco's afternoon radio program out of St. Louis for their first public debate of the campaign. Jaco had been angling for weeks to get the two men in the studio. Now that they were finally there, it was his job to hold them to the fire. After some preliminaries, he asked Carnahan the question that most needed asking.

"You extended Darrell Mease mercy at the request of the pope," he said. "How can you not extend that same mercy to everyone on death row?"

Carnahan answered in a tone of weary patience, like a teacher forced to go over the same lesson once too often for an inattentive class.

Look, he said, this was a personal request from one of the world's great leaders and, yes, he felt obliged to honor it. He was put on the spot and he'd tried doing the right thing. It was as simple as that. Did this mean, as his opponents were claiming, that he was soft on crime? A weakling when it came to the death penalty? Of course not. It was utter foolishness to suggest as much. And don't forget—it wasn't as if Darrell Mease would ever again be walking the streets a free man.

Ashcroft responded, but with surprising restraint. A governor's pardon, he said, "should be reserved to correct a mistake in the system." And he left it at that. This was his big chance for a knockout blow, and all he did was fire off a timid jab.

Perhaps, some observers speculated, Ashcroft was simply holding back until the final rounds.

Three days later, on a drizzly Monday evening, the twin-engine plane carrying Carnahan, Chris Sifford, and Carnahan's forty-four-year-old son, Roger, crashed in a craggy, wooded area near the town of Hillsboro, midway between St. Louis and Potosi. They'd been heading to a campaign rally in New Madrid, way down in the southeastern spur of the state. Roger Carnahan, who'd been piloting the plane, had reported an instrument problem moments before the crash. Rescue crews spent hours sifting through the wreckage, and early Tuesday morning officials confirmed that the three men were dead.

Carnahan was remembered in the newspapers for his old-fashioned virtues of diligence, humility, and honesty. His speeches may have been dull and rambling, his media appearances clunky, but he'd never shirked his duties, he'd never snubbed a subordinate, and he'd never tried snookering the taxpayers. He was remembered as a man who'd risen to the top while staying closely in touch with his small-town roots. The kind of man who'd spend weekends at his home outside Rolla, where he'd lived since 1959, shopping for his own groceries, getting his hair cut at the local barbershop, and washing the dishes after a family dinner. Perhaps most of all, he was remembered as the governor who'd risked political suicide commuting the death sentence of a born-again hillbilly from Stone County.

By the time of the plane crash Carnahan had significantly closed the gap with Ashcroft in the Senate race. Polls had the two men running virtually neck and neck. A week after the crash, the new governor of Missouri, Roger Wilson, announced that should Jean Carnahan's deceased husband actually get more votes than Ashcroft in the upcoming election, he'd appoint Jean to a two-year term in the Senate.

And so, of course, it happened. In November of 2000, Carnahan became the first deceased candidate in the history of the United States to win an election. This miracle he pulled off without so much as a cameo from the pope. In the end, the commutation seems not to have been held against him—not enough, at any rate, to prevent his reaching out and snatching victory from the grave. His widow, as pre-arranged, went to Washington in his stead. And John Ashcroft, proving himself an uncanny survivor also, picked up the pieces and was appointed Attorney General in the cabinet of newly elected President George W. Bush. The only man ever to *lose* an election to a dead candidate was rewarded for his efforts with a promotion.

SEVENTEEN

For Darrell, nowadays, it's the loneliness that's the toughest part of imprisonment. He still gets very few visitors, just Lexie, Larry, and the occasional stray from back home. It's been years since he saw any of his five kids, though they'll sometimes write with news of their own lives, the jobs, the romances, the small triumphs over adversity.

It's not that all the others he's left behind have forgotten him, or otherwise ruled him out. He's remembered fondly by a good number of people in Stone County, and truly missed by some. Quite a few of his old friends talk sincerely about going up to see him, saying they've been meaning to get around to it, but then they put it off and the months pass and they put it off some more. And it's not simply the long drive that stands in their way. Even more, it's the worry of what to say and how to behave once they get there; the horrible awkwardness of the situation. Sitting at Potosi with Darrell, a guy whose very nature screams out against confinement—the prospect is too much for many of his old friends to bear. Execution, they sometimes think, would've been kinder than life without parole. That way he'd be delivered of it once and for all.

His old friends needn't be so concerned. If they were actually to make the trip to Potosi and brave the checkpoints, the metal detectors, and the clanging doors, they'd almost certainly be guaranteed a lively conversation. In the main visiting center, small tables set up with two chairs or four, prisoners in standard-issue off-whites chatting with wives or girlfriends, absently dealing cards, getting a soft drink and candy bar from the vending machine, a sandwich from the microwave—in the visiting center Darrell rarely disappoints. He'll start off with religion, the New Testament's case against capital punishment, usually, and then switch to colorful, sometimes hilarious tales of his long-ago outlaw pals. For Darrell there's no necessary contradiction between these two halves of his existence. While intensely—*ferociously*—religious, he still feels deep kinship for many of the people he knew during his years of reckless freedom. The drugs he's renounced, the hatred and the violence he's renounced, but not in its entirety the outlaw life itself. It's where he comes from, and though he's moved on, there's much about the life and the people that belong to it that he still holds valuable.

So it's Matthew and Mark and Luke and John to start with; and then deliciously detailed stories of living outside the lines back home in Stone County, scuffling, scheming, gallivanting—the crazy, foolish, dangerous joy of it all. Saving souls, or shooting pistols: Darrell's perfectly at ease with either topic, though quite a bit more engaging with the latter. And there's not a hint of moroseness in his conversation, not a drop of despair. Why should there be? He knows with defiant, unflagging conviction that Potosi is merely one stop on the road, a lengthier one than he'd anticipated, to be sure, but a stop nonetheless, a place from which he'll soon be moving on.

But in the meantime there's the small matter of day-to-day survival, of coping with maximum-security confinement while waiting on the next miracle. The commutation has made some difference in this regard; not quite as much, however, as might have been expected.

In the months immediately after the commutation, Darrell enjoyed a fragile celebrity at Potosi. For years he'd been telling anybody who'd listen—fellow prisoners, caseworkers, even guards—that the skies could rain execution warrants and still the state of Missouri wouldn't get the satisfaction of killing him. With God as his lawyer, execution simply wasn't in the cards. If the blank stares were any indication, most people had trouble taking this seriously.

But then the pope came to town, and Darrell's boast came true. Not only had he escaped the death chamber, but he'd done so under circumstances that beggared the imagination. Prisoners who previously had him pegged as a religious flake or worse now found themselves revising their estimates. What was it about this guy? Why should the pope have singled him out for attention? He wasn't a household name, a controversial political prisoner, say, somebody the pope might naturally have been drawn to. Who'd ever heard of Darrell? He was strictly small-time, a local boy from a town you'd be lucky finding on a road map. And yet there it was: Darrell had insisted that he wouldn't be executed, and it was tough arguing with the results. So what was going on here? The talking heads on TV were saying it was a fluke, as if that really explained anything. Since when did flukes come this big? There was, however, another possibility: maybe, just maybe, it truly was a miracle. And if so, Darrell was definitely a guy who bore close watching.

No longer merely a number among numbers, Darrell became an object of wary, whispering curiosity. His fellow prisoners, while still not completely sold on him, were intrigued to see what might happen next. He'd already been the beneficiary of one surprise; perhaps there was something else in store. As the months passed, however, and nothing new materialized, Darrell's in-house celebrity gradually faded. The whispering died out, the curious glances abated, and before long everything was back to normal.

And Darrell, of course, was back in isolation. At first it was his long-running protest against doubling up, still no budging there; and then it was something else besides. A year or so after the commutation he was assigned work duty in the prison kitchen. He refused the assignment, saying that he'd developed a hernia and that hoisting heavy pots and pans on a (not infrequently) damp and slippery floor would put him at serious risk. Corrections officials said they'd arrange medical treatment for him, surgery if necessary. Darrell declined, not thrilled with the idea of going under the knife at the behest of officials who'd so recently been thwarted in their plans to execute him. So another standoff arose, and an additional reason for keeping him confined to the hole.

But then, about a year later, Darrell did something strikingly out of character. He actually backed down, relented—not all the way, but more so than at any point during his long imprisonment. While still refusing to take on the kitchen job, he indicated that he was now open to the idea of riding double, or sharing a cell. The privations of administrative segregation had finally proven too much even for him.

So these days, with the commutation several years behind him, Darrell is out of isolation, back in circulation, and making the best of doubling up. He's now able to purchase snacks and writing materials from the canteen. He can take his exercise in the yard. He can mingle with other prisoners in recreation, or drop by the chapel or the law library. And, of course, he can see family and friends in the visiting center—contact visits now, a handshake or a hug; not the behind-the-glass, over-the-phone affairs that he was accustomed to for so long.

But there's still the loneliness, and the endless waiting. Besides getting very few visitors, he misses the company of some of the death-row prisoners he'd gotten to know over the years. Bert Leroy Hunter, especially—Bert Leroy, Darrell's best friend at Potosi, was executed in June of 2000. Jeffrey Tokar, another good friend, followed almost two years later.

Jeffrey Tokar's execution went off almost unnoticed, with barely a ripple of protest. It was the twenty-third lethal injection in Missouri since Darrell's commutation. It seems so long ago now, the commutation, so terribly distant. Strange and distant, almost make-believe, a storybook episode from some lost and faded era. And yet, for the briefest of moments, it seemed to possess the power, the urgency, and, yes, the sheer capriciousness of revelation. It seemed that it might make all the difference in the world. If Darrell, why *not* everyone else? Why not indeed.

The moment was stalled by a hotly contested Senate race, in which the two principal candidates seemed determined to out-muscle one another on the death penalty. And then, on September 11, 2001, it was eclipsed altogether by an infinitely more powerful moment. In this moment of horror, and of shock, and of immense national grieving, there was neither time nor space for worrying about the fate of convicted killers on death rows across the country. The day for this, if it came at all, would have to wait.

As if this weren't enough, the nation was soon treated to the sorry spectacle of a sex abuse scandal in the Roman Catholic Church, with some of the country's leading Catholic bishops facing accusations of having covered up for predatory priests under their watch. The Catholic bishops, as much as anyone, had been hopeful of building on the commutation. They hadn't wanted it to end with Darrell. They'd been working and praying for the day when it might once again become front-page news, this time as the miracle in Missouri that helped put a stop altogether to the death penalty in the United States. Instead they themselves had become news, and in the process their moral voice was weakened and their credibility cheapened. How could the bishops be taken seriously as a voice of conscience in America, on capital punishment or any other issue, when they had proven singularly inept at keeping their own house clean?

So the commutation is rarely spoken about these days—by the bishops or by anyone else. It's long ago and mostly forgotten. For many of those who'd been hoping that its impact would extend far beyond Darrell, it now seems a wasted opportunity. It's the miracle in Missouri that got sidetracked, dead-ended—the miracle that could have been so much more.

Darrell, of course, thinks differently. All things in God's good time, he says. He'll be busting out of prison soon enough, and then the commutation will really start to pay dividends. He'll hit the streets preaching about the radical mercy of God and the fundamental evil of capital punishment. He'll tell the whole world everything he's learned since a retired bluegrass musician visited him in the Taney County jailhouse an eternity ago. People will initially think he's crazy, they'll try avoiding and ignoring him, but they'll never succeed in shutting him down. Eventually they'll find themselves listening, and also believing. After all, he's one of the very few who have made it back from the brink. He's a Lazarus of death row.

Down in southwest Missouri some things have changed quite a bit, others hardly at all. Cockfighting was outlawed by the state legislature in 1998, but it'll take more than legislation to do away with a traditional Ozarks way of life. There's still plenty of action to be found in open-air pits in the backwoods, and some of the world's finest gamecocks are still bred on remote properties up in the hills. Methamphetamine remains a terrible plague in the region, in some respects worse than twenty years ago. Most of the pioneering meth producers are long gone, either dead or in prison, but a new generation is proving itself every bit as resourceful, and elusive. Recipes for cooking crank, once a prized secret, are now readily available on the Internet, and many of the younger criminals operate out of mobile labs—small running vehicles, usually—that are difficult to track down and almost impossible to stake out.

Tom Martin and Jack Merritt spend fewer hours tromping around the brush these days. Both men retired from the State Highway Patrol several years back, and Jack made a successful run for sheriff of Greene County. One of his first moves in the new job, proving his soundness of judgment, was to bring Tom on board as chief deputy. Doug Loring and Carl Watson are retired also, and soaking up the good life on family farms near Willow Springs. Chip Mason is still living in the Branson area, where he heads up security for the Silver Dollar City theme park. All of these men, good and de-

cent men, truly Missouri's finest, were initially shocked by
the governor's decision to commute Darrell's death sentence. They disagreed with the decision but they accepted it,
made their peace with it, and moved on.

Others have moved on also. Mary Epps seems to have
gotten a fresh start, living and working in southwest Missouri, and raising a young family. Joyce and Donna, Darrell's ex-wives, are still haunted to some extent by their
"Darrell years" (as he's still haunted by his years with
them), but they, too, appear to have put the worst behind
them. Even Darrell's children, most of them, seem in the
process of laying the ghosts to rest and looking toward the
future.

For others, however, it's been more difficult. The commutation was especially rough on the Lawrence family, forcing
them to pick through the ruins of the triple homicide—to ex-
hume the horrifying memory of it, and the terrible sense of
loss. They felt betrayed, not unreasonably, by the deal struck
by the governor with the pope, and for some time afterward
family members were exploring the possibility of some kind
of legal recourse. Frankie, Willie, and Lloyd suffered brutal,
pitiless death by Darrell's hand. This is the harshest, most
unalterable fact of the entire saga, a fact which nothing—not
Lloyd's own ruthless criminality, or Darrell's conversion, or
the pope's intervention—can soften or excuse.

Some of the jurors in the case also felt betrayed by the
deal. They'd answered the call to duty, these ordinary
women and men, and they'd given it their solemn best. But
then the governor, at the stroke of a pen, undid a decision
they'd arrived at in fear and trembling. And why? they
asked. Because he was overcome by his papal moment?
Blinded by the light? Law and justice certainly had nothing
to do with it.

One of the jurors, a working-class man from Springfield,
spoke of the commutation, and the emotional strain he and
his peers experienced handing down the death sentence in
the first place.

"The facts in the case were absolutely clear-cut," he said.

"Guilt or innocence was never a question. We knew that Darrell did it. What was really coldhearted was the grandson. He should have spared the grandson. So the decision to give the death sentence was easy. The struggle came with combating our reservations about actually going ahead with the decision. This has to do with our natural inclination toward mercy. It's an inescapable part of our humanity. We've all done something we knew was wrong; we've all wanted a second chance. So now we were on the other side and we wanted to give Darrell a second chance. Most of us on the jury said, 'Boy, we wish there was an alternative. We wish one of the attorneys had presented an element which gave us a reason to hold off.' During deliberations in the penalty phase, just about all of us expressed this. But we weren't given the opportunity to say no. The death sentence was our only option.

"I don't fault the pope for asking that Darrell be pardoned. I fault the governor for doing it, and the reason he did it. He surrendered to the pope's influence. He let his personal feelings dominate his decision-making. As jurors we knew we were supposed to address the law and not let our feelings enter into it. It causes me to lose some confidence in our system when things like this happen. I am just one small person who was asked to sit on a jury and make a decision on the basis of the law. It would be tough for me to sit on another one."

The commutation was controversial everywhere in southwest Missouri, but nowhere more so than in Taney County. For some time afterward, the new county prosecutor, a dour man named Rodney Daniels, seemed intent on pursuing additional murder charges against Darrell. Darrell had been tried in 1990 on Willie's murder only, not Frankie's or Lloyd's. So why not go after him now on the other two killings and secure another conviction, another death sentence? See if the pope was up to bailing him out a second time? Jim Justus, an assistant prosecutor under Daniels at this point, told the press shortly after the commutation: "If my boss tells me to sic him, I'll go get him."

No new charges were filed, however, and as time passed the entire business was quietly retired. It may simply have been obligatory noise anyway, some tough talk to appease the local citizenry. The informal word around Forsyth was that county officials secretly dreaded the prospect of another trial featuring Darrell. Think of the glee the national press would take in it: here's a guy saved by the pope, and these vengeful hicks are trying to nail him to the cross again. Imagine the carnival atmosphere: anti-death-penalty crusaders ringing the courthouse, waving placards, chanting, preening for the cameras; and inside some Johnnie Cochran wannabe grandstanding before the jury, gunning for fame and fortune. It would be little Taney County against the world; little Taney County turned into a laughingstock. And imagine, finally, the damage to the tourist trade, all that negative publicity. The best option was to leave Darrell aside, and save the county a lot of expense and embarrassment.

So the subject isn't much talked about these days in the Forsyth-Branson area, at least in official circles. And the tourist trade shows few signs of slackening. U.S. 65, once a sleepy two-laner crossing the Arkansas line, is now a major thoroughfare bustling with out-of-state vehicles heading for the latest shows. On good nights the traffic on the Branson Strip is as thick as ever, visitors cruising from one end to the other and then back again, checking out the marquees, trying to decide between Andy Williams or Bobby Vinton, Mel Tillis or Mickey Gilley, or perhaps the Osmonds, the Duttons, or some other brighter-than-sunshine family act.

There are still places in southwest Missouri, however, where very few tourists dare to go. Darrell's hometown of Reeds Spring is just twenty-two miles from Branson, a short jump up U.S. 65 and then a meandering run along U.S. 160 into Stone County. Less than twenty-five miles away, and yet worlds removed from the comforting neon of Branson, the fancy theaters, the chain restaurants, the hillbilly theme parks. For most tourists Reeds Spring and the surrounding area remain uncharted territory—unfamiliar, secretive, bleak, and dangerous. It's hard and uninviting country; somehow too authentic, too close to the truth. Less than twenty-five miles from the nostalgic make-believe of Branson, it's a place where there are still real cockfighters, real outlaws, and real memories of things as they truly used to be.

The Eagle's Roost, formerly Betty's Tavern, sits nervously alongside Route 13 on the southern fringes of Reeds Spring. It's a place with a past, more than its share of knifings and ugly brawls over the years, and at least one cold-blooded killing. Never mind tourists—the Roost is a place that even local law enforcement wants no part of. Most of the regulars remember Darrell, or at least they've heard stories, and one Saturday night not long ago a number of them sat at the bar with an outsider and voiced their opinions.

"I'm just telling you one thing," a mangy, bleary-eyed guy said, "Darrell was a real good person. I used to run with Darrell. We'd go fishing and hunting. He was a good ole boy. He'd give you the shirt off his back. Something just went wrong with him. He snapped. He just did one bad thing. It was the drugs. Once he got in with the drugs, he changed. Also Vietnam—when he came back, he was never the same. Then when Lloyd Lawrence put out the contract, it drove Darrell crazy. It made him paranoid. I'll tell you, it would have made anybody paranoid. Once the contract is out on you, it's out there for good. The only thing you can do is to kill the guy who put it out on you. You've got to take him out first. Darrell had to do this. You would have done it, and so would I. The only bad thing Darrell did was killing Willie. He did this because he was so paranoid. But I'm telling you, Darrell was a really good guy."

The barmaid, a buoyant, chain-smoking woman in her mid-thirties, delivered much the same assessment.

"I've only been living here in Stone County a few years but lots of people have talked to me about Darrell," she said. "What was he supposed to do? Go to the local cops and tell them Lloyd had a bounty on his head? The Stone County cops are as crooked as a dog's hind leg. They've been getting kickbacks from the crank people for years. This is their main source of income. Everybody knows this. Darrell cracked under the pressure. I'm happy for what the pope did. Darrell didn't deserve to die. I think this is a message from God."

"Darrell did what he had to do and what nobody else had the guts to do," a guy in a hunting jacket a couple of stools down chimed in. "Lloyd would put hits out on people, and you know how they'd respond? They'd run scared. I've heard that when he had the contract out on Darrell, he also had contracts out on two other local boys J. D. Tolbert and Randy Gamble, I believe. J.D. and Randy didn't come looking for Lloyd. Only Darrell had the guts for that. And once he made the move, he was locked in. He had to finish the job."

"I knew Darrell growing up," a pretty, heavyset blond woman said. "He and my dad were good friends. It wasn't Vietnam that changed him. It was Lloyd and the drugs. Before that he was laid-back and friendly. He was a regular good ole boy. But then he turned real different, real strange. One time near the end my dad was standing outside the Nite Hawk with some people. Darrell pulled up in a limousine with tinted windows and got out. My dad grabbed his arm in a friendly fashion and said, 'Hey Darrell, how you doing?' He'd known Darrell all his life. Darrell looked at him like he didn't recognize him, broke his arm loose, and just walked away.

"And another thing," she went on, "a lot of people around here believe Darrell had help with the murders. They believe there was somebody I won't name—somebody he was crazy about—down there doing the shooting with him. Darrell confessed and took the fall because he didn't want this particular somebody to take any heat. I believe this myself. I believe this to be the case."

A young guy who'd been shooting pool off to the rear with friends, a young slim raffish guy wearing boots, jeans, black-brimmed hat, and black vest with no shirt, walked up to the bar, smiling crookedly.

"Did I hear somebody over here bad-mouthing Darrell?" he said.

"Nobody's bad-mouthing Darrell," the barmaid said.

"Anybody bad-mouths Darrell in here, I'll shoot him."

"I told you, nobody's bad-mouthing Darrell."

"Because here's the thing, outside of my father, Darrell's the best man I've ever met."

"Darrell's a better man than your father ever was," a grizzled guy in a trucker's cap said.

"My father wouldn't appreciate an outsider coming in asking questions about Darrell."

"Problem with you, you're too much like your father."

"Darrell's a great man. He's one of my heroes. There was a price on his head and he took care of business. He did what needed to be done."

"I haven't heard anybody here say anything different," the barmaid said.

"Anybody bad-mouths Darrell, I'll shoot him—"

He flicked open a switchblade and swiped it through the air.

"—or maybe I'll just stab him. And if I don't get around to it"—gesturing toward his friends by the pool table—"somebody else'll be happy doing it for me."

"Don't worry about him," the barmaid said, as the young guy sauntered off, first to the shuffleboard table, and then to the bathroom. "He's really a teddy bear. Problem is, he's sometimes meaner than a rattlesnake."

Outside in the parking lot, past midnight now, a middle-aged guy in jeans and a plaid shirt was standing by a dirt-caked pickup trying to fire up a lighter.

"He didn't do it," he said.

A pause while he gave up on the lighter and fished in his pockets for matches.

"I was in there drinking my beer and listening to everybody say their piece—"

He reached through the open window of the pickup, snapped up a packet of matches from the dash, and lit his cigarette.

"—and I'd normally just as soon keep my mouth shut. But I'm telling you that Darrell didn't do it. It doesn't figure. I know the guy. I've hung out with him. I don't think he has a malicious bone in his body. A guy like Darrell going down there and killing three people in cold blood? One of them a crippled kid? You tell me: How could such a thing have happened? And we're supposed to believe he used a shotgun? A guy who'd always been a pistol man? It just doesn't figure—none of it. A lot of us around here don't believe he did it. We believe he's been covering for someone."

He stamped out his smoke, got in the truck, and started it up.

"All right," he said. "I've said my piece. You can take it or leave it."

It's true—a lot of people in the Reeds Spring area don't believe that Darrell did the triple homicide, or at least don't believe that he did it alone. They don't believe it because they can't afford to. The idea of someone they'd always liked and respected, a guy who'd seemed the very embodiment of toughness and courage, the idea of Darrell lying in wait and ambushing three people—it's more than merely disturbing, it's downright subversive. It runs counter not only to their image of Darrell but also to their most cherished notions of masculinity. Hiding behind a blind and blowing three people away? Not confronting them, or challenging them—but simply blowing them away? One of them a defenseless teenager, all of them unarmed? This wasn't the way things were done in the hills. People settled scores, but not like this. And surely Darrell, a local boy through and through, would have done it differently.

So how indeed—how *could* such a thing have happened? The easiest answer is that it happened due to a conspiracy of circumstances. Take away Vietnam and it almost certainly doesn't happen. It was there that Darrell discovered drugs, and returning home his life began to unravel. Take away the dismal marriages, from which he emerged bruised, bereft, and aggrieved—it doesn't happen. Take away his baleful foray into the crank subculture of southwest Missouri—it doesn't happen. And take away Mary, their falling in love, and his subsequent fear for her safety—it *absolutely* doesn't happen.

Take away any one of these, and events follow a different course entirely. Then consider some additional factors: the culture of vigilantism in which Darrell was raised; his suspicion of local law enforcement, which sent him even farther over the edge; Mary calling home from Arizona and having it confirmed that Lloyd was on the prowl; the cultural idiocy whereby someone barely out of high school can waltz out of a gun shop with tools of death in hand; the run-ins with authority, the state trooper in California, the police in Cottonwood, that came to naught during that first nerve-jangling road trip. Alter just one of these factors and the entire business comes out otherwise.

As is so often the case with such matters, the crime was largely episodic. Everything—all these circumstances, all these biographical and cultural conditions—absolutely *everything* had to fall just so in order for things to go so tragically wrong. Remove one link from the lethal chain and there's very little chance that Mary ever drops Darrell off on Bear Creek Road.

Add to this Darrell's paranoia—the constant psychological backdrop to the entire saga. A by-product, possibly, of Vietnam and his two marriages, the paranoia was kicked into overdrive by crank, and then it raged completely out of control during those fateful first months on the road. The "danger urges" that would come upon him out of nowhere, like warning lights on a moonlit highway; the bizarre encounter with the park ranger in Arizona; the frantic scrambling to and fro—the enemy was everywhere, rapacious and devouring, lying in wait around every corner. Soften this just a bit, and Darrell and Mary might have set up house somewhere in California and eventually forgotten about Lloyd altogether.

But this is too easy, all this calculating and tallying, this enumerating of circumstances and conjecturing about states of mind. As explanation it falls sadly short of the mark. It maybe tells us why Darrell returned to Missouri and took that long walk up Bear Creek Road. It maybe even tells us why he killed Lloyd. But it doesn't tell us what we most need to know. Why Frankie? Why Willie? And why, afterward, the point-blank blasts to the head? Why six pulls of the trigger rather than just one—or none at all?

It's one thing to list the circumstances without which the triple homicide could not imaginably have occurred. It's quite another to say why in fact it did occur. Add up all the relevant circumstances, multiply them by three: this still doesn't explain why Darrell carried it out. All the circumstances in the world can't account for this. At the very most they put Darrell at the scene of the crime. Then Darrell himself takes over and does the rest.

It took courage for Darrell to return to Missouri fully realizing he was a marked man. It took courage for him to go up to Lloyd's farm with every expectation of facing not just Lloyd but also the hired help. At the moment of truth, however, courage seems to have given way to something else. Lloyd was unarmed—yet Darrell shot him anyway. And then Frankie and Willie. Why? Partly, no doubt, it was simply the stone-cold logic of killing. Once started, killing can be a hard thing to shut down. The occasion of killing takes on a brutal imperative all its own. Stalking the property all that time, his nerves jumping out of his skin, Darrell pounced at the first opportunity. He locked onto the job at hand, and once Darrell locked onto something he locked on for good. He didn't stop until *after* the killing was already done. He shot Lloyd, Frankie, and Willie, and then, having already passed the point of no return, he took the logic to its cruelest, most desperate conclusion with those last three shots to the victims' heads.

There was also, quite likely, another kind of logic at work: naked self-interest. Darrell killed Lloyd, his great nemesis, and then he turned the shotgun on Frankie. If he'd stopped with Lloyd, Frankie might have reached a phone and interfered with his escape plans. And when Willie turned back along the trail? What then? Easy: here we have Darrell's own admission. "The only thing I hate about this is Willie," he told Lee Stephens on the exit ramp to Springfield. "Willie would have recognized me. I had to do him, too." Darrell shot Willie because Willie was a potential witness.

Unadorned self-interest is seldom a pretty sight. Taken to these lengths, it's impossibly ugly. Which is why many of Darrell's old friends refuse to believe he committed the triple homicide. They don't remember Darrell as ugly. They remember him instead as a regular good ole boy—one of their own. They prefer keeping it that way.

Darrell's mom doesn't take refuge in denials of this sort. Hers is a strictly spiritual refuge. Lexie fully believes her first-born son did what he confessed to doing, and she believes he did so because, in her words, "Darrell was born for death row." Otherwise, she says, how could he have learned firsthand the evils of capital punishment? The triple homicide was God's mysterious way of preparing Darrell for a teaching ministry against the death penalty.

A mother's love is a boundless thing.

It's the only sign of its kind for miles around: a neon silhouette of a nude dancer off U.S. 160 just north of Reeds Spring Junction. Spank—no one calls him anything other than Spank—had it installed some years ago when he converted his gas station and convenience store into a strip club. With all the tourists flocking into Branson, a strip club—even an out-of-the-way one—had seemed a good idea. Surely at least some of those tourists would be itchy for a little after-hours action.

The years passed, however, and the tourists never came. Reeds Spring Junction was too far out of the way for all but the hardiest, and even the hardiest weren't hardy enough for Spank's. It was one thing driving by and admiring the sign; quite another working up the nerve to go inside. Spank makes a fair point when he says the tourists don't know what they've been missing. His place has an affably raunchy charm, and most nights it's actually one of the tamer spots around. Spank discovered early on that a five-dollar cover charge was all it took to discourage the worst of the local troublemakers from making a habit of stopping by.

Late that same Saturday night, after the rowdiness of the

Eagle's Roost, Spank's place seemed practically sedate. With the jukebox pumping classic Southern rock, two young women in G-strings were working the tables, swaying languorously, prying smiles out of their worn faces—trying their half-hearted best to coax a customer or two into the back room for a private lap dance. Three other women in skimpy outfits lounged at a small table near the bar, two of them nibbling on takeout fries loaded with ketchup, the third knitting a baby's sweater. Spank—big, bearded, and rosy-cheeked—was holding court at one end of the bar. At the other end two scraggly middle-aged guys who'd been staring into their beers jumped at the chance to talk about Darrell.

"Darrell's just about the only genuine prophet we've got down here," the first guy said.

"Darrell's an outlaw." His buddy.

"Yeah, he's that, too. But he's still a prophet."

"He's an outlaw prophet."

"He called it, you know. Nobody can say Darrell didn't call it."

"He swore he wouldn't get executed. That's what I heard. It looked bad for him, but who's going to argue with the results?"

"Yeah—and who believed him?"

"Not me. Not at first I didn't."

"How do you believe something like that?"

"You believe it when it happens."

"And now he says he's walking out. Who's betting against him now?"

"Not me. It looks bad for him, though."

"You don't bet against a proven prophet."

"And you don't bet against that pope."

"Yeah—how about that pope?"

"The pope saved Darrell's life."

"John Paul. He saved Darrell. What can you say about that pope?"

"I'll tell you. That pope—he's a good ole boy."

"John Paul—a good ole boy. That fairly nails it."

•   •   •

The Pope and Darrell. The Ozarks is a region rich in legends, fanciful tales of larger-than-life characters caught up in events not entirely of their own making. This particular legend has the advantage of being completely true.

AFTERWORD

In late January 1999 a reporter for *The New York Times* called my home in Toronto. He asked if I'd been following the papal visit to St. Louis. I said that I was only dimly aware of it. He asked if I knew anything about Missouri governor Mel Carnahan and his views on capital punishment. I said that Carnahan's name barely rang a bell. He asked if the name Darrell Mease rang a bell. I said no; it certainly didn't.

The reporter told me about the big news just then breaking in St. Louis. The pope had spoken personally with Governor Carnahan, asking him to commute Darrell's death sentence. He asked if I thought such a commutation would have a significant social impact. I said that his guess was as good as mine.

Nine months later a friend showed me the *Times* article where I was quoted, uneventfully, on the commutation. I'd completely forgotten about it. I was intrigued, especially by what was missing from the piece. I looked up other news articles and found much the same thing. Darrell was missing. The articles were strong on the pope and the governor but curiously stingy on Darrell. There were sketchy details about his crime, stray quotations from people who knew him—nothing that truly brought him to life. The pope and the governor had stolen the show; Darrell appeared in the articles as little more than a stage prop.

I eventually came across a small piece in the *St. Louis Post-Dispatch* that quoted fragments of a letter Darrell had sent Michelle Beth Mueller. "When I come out of here, I'll come out a talkin'," one fragment read. And another: "Fasten your seatbelt, it's fixin' to get wild. What a ride, God, what a ride." Here finally was Darrell, bursting out of the wings, if only for a line or two, full of bravado, not sounding surprised by the commutation, or particularly grateful, not sounding in the least like a guy who'd just been brought back from the dead. Now I was really intrigued. I wanted to learn more about Darrell. I wanted to investigate the story behind the headlines.

I drove to southwest Missouri and met with dozens of people in local law enforcement. I hung out at backwater taverns, clapboard churches, and sad-eyed strip clubs. I tracked down cockfighters, crank dealers, and old-time hillbillies. I dug up information at tiny county libraries and drank coffee with grizzled outlaws in dusky cafés.

Before long I was hooked. I'd spend a week in southwest Missouri, sleeping in my '89 Pontiac, sometimes grabbing a seventeen-dollar motel in Springfield, and then I couldn't wait to get back down again. Some people weren't pleased having an inquisitive outsider spending so much time in their midst. I was warned off, and occasionally threatened. A guy pulled a knife on me; somebody else opened his jacket and showed me a gun. Two guys in a pickup stopped me on Route 13 south of Kimberling City and said I was either too stupid or too brave for my own good. They said they were pretty sure which one it was.

On the whole, however, people were hospitable. They invited me into their homes and workplaces and answered my questions with refreshing candor. As often as not, they remembered Darrell with real affection. This was true even of some people in law enforcement. "Have you talked with Darrell yet?" Tom Martin asked early on in my research. I said that I hadn't. "Well, I know Darrell and now I know you," Tom said, "and if you get a chance to talk with him, I'm sure you'll like him."

For the first month or so, I seriously doubted that I'd get a chance to talk with Darrell. I wrote requesting an interview and he wrote back graciously declining. I sent a second letter saying that I respected his decision. Even if he'd said yes, I wrote, complete control of the project would still be mine. This time he replied suggesting that I drop by.

Tom Martin was right. Once I actually got around to meeting Darrell, I did indeed like him. I found him bright and funny and honest. Though inclined toward skepticism on such matters, I became convinced that his religious convictions were entirely sincere. I visited him often at Potosi, and he also sent me richly detailed letters elaborating on answers to some of my questions. Darrell insisted (convincingly) that he didn't care how he came out in the book. He asked only two things of me: that I include just one small passage on the spiritual angle to the story, and that I not be unduly rough on Mary. These were easy requests to honor: I was already committed to exploring the spiritual angle, and I had no interest in being unduly rough on anyone.

Darrell set no conditions on my work, and neither did any of the criminal justice professionals connected to the case. Jim Justus, Chip Mason, and Chuck Keithley gave me candid and lengthy interviews, with no strings attached. The Missouri Highway Patrol, asking nothing in return, afforded me complete access to their investigative files. Tom Martin, Jack Merritt, Harley Sparks, Doug Loring—all of these men spoke with me freely and forthrightly.

I conducted roughly three hundred interviews in Missouri and about thirty more elsewhere across the country. I turned over every stone, pursued every lead. I wasn't, however, able to speak face-to-face with everyone I'd hoped to. Mary Epps and her parents called off an interview at the last moment, leaving little doubt that they weren't keen on rescheduling. For Mary's involvement in the story, I drew heavily on trial testimony, police reports, depositions, interviews with lawyers and investigators, and, of course, my conversations with Darrell. I also spoke with a former schoolmate of Mary's and about a dozen other people variously acquainted with her.

I spoke personally with two of Lloyd's nephews and briefly by phone with his youngest son, David. David told me that he and his siblings had been advised by lawyers not to discuss the case with outsiders. I decided against pushing hard on this front, especially since I wasn't buying the whitewashed version of Lloyd that some people seemed intent on selling. I'd done my homework. Lloyd was what he was.

Bill Wendt was retired by now, and unavailable for interviewing. I spoke at length with one of his close associates, and I also obtained the complete legal dossier for the case.

I personally retraced every move that Darrell and Mary made on their two road trips. Everywhere they went, I also went. My conversations and correspondence with Darrell were enormously helpful in this regard, as were the Highway Patrol's investigative files, the trial transcripts, and the taped statement that Mary gave Jack and Chip in Phoenix.

Only one topic was off limits during my talks with Darrell at Potosi. He refused to discuss the crime itself, promising that this was something he'd go into at some other time and place. I reconstructed the triple homicide largely on the basis of Darrell's detailed confession and the extensive crime scene materials, which included still photographs, pathology reports, police files, and a reenactment video made by investigators for instructional purposes.

Much of the dialogue that appears in the book I recreated with the help (whenever possible) of multiple sources. For the crucial scene at Archbishop Rigali's residence, I had the benefit of interviews with direct participants from both the pope's side and the governor's.

Two sections of the book proved especially difficult. The first of these was Darrell's conversion, or spiritual epiphany, in the Taney County jail. Seeing this as the fulcrum of the narrative, and anxious to do it justice, I sent several draft pages to Darrell for his comments. He recommended one or two minor revisions. This was the only part of the manuscript reviewed in advance by Darrell or anyone else.

The other troublesome section came at the very end, where I attempted a final reckoning. Why had Darrell done what he'd done? If I hadn't gotten to know Darrell personally and seen for myself his positive sides, this section likely would have been easier to write.

Darrell's commutation was an international story, with wide-ranging implications for the debate over capital punishment in the United States and elsewhere. But it was also a resoundingly local story. While not everyone in Darrell's home environs approved of the commutation, most of those with whom I spoke seemed unwilling to dismiss it as a mere accident of history. In the intensely religious culture of the Missouri Ozarks, there are no mere accidents. Events of every sort, but especially extraordinary ones, are believed to reverberate with divine purpose. To suggest otherwise would betray not only a lack of faith but also an astonishing lack of imagination.

Executions in Missouri are customarily scheduled for just past midnight. As the clock wound down for Darrell, he stood virtually alone in believing that his life would be spared by miraculous intervention. In death-row time, it was almost midnight when the pope paid his historic visit to St. Louis. Not even the pope could have realized the full extent of the drama awaiting him.

ACKNOWLEDGMENTS

As background to the story, I consulted the following works: Mary Hartman and Elmo Ingenthron, *Bald Knobbers: Vigilantes on the Ozarks Frontier* (Gretna, Louisiana: Pelican Publishing, 1996); *History of Stone County, Missouri* (Marionville, Missouri: Stone County Historical Society, 1989); *The History of Reeds Spring* (Reeds Spring Historical Society, 1998); A. J. Bannister, *Shall Suffer Death* (Brunswick, Maine: Audenreed Press, 1996); Stephen Trombley, *The Execution Protocol* (New York: Crown Publishers, 1992); and Robert Jay Lifton and Greg Mitchell, *Who Owns Death?: Capital Punishment, the American Conscience, and the End of Executions* (New York: William Morrow, 2000). I also consulted various reports published in the *St. Louis Post-Dispatch*, the *Springfield News-Leader*, *The Kansas City Star*, and other local Missouri newspapers.

I am grateful to everyone who agreed to speak with me throughout the course of my research. A special word of thanks to Darrell Mease, Lexie Mease, and Larry Mease; Archbishop Justin Rigali, Joe Bednar, and Chris Liese; Terry Ganey, Michelle Beth Mueller, Dennis Graves, Tim Block, Patricia Rice, and Charles Jaco; Roscoe and Wanetta Keithley; Doug and Anna Loring; Chuck Keithley, Theron Jenkins, Jim Spindler, Jim Justus, and Chip Mason; Tom Martin, Jack Merritt, Jerry Dodd, and Harley Sparks; Laura Higgins

Tyler, Robert Maurer, and Kent Gipson; William O'Connor, Larry Rice, and Morris "Spank" Page; Amy Langston and Michael Glenn; the men and women of the Missouri State Highway Patrol; and Fred Pfister, the editor of *The Ozarks Mountaineer*.

Special thanks also to Margaret J. Cuneo, Rebecca E. Keenan, Brenda M. Cuneo, and the inestimable Shane D. Cuneo for their critical feedback and constant encouragement.

The Department of Religious Studies at the University of Dayton—and especially Terrence Tilley; James Heft, S.M.; Maureen Tilley; Sandra Yocum Mize; Una Cadegan; Bill Portier; and Joe Jacobs—provided crucial support during the early stages of the project; and the Missouri Department of Corrections and the staff at Potosi Correctional Center extended me every professional courtesy. Patricia Sharma, Marilyn Vitale, Marvin Reznikoff, Leanne Lowes, and my Fordham undergraduate students lent me valuable insight at various junctures of the research and writing.

Thanks most of all to my editor, Andrew Corbin, for his indispensable guidance every step of the way; to Siobhan Dunn, Sean Mills, and Karla Eoff of Doubleday Broadway; and to my agent, Claudia Cross.